The Effective Principal

Perspectives on School Leadership

Second Edition

Arthur Blumberg
Syracuse University

William Greenfield
Louisiana State University

Allyn and Bacon, Inc.
Boston London Sydney Toronto

To Our Kids

Barbara, Lester, and Susie

and

Geoff, Amelia, Ara, and Monica

The people from whom we've learned most about schools

Library of Congress Cataloging-in-Publication Data

Blumberg, Arthur, 1923–
 The effective principal.

 Bibliography: p.
 Includes index.
  1. School superintendents and principals.
 2. Leadership. I. Greenfield, William, 1944–
 II. Title.
 LB2831.9.B58 1986   371.2'012   85-30728
 ISBN 0-205-08740-X

Printed in the United States of America

10 9 8 7 6 5 4 3 2   91 90 89 88 87

Contents

Preface to the Second Edition

A colleague of ours once remarked, as he was talking about a recent book of his that had been very well received in the academic community, that a book is never finished. Even when the final draft of the manuscript has been sent off to the publisher, it is less than complete. Second thoughts, alternate ways of expressing oneself, or newly discovered bits of information always seem to intrude on one's sense of closure.

Certainly this sense of incompleteness accompanied our having "finished" the first edition of *The Effective Principal*. It was striking, as a matter of fact, as we realized that 1) what we had written represented a single point in the lives and thoughts of the school principals who were our partners in inquiry, and 2) that even before we had finished the manuscript, there had been changes in the careers of some of these people. Thus, the invitation to produce a second edition provided the opportunity, some seven years or so after our initial work, to continue our inquiry into the work lives of these principals—some of whom were no longer in that role—and make things a bit more complete. This was done, however, with the knowledge that when we had finished, the whole story would still not have been told.

The nature of the book and the message we were trying to convey suggested two major decisions about the structure of this edition. First, its essence, represented by the thumbnail sketches of the way each principal conceived of his/her life at work, would remain unchanged. The way they talked about it and the thoughts they had several years ago was not changed. Second, the contribution this edition could make would be to provide some information about what had happened and why to these people over time. Our thoughts here, quite naive in retrospect, were simply to enable ourselves and the reader to know these principals and their work better than we had been able to the first time around. Quite unforeseen and most fortunately, though, what happened as we followed up on them is that we achieved what we believe are some penetrating insights into the principalship itself and its effects on the humanity of the people who hold that position. In the final analysis, then, this second edition is important not only for what it tells us about the ways that some effective principals conceive their work, but also for its focus on the long-term meaning of that work itself as a career focus for the individual involved.

This book, then, is formally structured into two parts. Part I, As It Was, with some deletions and synthesis, contains most of the content that appeared in the first edition. The major deletions, made in the interest of space demands, involved not including two chapters on the development of the principalship and some focal research studies on that role. We compensate for that by including in the Suggested Readings section at the end of the book a much briefer bibliographic essay with those concerns. Part II, As It Became and a Bit More, has four new chapters. Two deal with the results of our interviews with seven of our original eight principals; one with value dilemmas faced by principals; and finally one with what we think could be a stimulating and productive focus of future concern with the study and education of principals.

Finally, a note is necessary about our collaboration on this project. When we first wrote together, we were members of the same university faculty. Talking and consulting together presented no problem. Greenfield has since moved on and is now a professor at Louisiana State University, while Blumberg remains at Syracuse. The interesting thing about this is that the distance seems not to have interfered with either our working together or our learning from each other. The latter thought—learning from each other—is really what collaboration is all about.

Preface to the First Edition

In a sense, this book is the story of a journey that we took, knowing where home was, but not sure of either what roads we would take or where we would end up. It was similar to a Sunday afternoon drive that families take (perhaps less frequently these days given the cost of fuel) to see the country-side, wander around, and possibly have dinner at a good restaurant if they happen to stumble on one—or, more likely, at the first hamburger stand that looms into view around dinnertime. More to the point, our purpose was to take an intellectual trip into the work lives of some school principals who, for one reason or another, were judged to be out of the ordinary by their peers or us. Thus, "home" for us was a rather simple matter—our curiosity about these people. Where we would end up in our travels was quite a different matter; it would depend on the human landscape we encountered.

What we found, as we journeyed through the work lives of these school principals was exciting, reassuring, and humbling. It was exciting for us to come to understand these people better, to see how each, rather uniquely, conceptualized and acted out his/her role. We were excited to learn more clearly than we had known before how directly a determined school princi-pal can affect the form and substance of what occurs in a school.

We were reassured and had our sometimes flagging confidence renewed in the institution of public education. It is no secret—the pollsters and col-umnists say—that the schools are currently suffering a confidence gap with the public. If the schools only did their job correctly (as they used to), if teachers were more concerned about teaching than how much they get paid, then youngsters would learn more and we would have less trouble all around us—this is the current mythology. There may be some truth to this mythology, but our study confirmed some things we already knew—that there *are* enthusiastic and dedicated people who are trying to make a differ-ence in the educational and emotional lives of youngsters in the schools.

Finally, and most definitely, we were humbled as we came to understand what is meant to be a school principal who was trying to make a difference, who was not content with serving as an organization maintenance person whose main purpose in life was to keep things running smoothly, with "keeping the peace." The amount of time and energy—intellectual and emotional—that it takes for a principal to make an impact on a school is startling. We became convinced that it takes a unique person to help give a school, first, an image of what it can be and, second, to provide the drive, support, and skills to make that image approximate reality.

We (the authors) were the primary beneficiaries of the experience of studying these school principals and writing a book about them. The book, though important, is almost incidental in the long run. What we learned about ourselves and about the schools is of a higher order of importance. In a sense, the act of writing this book together resulted in a renewal of faith for us.

In an odd sort of way then, and by hindsight, we wrote this book for ourselves. Others, however, should find its contents of interest. Professors and students of school administration should find it useful as a further means of understanding both the complexities and ambiguities of the principalship. Practicing administrators may find it helpful as it describes and conceptualizes experiences that most of them have confronted and continue to confront.

This book represents a collaborative effort between the two of us and the people who were the subjects of our study. Not simply inanimate repositories of data, they contributed most willingly to our analysis of the data that they had provided. We thank them for their time and their thinking.

Part I
As It Was

1

Principals and Schools: Rediscovering the Obvious

We begin with an anecdote told us by the principal of an elementary school:

> I started as a principal in August and this was the beginning of February. A kindergarten teacher came to me and asked "When would you like to pass out Valentines?" I looked at her and asked "When would you like to pass out Valentines?" She said "I thought during snack time would be fine." "Sounds good to me," I said. She followed up by asking me if I was going to issue a memo to that effect. I said "No, I hadn't planned on it. Teachers can do it whenever they want to." That was the end of the conversation.

As it turned out, the principal's matter-of-fact response constituted a crisis for the teacher. She wanted to do her lesson plans and fit the Valentine activity into them and she felt she needed the principal's direction to do this. There was no direction forthcoming, thus the crisis.

One may react to these comments with a smile, a laugh of derision, or, "My heavens! Is this what principals and schools are all about?" Reactions such as these, however, miss the point, which is to remind us how pervasive a principal's influence can be. There is more to it than that, though.

The principal went on to say that the previous principal had run a "good" school, meaning that it was peaceful and well-ordered. He set the rules and they were followed. That was what he was about, and in the process of playing out his role as he saw it, he socialized his teachers to expect that things would be done in certain ways. When our principal came along with a different set of expectations about what a principal should do and about the concomitant prerogatives of teachers, it upset things—at least for a while.

The point is that the principal does indeed make a difference in the life of a school, however that difference may be characterized. Even by doing nothing the principal affects the life of the school, if for no other reason than that by doing nothing he or she creates a fragmented system in which people work and survive as best they can. Roland Barth put the issue most succinctly in the following way: "It is not the teachers, or the central office people, or the university people who are really causing schools to be the way they are or changing the way they might be. It is whoever lives in the principal's office" (1976, p. 21).

Clearly building principals are critical figures in the life of a school. What is curious is that the educational world seems to treat this fact as a new discovery. The "effective schools" research, for example, strongly suggests—even if one downplays its relevance as too generalized—that the role of the principal is central to what the school is all about. Hence, there is a new concern about principals—a concern, we add, that has been obvious for a long time to anyone who thinks about the schools and what goes on inside them. Also, perhaps stemming from this concern, is a new development, something called Principal Centers, a concept certainly borrowed from the idea of Teacher Centers. Typically organized around a university base (the Center at Harvard apparently being the first), their general focus is to provide a collegial setting through which principals may engage in professional development activities, share the skills of their craft with each other, and develop a network of people with common concerns.

A development such as this, and others that undoubtedly will make their way into the world of the schools, can only be applauded. But we must be pardoned a smile that is related to the subtitle of this introductory chapter: "Rediscovering the Obvious." We hasten to add, however, that just because something is obvious doesn't mean people understand it or accord it the attention it deserves. Further, the "perch" from which one views a scene may cloud obvious parts of that scene. For example, if schools are not seen as purposeful organizations, but as simply aggregates of unrelated tasks and roles, it is quite possible that the principalship will be ignored as vital to school life. (We know of one school district where, several years ago, an outside consultant recommended that the office of the principalship be abolished.)

We know, of course, that schools are not always such simple aggregates. There are typically underlying (if not public) belief systems, goal orientations, ways of relating to both colleagues and students that characterize individual schools and distinguish one from the other, sometimes subtly, sometimes blatantly. This can be considered a school's *culture;* and it is our position—indeed the theme of this book—that the character of a school's culture is largely influenced by its principal. But this, as we have suggested, is "rediscovering the obvious," something that happens, perhaps, when times are stressful, as they surely seem to have been in recent years.

Narrowly conceived, this book is about eight school principals, who by reputation seemed to us (some of them are no longer principals) to be different somehow from many of their colleagues. The differences are hard to define. Certainly, if we may be pardoned a deeply felt bias, the differences would not be revealed by any sort of competency examination devised to find out whether or not a person would be a good school principal. Rather, the differences that caught our attention were those that came up during our talks with teachers, parents, district administrators, and our own students. We would hear, for example, of "someone you should find out more about." That is, this person was doing something, communicating something, or organizing things in a way that prompted people to say "That principal is unusual. Something is happening in that school."

What these remarks suggested to us was that—somehow—these eight principals were able to bring to bear on their work a particular view of their role, a certain set of skills, perhaps a type of energy, that needed to be talked and thought about; although not necessarily from the point of view that what they did could or should be copied—an impossibility to start with. What were these people like? How did they see themselves? Their job? How did they make sense of the sometimes elegant, sometimes humdrum, frequently hectic, and often frustrating life of a school principal? In retrospect, the essential question was, What did these people bring along with them—their intellectual and emotional baggage, so to speak—that enabled them to make the kind of impact on a school that was to be viewed so positively by others?

Two paragraphs ago we used the phrase "narrowly conceived" to describe the concern of this book, its focus on the work-world view of eight rather out-of-the-ordinary school principals. In this paragraph we urge you to reflect, as you read, on a broader concept—that of the principalship as a form of "work"—and to differentiate it in your mind from "labor" (Green, 1968). There is a profound difference between the two. Green notes that "We say, 'He *performed* a labor,' but 'He *produced* a work' " (p. 21). Further, agreeing with Hannah Arendt (1958) that labor is never associated with a product, while work always is, Green goes on to comment, "This difference is enormously important. It suggests that the concept of work is of an activity that *in principle* is aimed at the production of some persisting object or product" (p. 21).

Of course, what principals produce—the result of their work—cannot be seen as a tangible product. But it is observable as an attitude, an élan, a kind of concern for youngsters, perhaps, that permeates a school. So, it is with the *work* of principals—not their job, not their labor—that we are concerned. We want to know how some principals achieve a sense of accomplishment, at least at times, not simply a sense of having to labor at a task in an endless, cyclical, futile fashion.

What you learn here of the work of principals is necessarily incomplete. We are not bothered by this and hope that you will feel as we do. This incompleteness suggests that there is a bit of mystery to it all, which continually beckons the curious. There is nothing mystical about it. Rather, some people can work in ways that set them apart from others, ways that are simply "unknowable"—at least in any systematic, perhaps rational, sense of the word.

The methodology of any study is a function of the problem under investigation. Obviously, our concern mandates a qualitative approach, involving the use of in-depth interview. We selected eight principals: four elementary school principals, three male and one female; four secondary school principals, two male and two female. Our primary criterion was reputation. That is, we asked numerous teachers, principals, and faculty colleagues to nominate principals they knew who were making a difference in their schools. In addition, we were aware of a few people who in our judgment fit the same criterion. It turned out that we knew all the principals who were recommended; they all had some affiliation with our university. We wanted to be selective. We did not intend our study to be a broad-based inquiry of school principals *qua* school principals.

A further word concerning principals who "make a difference": all principals make a difference; what is at issue here is how some principals, who seemed to have had some highly positive qualitative impact on teachers and youngsters, perceive their work lives. "Qualitative impact" is an elusive idea. Given the idiosyncrasies among schools (and their sameness as well), we are hard put to define the phrase in any general way. Certainly, the selections we made reflect our own bias about what a school should be—a balance between a rather joyful humanistic experience and a determined focus on creating a productive learning environment. We think, however, that our choices were influenced by more than just our own values. In most cases, the people we chose received general *ex post facto* support, both from practitioners in the field and from our faculty colleagues.

Our interviews with these principals were simple and straightforward. We told them what we were interested in and that the primary criterion for their selection was their reputation among their peers. We simply asked them to start talking in an open-ended way about their life in school. Each principal was allowed to paint his or her own picture of the school world. The interviews were unstructured. We deliberately did not create a schedule of questions to guide all the interviews. Although we did raise some points that had been remarked on by one and not the other, we did not push very hard. Thus if one emphasized relationships with youngsters and another did not, we did not push the latter. There was, of course, considerable overlap in the circumstances talked about; but at the heart of it all was the notion that the views of these principals were their own, not ours. We wanted to get as close to the "eye of the beholder" as we could.

We had decided to let the interviews serve as a projective device that we could interpret. Beyond this was another decision. The study would not be comparative in any systematic sense of the word. Although we did engage in some synthesizing, it was not our goal to compare or contrast the interviewees with one another—for two reasons. First, it seemed important (to continue the metaphor) to let each principal's picture stand by itself as do paintings in a gallery. The issue, from our point of view, was to inquire into the internal dynamics of these self-portraits, not to compare one with the other along predetermined lines.

The second reason for not structuring interviews soon became apparent:

the people to whom we talked used different concepts to describe their view of themselves in their role. Each seemed to have his or her own theory of the principal's role, one that stemmed from his or her own personality, experience, and training. Thus it seemed wiser to let the individual principal's personal perspective dictate the course of discussion.

This interview strategy, despite the difficulties it presented (we wanted to synthesize the results), enabled us to deal with each principal as an individual without regard to anyone else. We were able to trace the themes each presented and thereby to produce an interesting, informative collage. The collage shows how leadership in a school can take many forms and still produce a productive learning environment.

Part of our study design called for a group interview with all the principals—after the individual interviews had been completed. Six of the eight attended. Each was provided with his or her "thumbnail sketch" and asked to react to it. We wanted to know whether or not our portrayals of them matched reality as they saw it. With a few minor exceptions, what we had written matched their conceptions of themselves and their work.

But the main thrust of the meeting, which lasted about four hours, was to inquire into what Levinson (1973) called the "emotional toxicity" of the work situation. That is, we were interested in the sometimes subtle, sometimes blatant factors in the work-life of a school principal that seem to take a toll on his or her emotional well-being. In a sense, we inquired into the "shady" side of their lives, one that rarely gets talked about publicly (Burlingame, 1979).

The essence of this second edition, then, remains unchanged. Indeed, it cannot be changed. What the principals talked to us about was what they talked to us about and there is no altering that fact or their words. We have been able, though, via this second edition, to pursue our inquiry about the work-life of these principals in particular and the work of principals in general in two new ways. With regard to the former, we decided that a lot could be learned from talking with these people once more. This idea took on more salience for us because, at this writing, only four of the original eight are still principals and two of those are thinking about applying for Central Office positions. What was going on in the minds of these people, those who left and those who stayed, was the question. Accordingly, we include two new chapters (13 and 14) that deal with interviews we held recently with seven out of the eight people who were originally involved.

Our concern with broadening our understanding of the principalship in general took another form: We made an assumption that one can learn a great deal about a type of work by understanding the nature of some of the conflicts of value that a person doing that work must confront. School principals seem rather continually to deal with one sort of conflict situation or another during the course of a day. Not all of them, of course, involve their own value system. But some do, and our suspicion was that, as we inquired into those that do, we would be rewarded by gaining a more finely honed insight into the demands involved in being a principal. We held numerous short interviews in which we asked, rather directly, "Will you tell us about some of the value conflicts you have faced in your work?" The description and analysis of this new data are dealt with in Chapter 15. Chapter 16, ". . . As the Principal Goes, So Goes the School . . ." concludes the book. It represents our ideas about the location of the motherlode of the school principalship.

A final comment. Perhaps the best way to use this book is to consider it as an invitation to a conversation. The conversation, we think, revolves around the idea that being an effective school principal is an incredibly complex task. It involves most centrally the bringing of one's intellectual and emotional history in contact with a desire to create qualitatively better education for youngsters—and having the skills to do just that.

With no further ado, begin by meeting, reacting to, and "talking with" Joan, "The Organizer."

2

The Organizer: A Whirling Dervish of a Problem Solver

Joan was the principal of an urban fringe-area elementary school. Talking with her about her work was an exciting experience, one we wish many more people than ourselves could have. She spoke quickly, pausing every so often to think, and then rushed on with her ideas. She did not hesitate to relate her successes; and, in a fascinating way, her intellectual excitement with her failures leaves the listener wrapped up in her story. We were somewhat in awe of both the volume and high tempo of her activity level. Not the least reason for which was our wonderment at where Joan, then aged forty, a principal who worked a twelve- to fourteen-hour day (she was also a doctoral student), got her energy. She really didn't know either. All she knew was that she had it.

> You know, I don't stop all day. I work at a pace that is very fast, but I don't ask other people to do that. My energy level is enormous. When I leave school and I think I've left something unfinished, as happened today, my mind just doesn't focus on new things.

Her mind did focus on the interview, however, and she provided a large volume of information about her style, her values, and her working hypotheses about engaging the diverse public with whom she must deal as she plays out her role as principal. The theme that seemed to guide Joan's personal life and the manner in which she conceived of a school—thus her role—were the same. This theme was that one makes the most out of life by learning how to solve problems as they occur. Joan believed that schools, particularly the elementary schools, provide an excellent opportunity for youngsters to learn good problem-solving skills. This emphasis doesn't deny the importance of learning the traditional skills. It simply puts the school program in a different frame of reference, one that, from her point of view, is more relevant to what life is all about. But it wasn't always that way. Joan had been trained in a rather traditional teacher education

9

school and had first gone to work in a school system that was noted, likewise, for being traditional. However:

> About ten years ago, I knew I had started to change. Maybe one of the things that started it all was an experience I had at Jackson School. I had forty-seven kids in the sixth grade with desks that were bolted to the floor. You couldn't move a muscle in the room. I asked the custodian if he'd please remove the last two rows of desks, but he refused to do so because he said there wouldn't be a seat for every kid. I said we could live with that but he still wouldn't do it. We didn't even have a permanent principal to whom I could appeal, so I was totally frustrated. It was then that I realized that I wanted very different things for kids than what was expected of them at that point. I expected kids to be thinkers. I trusted kids and I wanted them to be able to walk around the room and do different things.

The story continues and has an interesting ending, which is really only a beginning. Joan was frustrated at Jackson Elementary. The way out of her frustration came unexpectedly from a local university, which was starting a special program to train urban teachers. She was asked if she would like to join the staff as a supervisor. She did, and her horizons started to expand as she came in contact, collegially, with new and exciting people.

> I was really impressed. I sat in awe most of the time. I was really learning lots of things and not knowing I had learned them because I couldn't put them into practice right away. But I knew I liked what I heard.

But, nirvana came crashing down. The colleagues whom Joan found most exciting took other positions, and the situation became less attractive for her. Again, though, her dissatisfaction and frustration were alleviated by an unexpected source. The same college professor who became principal at the elementary school of which Paul (Chapter 9) was the administrator asked Joan if she would like to join his faculty. Again, she did, thus setting in motion, unwittingly, the circumstances in which she and Paul would become co-assistant principals and which would ultimately lead to her assuming a principalship of her own. Lest it be misunderstood, though Joan changed positions several times, these shifts were not made to advance to a higher organizational position with a higher salary. She seemed, rather, to be motivated by a desire for new and different learning experiences. Time and again during our interview, for example, she talked about learning new things, about what certain people had taught her, and about what she had learned from one or another set of circumstances, including those that she classified as unsatisfactory. Joan was a consciously insatiable learner.

After having served two years as an assistant principal, Joan was offered a principalship. The school, as we noted previously, was in a fringe neighborhood that had not stabilized with regard to its racial balance. Blacks were moving into the area in increasing numbers and whites were moving out. It wasn't a crisis situation, but the school, according to Joan, was in a state of turmoil.

The parents were revolting; the kids were revolting; and the teachers were all upset. I spent the whole summer meeting individually with parents, teachers, and as many others who were interested in the school as I could. I wanted to know how they saw the problem, how they conceived the school, and what they were looking for. What I found out was this: teachers avoided other teachers not because they didn't like them but because they didn't know them. They never came out of their rooms and didn't know what anybody else was doing. They were terribly threatened by parents coming into the school. At the same time the parents were incredibly threatened by the teachers. The kids hated school and I didn't know whether they got it from their parents or because they were so negatively reinforced while they were there. It was a mess!

The way in which Joan described the school and her initial activities speak quite graphically to how she conceived a school and the role of principal to be. The school is not just a building in which there are teachers, it is something that is in the minds and homes of the parents and the students. Its character exists in the relationships among teachers and among parents, teachers, and students. One gets the feeling, indeed, that the building was irrelevant to Joan's concept of a school. What's important is the character of the relationships that obtain within its walls and between it and the outside community.

Joan's high-tempo work style and problem-solving thrust also came through in her comments about her initial activities as principal. She didn't wait until the end of August to go to work on the school, but instead spent the whole summer talking with people. She didn't wait for problems to come to her. Rather, she sought them out. She knew the school had problems, but wanted to get the facts for herself and diagnose the situation in her own way.

Interestingly, while Joan was telling about her early activities as principal, she displayed no feelings of ambiguity concerning her role. For Joan the issue was simple: there were organizational and educational problems to be solved and one might just as well be about solving them because they weren't going to solve themselves. If issues of role or role conflict arose, they would be dealt with like any other problem; get the facts, look for alternatives, and act. Always the theme for Joan was problem solving and action. But first get organized, get the facts.

A more abstract way of describing Joan in her role as principal is that she was almost a pure practitioner-empiricist. Her strength seemed not to rest with her ability to conceptualize, a priori, her role and her school as an organic social system. Indeed, when confronted with questions that focused on the way she conceptualized things, she appeared a little uncomfortable, feeling more at home with a problematic situation to which she could apply her energy. This does not mean, of course, that the way she acted was not guided by some sort of philosophical or theoretical set. It clearly was, but that set seemed to derive from the nature of the data she collected and not from some preconceived notion of what ought to be. She was clearly a situationalist, organizing her actions and program proposals to the demands of the here and now, and not to some grandiose educational plan for the future. Instances of this style were plentiful, many of them stemming from her own fact-gathering efforts of that first summer. For example, relative to the teachers:

> The place was so uptight. No one talked with anyone else. So I spent the whole first year knowing that what I was going to do was work on plain old human relationships. I taught a lot that first year with other teachers. I simply wanted to show people that there were other techniques, that there were other relationships that one could build with kids without holding the reins so tightly that they couldn't get up from their seats to move around.

If the problem, then, was that the teachers weren't talking to each other, one solution was to model different behavior, and start talking. But not talk for talk's sake; and, this is where Joan's values came in. Although the desks weren't nailed to the floor as they were at the school she taught in several years before, she saw the teachers dealing with their classes as if they were. So, she worked with them in an effort to induce some change in teaching style and to open up communication. In the process, Joan gained credibility among her staff, because they became aware that she could not only manage the school but also function very effectively as a classroom teacher.

An additional clue concerning how Joan saw herself slipped in almost unnoticed in her comment above. That is, she said that she taught a lot with "*other* teachers." This comment tells the story. Joan was basically a teacher, and it's through teaching, whether with youngsters or adults, that most of her personal and professional satisfaction derived.

Another example of Joan's problem-solving thrust, this time with the faculty as a group, becomes clear as she went to work on the learning environment of the school:

> We all got together and listed all the kinds of problems that stopped kids from working in a really acceptable learning environment. We then brainstormed the different kinds of ways we could alleviate those problems. What we decided was really important was to make problem-solving skills an integral part of the instructional program. If we didn't help kids learn to problem-solve there were lots of things they wouldn't be able to do.

And, by problem solving, Joan meant:

> To start with, just to be able to identify the problem. What we first found out was that kids would be arguing and they wouldn't even know what they were arguing about. So we helped the kids define their problems. We helped them to learn to separate problems from symptoms and now most kids are really fantastic at that. Then we sat down and talked with them about all the things that come into play with their problems and all the solutions. But we never told a kid which way to solve a problem.

It was difficult to hold Joan to a specific point. She raced on, but in the process revealed more about those things she held to be of value. More importantly, there was little incongruency, if any, between her values and her behavior. What she said she believed in, she implemented or tried to implement, not by exhorting or making new policy, but by engaging with other people—on a one-to-one basis or in groups—and teaching, always teaching.

The style of teaching in which Joan engaged is not the stereotypical classroom variety. It is here-and-now problem-oriented, and the teaching methodology she employed got people working together on the problem. Her school, in a way, was an experiential learning laboratory. Thus, sensing a need to change the character of the school's learning environment, she did not promulgate a new policy or develop a lofty goal statement. Rather, working collaboratively with the faculty, she was able to help them identify, own, and commit energy to an issue that affected their lives every day—the very humanity of their school.

One of the things that Joan quickly found out about the nature of the humanity of her school was that the primary mode of dealing with behavioral problems of the youngsters was a punitive one. The school had an aura of negativism. It was cyclical in nature, usually starting at the beginning of each week. What seemed to occur was that numbers of youngsters would arrive at school on Monday morning, upset and sometimes angry. Their behavior in their classes would become disruptive, and teachers' dominant mode of dealing with them was one of negative reinforcement—punishment. The teachers and students became aggravated. Teachers didn't teach and students didn't learn. The result was a disrupted school at the beginning of each week, not a pleasant prospect to confront for principal, teachers, youngsters, and, ultimately, parents. The framework within which Joan chose to view this problem provides additional insight into her concept of the role of the principal. A stance that she could have taken, for which no one would fault her, would have been to view each problem that developed as an independent, unrelated matter. This stance would lead to individualized action—dealing with the child, and with the teachers, or both. Hopefully, the problem would be solved for the moment, at least, and the process would be repeated at the next eruption.

Joan chose not to take this point of view that called for isolated remedies. Rather, her position was that, although it was clear that the problems were caused by individual actions and reactions, the ultimate consequences of it all were borne by the school as an organization. She said:

If we (i.e., the school) didn't take care of those problems, then the teachers would have to keep on dealing with them and the result would be a disruption of the whole instructional atmosphere.

It is extremely important to note that the we referred to in this statement did not refer to the transfer of behavioral problems out of the teacher's hands and into those of the principal, which would have meant maintaining the individual focus in the principal's office instead of the classroom. The meaning of *we*, then, was the school as a system that had an identity of its own that included but was not the sum of the identities of all the individuals involved. The conceptual import of this for the situation Joan described is that human problems that impact and affect an organization as a system demand resolutions that are organizationally based, and not resolutions that deal with the problems as isolated phenomena.

In this case, the steps taken to work out the problem of behavioral disruptions in the classroom took the form of a structural change that had two different but related facets. Joan's words describe best the action that was taken:

> First, we instituted what we call a parent "drop-in" time two days a week and at different times so that parents who couldn't work it in one hour might be able to at another. We wanted them to feel free to come in and talk and not even necessarily about kids, but anything. We also asked them about problems that may have occurred over the weekend and if they would take the initiative to tell us about this so we could be prepared to deal with them. This has been pretty successful.
>
> The other thing we did was to make the first hour of each day available for any kids who wanted to come down to the office and check in with us to talk a bit. Sometimes a kid will say, "I had a problem with so and so and I think it's really going to be a bad scene today." Other times they will say, "It worked out, everything's okay, the problem's over." We try and bring the kids together and talk about problems. Sometimes all they want is somebody to listen while they talk. We don't have any hard data about how this is working. But we do know that teachers feel a lot better.

Patterns in Joan's style, then, repeat themselves. Recall that the first thing she did upon her appointment as principal was to start by reaching out to the community, even before school started. She did this because she needed information and wanted to establish healthy relationships with parents. When another situation developed that seemed to require help from the community, she was back there again, reaching out both to get information and to build relationships. The recurrent emphasis on "problems" is also there. And, lest the reader get the wrong impression, we hasten to add that Joan was not a "down in the mouth" problem-burdened person. To meet her results in precisely the opposite picture—a person who looks for and sees opportunities for growth and learning in practically all *problematic* situations. One might say, indeed, that her orientation was not to focus on problems *qua* problems but to concern herself most centrally with the process of problem solving; of organizing facts and resources in a way that gets the problem identified and eventually solved. We came to think of Joan as "The Organizer."

Joan's comments relative to dealing with disruption in classrooms offer another form of insight into the way she saw the role of principal. At issue was her willingness to create new organizational structures for problem resolution, her willingness to step outside the regularities (Sarason, 1971) of school life in order to fit solutions to the demands of the problems. For example, the curricular pattern of schools does not typically provide for the first hour of the day being devoted to youngsters who have personal things they want to talk about. In fact, many principals would negate the idea because "it isn't done" or "there is no precedent for this" or, "the children should be in the classroom." Concern for what is or isn't done, or for whether or not there is a precedent to a particular action was not central to Joan's thinking. What was was the idea of organizing the resources of the school and community to do things. If these "things" required changing accepted routines and patterns of structure and interaction—well, they had to be changed, because that was what had to be done.

But things don't happen overnight, and Joan was the first to acknowledge the slowness of change. Much as she would have liked changes to occur "yesterday," she was a realist with regard to the time it takes to induce meaningful normative changes in a school. In speaking about the success of the daily hour devoted to kids who have things on their minds, she said:

> We are talking about three years of training when you've been working with kids, teachers, and parents. We've tried to help kids understand that there are acceptable ways of dealing with problems at school and ways that are unacceptable. And we've tried to help parents learn to problem-solve with their children. Sometimes the kids have even helped their parents learn skills. We hear sometimes of kids taking their parents over to other parents to see if they could bridge some gap that's developed between them. But it all takes time. It's taken three years, but in that time the idea has become a really important part of our school.

The teachers also had to be part of the problem as well as part of the solution, for both common wisdom and the results of research clearly indicate that programs in schools don't succeed unless the teachers are involved and lend their support. To gain support from teachers, she involved them in their own learning. Joan's position was clear as it applies to the problem of disruptive behavior in the classroom:

> I never try to hold a conference with a child who has had a conflict with an adult unless the adult is present. There are two reasons for this. First, I don't think you can solve the problem without the person being there. Second, when the teacher is there, it's an inservice session for that teacher on problem solving. The focus is on building relationships. Kids can learn to build relationships with teachers and teachers with kids if they solve problems together and are open with each other and don't behave impulsively. For example, a teacher grabbed a kid who appeared to be misbehaving. The kid said, "You grabbed me and you didn't even ask me first." And the teacher said, "Yes, you're right. I had other problems on my mind. I had no right to do that." And we do the same thing with parents when they have problems with teachers over their youngsters. We inservice the parents.

So, once more, Joan was always teaching. Curiously, though, it seemed that the people with whom she worked in problem situations felt less that they had been "taught" and more that they had "learned." At least part of the reason for this impression is that Joan saw situations as opportunities for her own learning—and that attitude gets conveyed to others—as well as opportunities for her to teach others. Her enthusiasm and energy seemed to spread to others who worked with her. Probably one of the primary reasons for this was that, as noted earlier, her behavior communicated centrally that "First I, too, am a teacher."

Some effects of Joan's ideas, energy, and enthusiasm seem to have occurred in her school in an unplanned-for way. Recall that her initial observation of the climate of the school was that it was punitive and negatively reinforcing. Further, there was little communication among the staff. Her first goal as principal was, as she put it, to work on "plain old human relations" so that the degenerative cycle in which the system was caught could be reversed; so that the total school community—teachers, students, and parents—could start to experience success instead of failure; so that school could be a place where something good happened and not merely a place where people—particularly teachers and students—tested their survival and endurance capabilities. Within the context of this chapter, some bits and pieces of evidence suggest the reversal had taken place. For one thing, the disciplinary problems:

> The first year I walked in, the first month, in September, I had 127 kids referred to me for discipline problems—in my office. This last September (the third of her tenure as principal) there was a total of nine for the whole month.

And, with regard to changing from a negative to a positive reinforcement model:

> Teachers and kids come down to the office now with notes that say "Yippee" or "Hooray" or "Good News" for example when a particular problem kid has passed a grade level test. Or, I'll get a note saying, "Come to my classroom. We've got a great thing going!" Or, they're free to say, "Hey, I tried something in my room today and it didn't work. Do you have any ideas?" And, they're also quick to say, "Look, I've got a really tough home visit today and I don't think I can make it alone. Is there anyone who can go with me?"

Things changed, indeed, in Joan's school, though she would be the first to say it was only on the surface, or perhaps just beneath the surface, that scratches had been made. The system that was once closed seemed now to be quite open. Teachers became unafraid to talk with each other and with the principal, about their successes as well as their failures and their anxieties. What had been a distasteful social climate became quite tasteful.

The ingredients of the change recipe? Some are matters of personal style, including a bit of charisma. Some seem to be matters of intuitive organizational pragmatism for, as was indicated earlier, Joan was fairly atheoretical in any deep academic way. On the style side of the coin there was her energy, enthusiasm, problem-solving skill, optimism, sense of fairness, and sense of what is needed in a wholesome learning environment. Relative to her pragmatic side, what came across strongest was her intuition to reach out to the affected parties and their problem and to involve them in its solution. There was another facet of Joan's way of working with her faculty, however, that caused learning and change to take place. It amounts to a creed, spelled out best in her own words: "I will not do it for you but I will help you learn it."

As one listened, it was almost as if the words were tattooed on her forehead. She learned it from her primary role model, her former principal.

> The *one* thing he taught me was that you don't do things for other people. You sit there and help them learn. That's what he did with me. He would sit in my kitchen, if need be, until two o'clock in the morning to help me learn. If I had a program idea that needed money, he'd say, "I'll show you how to go about raising the money, but I won't do it for you."
>
> But when I became principal, knowing I wouldn't "do it for them," for a while it was awful. I would confront a teacher about a problem and say, "Could it possibly be your problem?" I'd watch the teacher get very offended, and instead of dealing on the factual level, deal on the emotional level and say things which were very cutting and hurt. I would sit there and grind my teeth so as not to get caught in the game that they were always losing with the kids. But it hurt and after the teacher left I cried. I cried a lot that first year.

Trying to do what Joan was doing takes its toll on a person. If a school principal chooses to embark on a design to change a school in ways that matter, the energy, enthusiasm, and skills of the principal need to be combined with a certain toughness—a toughness that lets a person take the hurt, but not engage in hurting back, a tactic that would be self-defeating. Joan's thinking seemed to go like this: "In this confrontation, what is happening could develop into the same kind of situation that occurs between the teacher and the kids—an emotional win-lose game where, ultimately, the issue is, who has the most power? I don't want that to happen here, I don't want to win. I want the teacher to learn." Ergo, Joan refused to play the game, did not respond in kind, waited, perhaps cried a lot, but things did start to change.

The change that Joan started to induce can be described in organizational terms. Briefly, it was an effort—and a conscious one though it did not appear so—to move the locus of decision making in the school from the principal to the teachers, on all matters in which they played a central role. Included were such things as curriculum, instruction, and discipline. Joan's role was that of initiator and problem-solving organizer and consultant. She refused to play the role of problem solver *qua* problem solver. She also had a built-in support system, a small cadre of teachers (one of whom became her assistant principal) that moved with her from her former school when she assumed the principalship. They understood and supported her goals and value system. They were able to communicate together quite openly and thus served as her alter egos. That is, they helped her maintain contact with realities of a situation that might escape her, particularly when she wanted things to happen quickly. For example, Joan's first encounter with her new faculty as a group was a shocker for her:

> From the first words out of my mouth I knew that they didn't even understand the difference between cognitive and affective. I was appalled when I first talked to the staff, used those words, and looked across a room of blank stares. I knew I had to back up twenty paces. Mary and Susie got hold of me and said, "Look, here is what we see and we just want you to think about this. You can't move too fast because if you do you'll lose people. They'll become dissatisfied and frustrated. You won't even get a chance to test out your ideas." It was good for me to hear that and I asked them to pull in the reins whenever they saw we were running too fast.

Besides the potential for "losing" people because of her need for quick action, there were two other unintended consequences of her high energy and pace. One was the possibility of her staff becoming exhausted, "burned out." The other, as exhaustion set in (as it did from time to time), was their becoming involved in a curious type of self-induced organizational trap.

> It's hard. We get one hour a week for team planning. Teachers are with me every single week night. And anywhere from ten to seventeen of them are there on weekends. I'm concerned about getting burned out and I'm concerned about their getting burned out. I've seen it happen and watched teachers fall by the wayside. We're trying to find ways of dealing with that.

And, her description of the trap:

> All of a sudden, in February, I found I had to get out of there for a while. I was getting into a bind, falling into a trap. What it was, was that the teachers were getting exhausted and fell back into their old ways of sending problems down to me. And I was exhausted, too, so without even knowing it I started to deal with the problems myself. I was not liking myself and I wasn't helping the teacher because the problems kept recurring. It was a bad scene.

Fortunately, this situation occurred before a vacation, but the vacation was only part of the solution. What Joan did was to ask the staff if they'd mind coming to an unscheduled staff meeting. At that meeting she leveled with them about her own feelings of exhaustion and what she saw as the consequences, the kind of trap she had fallen into and what it all meant for the school. The staff responded in kind and talked about how low they felt and the reasons they felt that way. This sharing had an important impact, because it removed the temporary feelings of isolation from each other that faculty members had developed. As the meeting progressed, a sense of relief became apparent, and tension was reduced as the total staff came to realize that it was "all right" to be temporarily burned out, to be angry, and to wish desperately for a vacation.

Joan's problem-solving style was evident, once more, though perhaps in a subtle way, in this situation. The dominant strategy of most administrators faced with similar circumstances would probably be to ignore it or to be paternalistically exhortive to the faculty: "I know you're all tired but give it all you've got. Vacation is next week." Joan acted differently. She disclosed her own feelings because they were facts that were important to the situation. By that disclosure she enabled her staff to do the same and, in the process, get more facts. But most important, this mutual revealing of self enabled all involved to build a more solid sense of community. The difference in feeling tone after the vacation, in Joan's words, "was incredible." People knew that they had been understood as people.

We sensed through listening to Joan and writing about her that she was totally immersed in her school. As she talked, we felt physically transported from the place of our interview (a university office) to the school building, such was the involvement we felt with her teachers, students, and parents. The contagious effect of the behavior that was described earlier spread to us as well. Joan's job as principal, however, like all principalships, required interaction with certain relevant others within the school system—the Central Office, other principals, and the cadre of curriculum specialists and supervisors employed by the Central Office.

The impression usually gained from talking with most school principals is that the best strategy to employ in relating with the Central Office is to maintain distance. The existence of the Central Office cannot be denied, of course, but principals seem to see it, at best, as a rather bumbling bureaucracy. Each will acknowledge that there are some individuals in the bureaucracy who can and desire to be helpful, but that, by and large, it is best to avoid dealing with that part of the system whenever possible. One only gets bogged down in unmanageable policy or political constraints. Joan saw this side of her relationship with the Central Office:

Well, a policy decision will come out. You know that it's something that's absolutely ridiculous. We have to decide, do we ignore the policy and go on doing what we've been doing or pay attention to it? Probably we'll ignore it because nine times out of ten they are not going to know you're ignoring it anyway.

Joan dealt with the Central Office by playing the role of practicing bureaucrat herself. She was aware of how the system worked, seemed to feel that the bulk of policy decisions that emanated from "downtown" were either unworkable or made no sense in the day-to-day operation of the school, and was keen enough to sense the one-time-in-ten that she had to pay attention.

There was another side to Joan's dealings with Central Office, though, that seemed to reflect her reaching-out, energetic problem-solving style of running her school. The following rather lengthy comment tells an interesting story:

The first year they were extremely helpful to me. I used them for transportation purposes, for gathering information about policy that was unclear to me. I used them to find out how to get around policy. Amazingly, there are people down there who tell you how to circumvent policy without getting hurt. I spent a lot of time meeting with secretaries, particularly the secretary of the supply person because I wanted to know who I was talking to on the phone when I needed something. I spent half a day at the maintenance shop getting to know the carpenters and painters. Mainly, I wanted to become familiar with people, finding out what they could do because you never find it out from the manual. This has all paid off.

The second year I learned whom to trust and whom not to trust. The first year that didn't seem to matter, getting clarification and getting to know people was more important.

Everyone is willing to help a new administrator if you just say, "Look, I'm new, I need your help." It works. It's beautiful. and I wasn't just playing at it. I was kind of helpless in terms of not knowing how things worked.

About the trusting. It had to do mainly with which people passed along different kinds of information and to whom. For instance, I'd go down there and say that I really would like to solve a problem with James Jones and ask how I should go about that. Before I ever had a chance to find out how I should go about it, James Jones knew I had a problem. I didn't like that. I also found out whom I could count on to be "too busy," and who would see me when I needed help. It hasn't happened too often but enough so that I know what to do.

Like almost everything else related to being a principal, then, for Joan the circumstances of having to establish relationships with Central Office constituted a problem to be solved. And she employed her typical proactive style, once more, which seemed to go something like this: First, don't wait for the people to come to you. Go to them, reach out, as she did with the parent community and teachers of her school. Second, get the facts and get as many different kinds of facts as you can. Go to the people and ask them—and don't be afraid to tell them that you don't know how everything works. Third, become familiar with people as people so that you can relate to them not just as principal to carpenter, for example, but as Joan to John.

But Joan was not naive. Much as it seems that her preferred style of relating to people was one of openness, it became clear through her dealings with Central Office that it was unwise to be as open as she wished if she wanted to maintain control over her prerogatives. She had to become circumspect about her openness, to strategize a bit about whom to talk to and about what. One must play the bureaucratic game, at times. She disliked doing this but her contacts "downtown" were infrequent enough so that "playing the game" did not become a major problem. In any event, the battles that would have to be fought to create a more open system in the Central Office would be too costly for her, relative to any payoff she might receive. It seemed sufficient for her to be aware of the politics involved, thus leaving her free to pick and choose her avenues of entry into the system.

If the basis of mutually satisfying and productive collegial relations is a giving and receiving of help and counsel, from Joan's point of view her relationships with her peers—other principals—seemed to be out of kilter.

That is, it appeared that she gave a great deal more than she got. Things were out of balance.

> I have contact with certain people for certain things. When someone has a problem they come to me. For example, if they're developing a new report card. Well, we already did ours. They'll say, "Hey, can I have a copy of your report card?" Okay. Or, "I understand you are working in teams. Could we come over and see your teams?"
>
> But if I want to get ideas or talk about roles or other things, administrators always seem to be so overinvolved and they tell you they don't have time.

The curious thing was that, although Joan apparently did have the time to give to other administrators, even though she was incredibly busy, she believed that most of her colleagues had no time to give in return. She believed that, indeed, they were as overwhelmed with work as they said they were, but for reasons of their own making. Her notion about this is a dreary indictment of the leadership and management in the schools with which she was familiar.

> I think principals have done themselves in. They don't know if they have any power, don't feel they have a lot of administrative power, and yet feel the responsibility is overwhelming. So, they can never get out of the building because in order to feel good, in order not to be feeling guilty, they feel they've got to be running the whole show.
>
> And, they do it. No wonder they don't have the time. For example, if the teacher's contract says that teachers can't do hall duty. So the principals say, "I'll have to do it. Well, I don't do hall duty and I don't intend to unless everybody does it.
>
> Another thing. I don't think principals are very good problem solvers. Maybe they solve problems for teachers by taking on the problems themselves, but that doesn't help them as principals. It just takes more of their time and makes the teachers more dependent on them. The whole point is that they take on so many kinds of responsibilities that are not theirs, from hall duty to solving teachers' problems. No wonder they don't have time!

These comments relate directly to those Joan made earlier about getting herself in a trap of her own making. Her point was that it was precisely at the time that she started to take on role responsibilities that were outside of her definition of what she should be doing that the job became overwhelming. Further, she saw most principals doing this and almost guaranteeing for themselves an extremely burdensome situation. Put another way, Joan saw most principals behaving as if their schools were Catch 22 situations—no alternatives, no exits. But the life of a school principal need not be that way if he/she seeks alternatives and has some problem-solving skills, according to Joan.

If Joan seemed less excited about her relationships with other principals, the opposite was true for what transpired between her, her school, and the cadre of curriculum specialists/supervisors based in Central Office. This is a bit unusual; most principals and teachers prefer to hold these people at a distance, perceiving them as harmless at best, insensitive evaluators or spies at worst. Joan described the situation at her school in the following way:

> First, I know that we couldn't do all that needed to be done by ourselves. The outside people could be helpful to us if we knew exactly what we wanted. If we were straight on this then they would be responding to us and not us to them. If they brought us stuff we didn't want, we realized we hadn't communicated well.
>
> Supervisors, by the way, are very seldom asked to come in and support schools. And they are very, very eager to do that if you are inviting them in to participate. It's just incredible. They are so eager to come to our school, and that's because everybody wants them there. The teachers don't see them coming in to evaluate. Sometimes I would like them to because there are times when we get so close to a problem we don't know when we're making big, gross mistakes.

Elements of Joan's organizing style and outlook became clear again, almost sentence by sentence. First she had to sense the need, recognize that there is a problem. Then she tried to get the facts, which led her to know what kind of help she needed. Then she reached out for help and people responded because they knew that they, their resources, and their involvement were wanted and that no political game was being played. This process involved a certain feeling of fallibility, illustrated by "If they brought us stuff we didn't want, we realized we hadn't communicated well." The sense of fallibility is also illustrated in Joan's comments about wishing the outside people would, at times, evaluate. That they don't evaluate may be reflective of their feeling that if they did they would no longer be welcome.

There was another part of Joan's world view as a principal that leaped out at us as we analyzed her comments about outside supervisors. It seemed to account for a good bit of her success. It is implicit in the number of times she used the word "we" or "us" when she referred to the school. In the first paragraph quoted above, for example, these words accounted for 20 percent of all the words she used. The point is, of course, that they were not used in an editorial sense. On the contrary, they communicated a sense of community and involvement. When Joan said "we" or "us" she appeared to mean that, precisely.

Finally, and in a somewhat different vein, with regard to the relationship of supervisors to schools in general, Joan may have put her finger at the crux of the problem. The outcome of supervision in the schools is not an overwhelming success story; far from it (Blumberg, 1974). Mostly, it seems, the mythology associated with supervision suggests that supervisors are not very helpful, and that the best strategy for teachers to employ with supervisors is one of avoidance. But many supervisors, according to Joan, have a lot to offer, and the best strategy then becomes to get them to respond to your needs, which, apparently, they are eager to do. The way to develop this mode of response, thus eliminating a potential defense-inducing situation, is to know what is needed and then reach out for help. We doubt that

Joan conceptualized the relationship this way, but that's the path in which her intuition led her.

It's difficult to know where to end this discussion of Joan, or if indeed there can be an end. The infectious enthusiasm, the sharpness of insight, the huge amount of energy that she communicated all seemed to lead us on. It is like trying to find an end to perpetual motion. There's much about her as a principal and as a person that we've touched on only lightly, and much that we've not mentioned at all. For example, we did not mention that she made sure she was in at least two classrooms every day to observe what was going on. She made a dozen or so home visits every week. Where did she get the time to do these things? Aside from commitment and desire, it seems clear that time becomes available because of her concept of her self as principal. We paraphrase her sense of her role in the following way: "I am an organizer of problem solving. I want to help people learn how to solve the problems that confront them. I will not solve their problems for them, because when I do that, I treat them like children, not adults."

Perhaps, then, this last comment provides the key to it all. Implicit in it is the notion of an unfinished task; a task, in fact, that will never be finished because learning adult behavior is not a finite thing but an open-ended spiral of ability to confront and deal with human problems that become increasingly more complex. And that seems to be what Joan, The Organizer, is after—for herself and for others.

3

The Value-Based Juggler: Up Front with Kids' Interests

George, in his early thirties, was principal of an eight-hundred-student high school in a small town in a rural area. He had been principal there for about three years. He had been assistant principal, charged mostly with the discipline function. In addition to his disciplinary duties, he shared a great deal of responsibility for inducing a change in the school that moved it from a rather traditional program to a flexible-modular schedule mode. He believed this experience had a great impact on his learning and development. His principal became a valued mentor and the experience itself was a "hands-on" learning opportunity for him to translate theory into practice. In addition to his full-time job he was also a doctoral candidate in educational administration.

In the course of our interview with George, one thing fairly leaped out at us. It was the continual and strong reference that he made to his value system—would it be good for kids?—when it came to making decisions affecting both the substantive education of youngsters, the quality of their life in the school, and the quality of his relationships with the faculty. When George saw that an issue under discussion was related to his values—as different from one that required simply collaborative effort to resolve a problem in which his central values were not at stake—adherence to these values became the point from which he would rarely give ground. He held this position even though it meant, in some cases, the violation of policy or incurring the ire of his superintendent. He characterized his guide for making decisions by saying, "I think a lot of it comes from right inside." And "from right inside" applies to matters as *seemingly* mundane to the outsider as whether or not to hold graduation exercises out-of-doors and risk the threat of rain, to the question of how and under what conditions to integrate special education students into regular classrooms, to dealing with bomb scares. For example, George said:

> If I get an idea in my head, right or wrong, I tend to pursue it and try to convince other people or groups regardless of whether or not it's the faculty, parents, kids, central administration, or what have you. Let me give you an example. It's been

25

my worst experience *ever* as a principal. Graduation has traditionally been held outside on the football field which is a beautiful setting. (The school is nestled in a scenic valley.) Four out of the last seven years have been rained out. A year ago I attempted to switch graduation indoors. The students said "NO!" and against my better judgment I gave in. Not only were we rained out, we were flooded out. We regrouped two hours later in the gymnasium, and then that area of the building was hit by lightning. It was a bad scene.

My judgment on it was that *that* was not the way to conclude thirteen years of education. If graduation is at all meaningful, then let's do it right. The following year I made a dictum—come hell or high water it's going to be inside. I told the superintendent and the president of the Board of Education. "Next year you are going to have to get another principal if you want to hold it outside. It's going to be indoors." And they both concurred.

It's important to note that the central issue was not that the rain and lightning created a mess. Rather, the upset in the physical setting was terribly disruptive, as well, to George's values. Recall the comments above, ". . . that was not the way to conclude thirteen years of education" and "If graduation is at all meaningful, let's do it right."

George's value system came into play with a vengeance when he perceived bureaucratic regulations (by inference, irrationality) going counter to the educational philosophy of his school. A case in point occurred when a county-wide educational service organization wanted to change the basis upon which special education students from George's school would be admitted to its program. George's school had long been committed to total mainstreaming. The service organization wanted to screen youngsters because their teachers "did not want these retards in their classes." At issue was whether or not George would go along with this new procedure, which he learned of upon returning to his office late one afternoon. He didn't. "I went right to the superintendent and met, until 5:30 that day, with the superintendent, the special ed teacher, and the director of special ed. We changed the procedure for screening. If they hadn't, I would have put the kids on the bus that next Monday morning and let *them* send the kids back to our school."

It would be wrong to gain the impression from these two examples that George was an administrative troublemaker who thrived on seeking out opportunities to fight the authority structure. Nor was he a person who seemed to need to assert his power in a startling manner. Quite the contrary, he came across in a very soft, often quizzical way, giving the impression that as he takes positions he is also mulling over alternatives. He juggles things around, balancing values against each other. But once he has taken a stand, it seems clear that he is ready to deal with the consequences. "What's right is right, particularly when the kids are involved." Put another way, when his primary reference group, that is, the group that will be most directly affected by his decisions, is the student group in his school, George's administrative stance appeared to be a strong one buttressed by his internal value system, or, as he put it, "some general statements about education." Indeed, we've come to think of George as "The Value-Based Juggler."

"Some general statements (values) about education" also served George well as he played the educational leader role in his school, as distinguished from the managerial role. For example, he was opposed to grouping or tracking students on any basis that would separate them and thus create an intellectual elite. When he saw a department or faculty member making such a move, "I move in the opposite direction." George, then, was clearly different from the stereotypical school principal concerned with routine administrative matters. His fingers seemed to be on the pulse of all areas of school life. But his activity didn't stop with pulse-taking. The latter seemed to be a prelude to action, particularly if he didn't like the rhythm or direction of things.

What made George different? Two factors appear prominent. First, he had, as we all had, some important role models in life. Perhaps the most important was the principal under whom George assumed his first administrative position. His style was very different from George's. Whereas George came across in a soft and rather quizzical way, his former principal was seen by many people as brash, dominating, and exceedingly active. They were as unlike as apples and oranges. It seems that George, probably in an unplanned-for way, abstracted from his mentor's world view those things that could conveniently and comfortably fit into his own internal system. Thus, there was simply no way that he could emulate the brashness or the aggressiveness of his model's behavior. In current parlance, he would have "bombed out." What happened is best described in George's own words:

> When I came on board with Frank, theory to me was highly impractical. (My whole master's program was a series of seminars with experienced administrators—real old-time superintendents. And they were not theory oriented. But it was a good experience.) I was a person who was interested in the practical aspects of running a school; implementation, getting the job done, and to hell with theory. Frank and I argued about that for a couple of years, until we implemented flexible modular scheduling, and I saw how theory was like being there at the birth of the earth. I mean, you saw things happen the way theory predicted they would. And so I began to get highly interested in what moves people in organizations, what are their needs, how do you meet their needs, and how do they vary from time to time.

George's experience with his principal was a critical turning point in his professional life. It marked a change from his initial conception of the principal's role, which was "How to Keep the Machine Running Smoothly," to one of a school as an organic system that made some sense intellectually. This latter gave George a sense of power to influence things. Rather than conceive of himself as concerned mainly with, and sometimes overwhelmed by, administrative routine (though he acknowledged that a good bit of the job was just that), he began to see that by understanding the nature of the school, of teachers and students, and of the dynamic interaction among them, he could make things happen in ways he had not thought of previously.

The most telling sentence of his comment is, "I saw how theory was like being there at the birth of the earth." The comment seems to fit in with his basic, pervading concern with values. It is not so much that the theory is value oriented, although it may be, as much as it is that sound theory (if there is such a thing in education) can provide an anchoring point for action, as much as values can. Thus, in George's case, it seems the dynamics of his concern with values and with theory as action take-off points appear complementary. Each provides him with a solid reference system for his behavior and decisions.

It would be a mistake, of course, to make the interpretation from the preceding discussion that George's only guides for action stemmed from his internal system. Quite the contrary, he related to, used, and seemed to be continually aware of the variety of reference groups with which he was in almost daily contact. In a general way, his strategy for dealing with these groups is summed up in the following comment:

> One of the things I learned from my former principal is that I put the knife in the ground and see which way the herd is running. Then I either build a stone wall or a bridge depending on which way I want them to go. But first I get the rumblings from different people—teachers, faculty, students. When they come from all around me, I usually try to find out what is the central direction from which they come. This searching out gives me more time to plan rather than just react impulsively.

This statement is a revealing one. First, it should leave no doubt in the reader's mind concerning who he sees as controlling the school. It is George! And this appears so whether the issues are clear-cut or vague. In the former case his actions were quick, i.e., the graduation problem or that concerning the special education students. Where the situation was not so clear his actions were quick and firm, but they were of a different nature. They were process, not content, oriented. Thus, he "puts the knife in the ground" not with the view of being a spectator to whichever direction the "stampede" may take, but to enable him to control things in the school.

The statement is also illuminating in another way. His use of the "herd" and "putting the knife in the ground" metaphor presents an interesting speculation about the way he, and perhaps many principals, see events in their schools. That is, it seems likely that, particularly in high schools, things may start to happen that have herdlike and stampedelike characteristics. Clearly, when circumstances such as these start to occur they tend not to be initially amenable to rational discussion. To use another metaphor, what George seemed to be saying was that, when a flood is imminent, one must gauge its direction, crest, and the weak points in the dike, lest sandbags are put in inappropriate, useless places. It would be a mistake to think that George conceived of all the human problems and movements in his school as having an undifferentiated, stampeding, herdlike quality. But, probably, sometimes they did.

In a way that is not conceptually neat and tidy, George conceived of his role as split between that of the educational leader and the organizational maintenance man. These two roles carry with them a different set of behavioral demands, according to George. To be an influential educational leader in his school, to effect change, to move his teachers to grow and become better, the requirements are to be a salesman who knows how to make trade-offs. In order to get something you have to give something. To maintain the organization in a stable condition, it's necessary to perform a balancing act between and among the various competing groups pressuring the principal to support their primary interests.

An interesting and realistic picture was given by George relative to the demands placed on him as a principal (possibly most principals) to be the educational leader of his school. He said:

> I think in the area of leadership, real leadership, the principal has a free hand. For example, nobody's pushing the principal to a new curriculum, nobody's pushing for a new schedule or a new program for students. There is no push for new budgeting techniques. You don't have a parent group come in and say, "Hey, let's get X program started at the high school." The faculty doesn't push you either. Even if one department has an out-of-proportion slice of the budget, there's very little pressure to change it from other departments because they see it as just too big a task.[1]

The case seems to be, then, not so much that there is a leadership vacuum as there is a lack of any strong concern by potential pressure groups that acts of leadership—suggesting new structures, proposing new programs, and so forth—take place. From George's perspective, then, his job would be secure and the school community would offer him positive feedback if he did little else but focus his energies on maintaining the school in a stable condition, handling discipline problems evenly, and keeping the faculty happy. In other words, keep the peace! There is little pressure to lead.

There is, in fact, a lot of peace keeping to be done if that notion is interpreted as paying attention to keeping the school routine well oiled, so that the parts will mesh with as little friction as possible. And to do this, as was noted above, required that George perform a balancing act between competing forces, a different role for the principal from when he is interested in promoting an innovative educational idea where he sees himself as a salesman whose sales ability stems from his power to make trade-offs. Operationally, there are differences between the kinds of behaviors required. When George wanted to get a teacher or a department to try something new, or to think through the efficacy of a particular program, for example— anything that deviates from the normal faculty function of teaching *qua*

---

1. It's important to remember that George was talking about *his* situation. Although we are aware of some circumstances where building principals do receive pressure from the superintendent or from parents, but rarely from teachers, to develop new programs, our experience suggests that the lack of such pressure is much more the rule rather than the exception.

teaching—he must offer something in return. Sometimes it might involve an extra period of planning. In large matters, it might mean giving the teacher as much as four weeks of summer work for which the teacher would be paid. In other words, it seems clear that he perceived the success of his leadership initiatives as being in large measure related to the extent to which he had access to and control of the organizational reward system.

The situation relative to the demands placed on George for organizational maintenance is much different—up to a point. That is, as long as the school is running smoothly, as long as the scene is relatively peaceful, no specific demands were made. It is only when something disruptive occurs, stemming either from the faculty or the students, that the pressure comes on. The force of this pressure, of course, depends on the extent and longevity of the disruption. And it is in these situations that he goes into his balancing act.

This reference to the balancing act is not an unreasonable one, raising as it does the image of a tightrope walker needing to counteract the forces of gravity on either side of the wire. This image particularly fits the discipline situation in the school. George steps off a stable platform and starts to walk the rope in September. The close of school in June represents the stable platform at the other end of the rope. As he walks the rope, trying to keep his balance and thus maintaining stability in the school, two major "pulls of gravity" are tugging at him to fall to one side or the other. One pull is the pressure from the faculty not to loosen up on controlling students through disciplinary actions—the one thing, according to George, that would really irritate the faculty. The other major pull, naturally enough, comes from the students; to tighten things up would really irritate them. To continue the image, it's probably hardest to maintain the balance when the rope is slackest, at about the middle—during what principals refer to as the February slump.

There are, of course, times when George has to engage in short-term balancing while in the midst of selling and trading off. For example:

> We have a college English program in lieu of senior English. It was taught by teachers from Jones College when it was first established. We would get sixty kids signed up for it, send them to class, and the next day thirty would come in and drop it. What was happening was that the faculty was killing the idea, because we were using teachers from Jones, thus implying that our own teachers weren't good enough. To counter this, our teachers would say, by one means or another, to our students, "You're a good academic student. You're going to get a lot more from my senior English class than you'll get from Jones College."
>
> What we did was to go to Project Upward at Calhoun University. They trained our own teachers who also received inservice credit for the summer training. Our faculty then did the teaching and our kids still got a college level freshman English course. Our teachers were no longer under the threat of not being seen as smart enough, and they also received status in our own organization.

In terms of the trade-off/balancing act notion, then, here is what appears to have happened. A new program had been established which, by its very being, and despite the fact that it made no demands on the faculty, had started to throw the system—stable faculty-school relationships—out of kilter. The system was being disrupted, and it appeared that the fall-out of the disruption would signal the demise of the program. This was the prospect, even though all parties involved agreed that an advanced English program for superior students was a good idea. The problem was to bring the system back into balance and to maintain the *concept* of the program at the same time, which was done by trading off. In effect, what was communicated to the teacher was, "If we invest in Project Upward and all that it entails, including your time, will you support the program?" The answer obviously was in the affirmative. Trading off, in order to keep the system in balance, paid off.

It seems clear that, for the most part, George was and primarily conceived of himself to be in the business of dealing with groups that have different needs and points of view. Whether by compromise or by rebuff, George wanted to accomplish at least three things: (1) to maintain the system in balance; (2) to create new opportunities for learning for youngsters; and (3) to enhance his own self-image as a value-oriented administrator whose primary concern is students.

The remainder of this chapter offers a glimpse into the perceptions that George had of the groups with which he had to work, which affected his decision making, or which affected his behavior in more subtle, sometimes hardly perceptible ways.

Through the course of our interview with George he identified nine different groups that, in one fashion or another, he related to as he administered his school. It's important to note, though, that his initial response to questions about his reference groups indicated that he had no formal way of thinking about and dealing with them. Indeed, the idea of having a role set (Katz and Kahn, 1966) composed of a variety of disparate groups sometimes with conflicting interests, was not something that was central to his understanding of his role performance. This is not to say that he didn't see himself dealing with different groups. Indeed, he did. But, at the time of our interview, the formal notion of a reference group theory of administrative behavior was not at all focal to George's thinking, even though it seemed clear that he operated on the basis of just that sort of theory.

George, either through his own initiation or as a result of our questions referred to nine different groups: (1) faculty and department heads; (2) parents; (3) students; (4) the "C" students; (5) close colleagues; (6) the community; (7) the Central Office; (8) other administrators in his system, and (9) the School Board.

The faculty group, of course, was most salient in George's thinking, but in an interesting sort of way. The faculty is a group to be served, but more important, to be used. Used in the sense that he understands that there will be no movement in the school, no program development, no innovation unless the faculty is supportive, which is not a new idea. However, George's clear articulation leads him to a basic strategy for working with the faculty: the power of the faculty to block or support the implementation of new ideas requires him to maintain the faculty in a state of receptiveness. This strategy gets translated, behaviorally, into a nonunilateral conflict-resolving stance. This stance calls for openness and a careful weighing of the costs and benefits of each particular issue so that the stability of relationships can be maintained and so that the faculty has an image of George as a fair-minded administrator. But he did not back off from making decisions that might upset the faculty. Indeed, he was not the faculty's pawn, but a question seemed to have been in the back of his mind: "Is it worth it?" A case in point:

> I remember sitting down with the assistant principal to talk about a specific kid. He was bad news. Nothing we had done with him—befriended him, nurtured him—had worked. The question was whether or not we were going to keep him in school or move him out of school. We made the decision to squash him for the betterment of the system. In other words, we decided that the cost of keeping him in school, in terms of faculty reaction, would be too great.

Don't get the impression from this illustration that George's main concern with the faculty was conflict avoidance. Quite the contrary, he seemed not to shy away from conflict, nor to be unable to make decisions contrary to faculty wishes. The essential question, to repeat, is "Is it worth it?" both in terms of short- and long-term fall-out on faculty-administrator relationships. Put another way, the question is, "How big a withdrawal from the faculty 'goodwill account' will result from a decision that runs counter to the direction the faculty desires?"

George was also aware of and used the power structure of the faculty—the department heads—in a rather straightforward manner in matters of personnel problems or program concerns. "If you want to get something going in your school, you want to get people involved who are part of the power structure. If you had a committee functioning without any department chairman on it, they would find it a hard row to hoe." Not many principals would argue with the "rule of thumb" that's implicit in this statement—involve the people who will be concerned with the decision and who have the power and influence to implement it. George, in this respect, seemed not to be out of the ordinary. But what may have been at odds with most administrative practice was his position on termination:

> If you are firing a teacher, there's a whole bunch of groundwork that has to be laid (so far there is nothing unusual in this). The department chairman, the teacher in question, and the *other people on the team.*

The parenthetical expression and the italics in the above comment are ours and need explanation. Indeed, any school administrator will support the proposition of needing to lay a lot of groundwork if a teacher is to be fired, particularly in this day of increasing militancy of teachers' unions. As ironclad a case as possible needs to be made, even in situations involving nontenured teachers. What caught our eyes, however, were the words we italicized—*other people on the team.* At issue here is the concept of an open, disclosing organization (Steele, 1975). In his delightfully pointed book *The Open Organization,* Steele raises time and again the problems that are generated by organizations whose norms are generally of a nondisclosing, play-it-close-to-the-vest nature. Such organizations (and unfortunately this probably includes the majority of schools) typically develop taboos against discussion of certain types of problems. Usually among these tabooed discussion topics, at least in the formal systems, are problems related to career decisions about personnel in the organization—promotions, hiring, firing, and so forth. Most discussions having to do with such things are carried on in secret with only a few being privy to them. One of the results of taboos such as these is that an inordinate amount of emotional, nontask-oriented behavior is channeled into maintaining them.

Back, then, to George. As he thought about such a critical personnel decision as terminating a teacher, it seems that part of the strategy for laying the necessary groundwork also meant his breaking the taboo involved. But he probably didn't have breaking the taboo on his mind, nor did he even faintly realize that this particular way of working helps to break down unproductive taboos. But, it is safe to predict that in George's school it was possible to hold public (or quasi-public) discussions on topics considered *verboten* in others.

The theme of George's concern for students as students, their welfare and learning, has been communicated on several occasions in the previous pages. We find nothing unusual in that and, indeed, would have been surprised had it not been present. Two more specific comments, however, clarify his concerns about and relationships with students. The first was given during the discussion of the way his value system, beliefs, and ideals affected the decisions he made and directions he took. In response to questions about the origin of some of his educational values, George said:

> If you want to, you can trace it all the way back to concern for the "C" student in high school.

The "C" students, the "average" ones, the "silent majority"—in a way the great mass of students that he saw as neglected, even though that neglect may be benign, appears to have been salient in George's mind. There are programs for the educationally handicapped and, sometimes, advantage piled on advantage for the educationally gifted (the rich get richer). But no one, or so it seemed to George, pays much attention to students who are just "average." "What a contradiction we are faced with," George seemed to be saying. "On the one hand, the 'C' student body is huge, the most potentially powerful group of students in the schools. On the other hand, we ignore them, for the most part, and simply assume the system will take care of them. They will put in their time, leave, and the school will probably have had little effect on them." George wanted to change this and many of his decisions had that "average" student as a reference point.

The second student condition to which he responded had little to do with the academic side of school. This condition is apt to occur when students are agitated and:

> When they are organized. When they have power. When they are going to be sitting up on that hill across from the school if you don't do something.

George, then, was not an unrealistic educational reformer. Although his concern for high quality learning opportunities is a thread that ran continually through our discussion, he was also fully aware that the needs of the adolescent culture often run contrary to those of the adult culture. Further, there is always a possibility that this frequently covert and passive conflict may quickly turn overt and active, a situation he wished to avoid or at least channel productively. He seemed to have his communications networks open, and was rarely caught by surprise by student action. He was not beleaguered by students; rather, he seemed to acknowledge that there was always the possibility that he would be, so he stayed on top of things in order to forestall that possibility's becoming a reality.

In George's perceptions of and relationships to parents, he used them as a source of both passive and active support. By passive support, he meant working and communicating with the parent group so that their reaction to change, curriculum innovation, in particular, is minimally resistant and, hopefully, very supportive. He clearly did not use or intend to use parents as a source of new ideas, and his perceptions were that they don't want to be used that way.

George sought out the active support and problem-solving skills of parents on issues that may or may not be related to curriculum. The drug problem, for example:

> The parents did a fantastic job in helping out on the drug policy. We had no policy on drugs and one of the big issues was the search and seizure of drugs that students might have on them in school and in their cars in the parking lot. It was a touchy problem even though we were legally within our rights. We ended up with parents saying, "Yes, we want that" and so we were able to get signed releases from anybody who parked in the lot with no problem.

But George indicated that organizing the parents and getting them involved does present a problem, particularly in secondary schools. The PTA seemed ineffectual, as is commonly the case. Another feature complicating the situation was that George wanted to have students in on school committee action and he was hamstrung by the attitudes of some teachers who said, "When students walk into this committee, I walk out."

The answer to this situation was an end run. We formed a Parent-Teacher-Student Council, which was outside the formal organization of the school, but it wasn't a tea and cookies PTA. We met to discuss problems that involved parents, teachers, and students. Primarily, it was a sounding board for faculty meetings and department chairmen. It worked.

Despite what appeared to be the viability of this group, the impact of parents on the school, and on George, seemed to be a hit-or-miss phenomenon. It is difficult to get them involved because "they are satisfied as long as nothing bad seems to be happening to their kid or as long as the school isn't blowing up." How to get them involved? George's caveat was:

When there's a situation in which they have an interest, do something they don't like.

This is an interesting comment. It suggests that, at times, he played the role of Agent Provocateur—rather deliberately, it seems. But that role isn't recommended for a principal who feels insecure in his position and who, at times, does not enjoy a good fight.

Other reference groups seemed to minimally affect the world view that George had of himself as a school principal, or the nature of his decision making. He saw the Central Office primarily as a force to be coped with in order to insure freedom of action. On occasion he used the superintendent as an arbitrator of differences between himself and another administrator, but usually he preferred to keep the superintendent at a distance. As far as other administrators in his system were concerned, George gave them rather short shrift. Directly, and to the point:

I find it difficult to relate to other administrators, how they act or how they feel. I don't respect the way they operate. They are different than I; dull, dumb, noncreative, authoritarian, not open, mainly concerned with how to survive in the system. My concerns are decreasingly survival oriented and more and more directed at getting some personal satisfaction out of what I'm doing.

This facet of George's work life is clear. The price he paid for his attitude toward his colleagues may have caused him to be a bit lonely. However, it seems to have been a price he was willing to pay in order to avoid being bored and angry with associations he didn't desire.

George's relationship and feelings about the School Board were similarly direct and uneqivocal. Responding to a query about the importance of the School Board to his work, he said:

Not reallly, I'm long over being frightened of the Board. I think it's important they understand what we're doing, but that's about it.

In a fashion complementary to the earlier part of this chapter, on the way George's value system continually acted as his guide for decisions, George talked about his relationship with community groups. No Rotary Club for him! Because ". . . they didn't ask me until I became principal and I figured if they wanted a principal they could get somebody else." But:

> My personal involvement is with the ministerial association, which I find to be kind of powerful for me. I feel like God is living, you know, to have on your side. That is kind of Machiavellian, I guess, but that's the way it is.

And that is what George was all about!

4

The Authentic Helper: I Am Myself—and Comfortable about It

Ed, in his early thirties, was an elementary school principal. When we interviewed him he was in his third year as principal of his school, situated in an industrial suburb of a medium-sized city in Connecticut. We requested the interview because we had heard, of all things, that he was introducing Gestalt therapy techniques into an elementary school setting—unusual, to say the least. It is not that Ed was bent on turning his school into a mass, five-day-a-week therapy session. Nothing could be further from the point, for, as he indicated, his primary concerns were with the quality of the curriculum and instruction carried on, not therapy. But his therapeutic focus came out in a number of ways. For example, some of the goals of therapy (in this case, the Gestalt variety) are to enable people to become more aware of themselves as human beings, to be open to their own emotional awareness of self and others. This fit well into the way Ed conceived of and dealt with himself and others. For example, here is Ed's response to a question on how he played out his role:

> I guess, if anything, I don't perceive of myself as being in a role. I try to be as natural as possible, and natural means to me being as authentic as possible, or as genuine as I can be. It means being aware of what I'm feeling, and, if appropriate, letting people know in terms of both positive and negative responses. I really enjoy my humor. I use that a lot with children and teachers. I'm very comfortable with the warmth I possess and I will physically show warmth to children and teachers. I think that's very important. My primary identity is that of a human being who happens to be principal of a school.

The tone, then, is quickly set, and rather unequivocally at that. He rejected, first of all, the notion that, merely because he happened to be the person who had responsibility for the operation of a school, he should behave differently with people. The key concept that seemed to guide him in his behavior was authenticity, genuineness, and being comfortable with what he saw himself to be. This stems directly from the therapeutic milieu and, derivatively, from the human potential movement. It is unusual—in fact, Ed spoke of himself as an unusual principal—for a school principal to articulate this concept so clearly as a guiding principle. But principals are not a lower order of humanity. Rather, the notions of formal role, role preroga- tives, role expectations, and so forth, which seem to influence the behavior of most people, include principals. But not so with Ed, it appears. First and foremost he is a human being whose theory seemed to work, as he engaged with his own humanity and that of others in a genuine way; regardless of the position he holds, things fall into line in a productive fashion.

The notion of genuineness implies two dynamic factors. First is the ability to be aware of both the feelings and the ideas that a particular existential experience causes, to be able to identify those feelings and ideas, and own them as part of oneself. This is not an easy task. For example, professionals in human relations training practice frequently indicate that having to be "in touch" with one's feelings can be formidable. Somewhat tragically, it seems, a great number of people have been taught that the way to get along in life is to suppress their feelings, and if they can't suppress them, at least not acknowledge them. For Ed not to acknowledge as his own the feelings he experiences would be a violation of his basic sense of self.

The second factor associated with genuineness—behaving in a manner that is congruent with a person's feelings and thinking—is tempered a bit in Ed's comment. Note that he talked about letting people know how he is feeling, positively or negatively, "if appropriate." There is a complex issue involved here. A person who is as personally and interpersonally aware and as skillful behaviorally as Ed seems to be can wield a tremendous amount of power, interpersonally, irrespective of the position that person holds. The power stems from the fact that most people seem to have difficulty dealing with their feelings openly. Correspondingly, they also experience discomfort when others are open. At times they become immobilized, unable to deal with, for example, congruent expressions of anger or love. It is much easier and less threatening to play the games learned in childhood. Ed's "if appro- priate" stand, then, is important, for the last thing he wanted to do, even though he easily had the ability to do it, was immobilize another person.

Genuineness, however, is not enough. People must be comfortable with what they are, so that they do not become headstrong, with a sense of self that doesn't fit with how they want to behave. Thus, Ed saw himself as having warmth, being comfortable with it, and finding ways to express it on the job. But he applied the idea of comfort not only to himself. Ed applied the idea of being comfortable with self most centrally to his interaction with teachers as he worked to help them.

In sum, Ed refused to define himself as a principal in bureaucratic terms. Instead, he talked about his job in terms of his personal interests.

> I'm interested in instruction and curriculum as well as developing a climate where children feel good about being here and teachers feel good about working here.

I'm very much interested in human relations, in helping relationships, not only between teachers and children, but also teacher-teacher, administrator-teacher, and most specifically, administrator-child.

And he elaborated on his concerns about youngsters.

I see kindergarten children coming into the building, very alive, feeling-centered, very bubbly for the most part. And then I see things start to change, maybe after the second or third grade. They seem to become less aware of their feelings, less bubbly, less alive. By the end of the fifth grade when they leave the building—I hate to use the word—they seem deadened. Hopefully, if we can somehow work with their feelings on a daily or weekly basis, throughout the year, I will see the fifth grade kids smiling.

The clues to Ed's view of himself and to his views of what a school should be are congruent, logical follow-ups on his initial statement concerning genuineness and comfort. For example, feeling good about himself and what he does rather naturally leads to his desire for the children and teachers in his school to feel good about themselves. The aim is not only to enjoy school, but also to enjoy each other. Of course, it probably is true that most principals would offer the same opinion. Who wouldn't? What is important here, though, is that Ed was not asked. That is, the comments he made about children and teachers feeling good about being in school were his first remarks. Indeed, this thrust is central to everything he does. How central was revealed in his comments concerning the "bubbliness" of kindergarten youngsters, and how this bubbly pattern seems to dissipate in time. Perhaps it is trained out of them, as they are socialized in the school world, until at the end of the fifth grade—at ten years of age!—they appear to Ed to be deadened.

Ed's interest in developing helping relationships in his school, particularly his focus on the relationship between administrator and child, can be seen in his thinking about the typical perception that school children have of principals:

I think that the administrator has been looked upon as an authority to be feared by most children. For example, this really happened: A new group of kindergarten kids came into the building. The teacher introduced me and asked them what they thought the principal did. The response was, "He spanks people."

In *Escape from Freedom,* Erich Fromm (1941) remarked that problems related to the associations that people have with authority constitute the major moral issue of our time. That is, until authority figures let themselves be treated as human beings, and until hierarchical subordinates are freed from their fear of authority, humankind will continue to behave immorally, in the sense of relating to a person in a way that denies his/her humanity, focusing instead on issues of power.

Although Ed didn't frame his concerns about authority in terms of morality, that issue does seem to have been present in his thinking. His focus on "treat me as a human being who also happens to have responsibility for this school" puts the problem squarely. Interpretatively, the notion seems to be that the more people focus on his role and de-emphasize his person, the more dehumanizing and thus immoral the situation becomes for him. For Ed, the centrality of the whole education process resides at the point of helping people, particularly students and teachers, to become more aware of their emotionality. And once aware, a person can be more free with himself/herself and others. The person becomes freer to be what he/she is— clearly a moral goal. Ed approached the issue of his own freedom when he talked about the way he allots his time during the school day.

> I find that I spend 25 to 30 percent of my time on work such as budgeting, scheduling, transportation, cafeteria, and so forth. That's plenty. That leaves 70 to 75 percent of my time that *really is free.* I guess I could sit in my office and waste the whole day by expanding the managerial aspect of the job to 60 or 70 percent. I *choose* not to do that, most of all because I find it boring as hell.

And at another point, by way of elaboration of his last sentence, he said:

> For the most part, the expectations I respond to in my position are my expectations of myself rather than someone else's expectations of me. In other words, because someone expects me to behave in a particular way because I am principal of the building does not force me to behave that way. There's no reason for me to be the way others want me to be.

Basic to all, then, is the matter of individual choice, and Ed left no doubt about where he stood. Indeed, as will become clear in this chapter and throughout the book, Ed's choice was to be primarily an authentic helper. A principal can choose, for the most part, how he/she wishes to organize his/her work-life, that is, choosing which things will have priority. If a principal spends the majority of the day engaged in managerial functions— "administration"—then, according to Ed, that's a matter of individual choice and that principal shouldn't complain about being overburdened with such matters. The wound is self-inflicted. The gospel, according to Ed, is that if you really want to be free, but you aren't, the problem is that you've conceived of your job in a way that mandates your responding more to the demands of others, rather than to those you hold for yourself. There's a large amount of truth in this position. For example, there are many principals who appear to be positively overwhelmed and exhausted by what they see as the necessity of spending their days almost totally in their offices working on "nitty gritty."

Yet, the principals written about in this book seem to tilt the balance quite the other way. It's not that they do not work hard. Indeed, they do. But they spend their time differently. From Ed's point of view, it's a matter of choice, whether the people involved in the former work style are aware that they are, indeed, making the choice or, perhaps more important, that they have the choice to make. Ed made the point clearly when he indicated that, if he wished, he could have more than doubled the time he spent on routine administrative matters. Aware of his own needs and responding to them first, he simply chose freedom. And underlying the notion of choice, though he didn't articulate it, would appear to have been the idea that if Ed could present a satisfactory model of choice-making for freedom to his faculty, then the human values inherent in the process would infect them.

Being free, of course, is only the start. The critical question is what to do with freedom. The answer rests in a statement of people's interests and the roles that they see themselves playing in order to actualize those interests. We have already seen that Ed's interests were in instruction, curriculum, and the quality of human relationships between and among principal, teachers, students and parents. Relative to his role, he defined it and his strategy for implementing it in the following terms:

> always a helper . . . but the most common problem that occurs is a situation of my wanting to help someone and that someone not wanting help. So what I've tried to do is to create a climate within the building such that people see they'd like to change, feel they can change because the atmosphere is conducive to change, and can or will come to me as the potential helper in the building.

Carving out such a role can be a many splendored thing, but as Ed indicated, merely because that is the role he wanted to play was no guarantee that his offers of help would be accepted. This point is painfully evident in the schools with regard to supervisor-teacher relationships. Historically, for example, the relations between teachers and supervisors have been characterized by mistrust and defensiveness (Blumberg, 1974). Ed's school, when he became principal, was no exception. He commented on this state of affairs on two separate occasions:

> At the beginning of my tenure, there was no helping base. I was looked upon as a very young, maybe inexperienced person. The feeling seemed to be "Who is that authority coming into my classroom and telling me what I should do?"

and

> I walked into a building that was devoid of trust. It was a very cold climate. The perceptions of administrators were very suspicious and negative. I wanted to have some data to guide me, to help me work with the faculty. So, I used two types of survey instruments. One dealt with "how it feels here" and the other was a leadership profile. I've readministered them and things have changed, on the feeling level and with regard to perceptions of me as an administrator.

Ed put his finger on one of the primary blocks to changing and improving the character of the teaching-learning process. Again, historically and systematically, schools seem to be resistant to change. Administrators and teachers, perhaps for ample reason, tend to be protective of the territory they are willing to grant each other. Encroachments on the territory of the other have been typically greeted with suspicion, distrust, and defensiveness.[1] So, in some reiteration, the situation that Ed confronted when he became principal was not an unusual one. It was the rule rather than the exception.

It is interesting to note that Joan (Chapter 2) saw herself dealing with essentially the same situation during her year as principal. She said, "I knew I was going to have to work on plain old human relations." Ed said, "I wanted to build trust on their part." His approach to the trust-building task contained two elements. One was in his organizational role as administrator of the school. The second was his personal style of relating to members of his faculty. Relative to the latter, the problem, as he saw it, was to enable teachers to start to identify with him as a person who was nonthreatening, with whom they could be open, and to whom they could bring their problems, confident that they would be listened to. So,

> I guess, at first, it was mostly just a type of democratic acceptance of them as people, without any pressure from me. I wanted to feel out what kind of instruction was going on in each classroom. I realized I had my own biases toward instruction, but I tried not to let those biases interfere with my observations and relationships with a teacher. The first year I really didn't attempt to make any changes per se in a particular teacher's classroom style. I guess I wanted to build a feeling of trust on their part.

Ed was caught in a bind that was induced by his own value system. On the one hand, he understood that, in order to establish the kind of relationship that would let teachers trust him, he had to move slowly, to observe, listen, and be nonevaluative in his interaction with teachers. On the other hand, he observed things going on in classrooms that ran counter to what he valued in teacher-student relationships and the teacher-learning process. Ed realized that if he were ever able to play the role he wanted to play, the changes he would like to see would have to wait until he and the teachers could communicate openly with each other. Given the intensity of his feelings about the nature of productive classroom learning climates, he went through that first year with some inner conflicts—seeing some things he really wanted to change, but knowing he had to pull back lest he destroy what he was trying to build.

Was Ed being phony in all this? That is, believing in the necessity of being authentic with people, wasn't he being somewhat dishonest in not letting teachers know that some, perhaps a lot, of what he observed he thought was counterproductive? A "human relations purist" might answer in the

---

1. The counterpart of the teacher's distrust is illustrated by a remark one of the present writers heard an administrator make as he rejected a teacher union's invitation to attend a session on teacher evaluation. He said, "I'll be damned if I'll let them tell me how to evaluate teachers!"

affirmative. "Tell them where you are, gently if need be, but be sure to level at all times" might be the motto of the purist. Ed's position was different. Authenticity is a two-way street, and both parties have to own it as a value and a communication skill. Further, the development of the value and accompanying skill is an experiential learning process. And further still, as we infer from Argyris (1976), most people learn that the way to get along in this world is to be nonauthentic—to not let people know what they are thinking and feeling in ways that might reveal themselves. The risks are too high, because, as a person reveals himself/herself, he/she becomes more vulnerable to others.

Again, the question is whether or not Ed was being phony when he observed and listened, but did not reveal himself to the teachers. We think not, given what his goals were during that first year as principal. What he saw and heard became part of his data bank for future use. In a way, there was a parallel between Ed's strategy of working with teachers that first year and the manner in which he dealt with the school as a human organization. If, for example, his work with teachers is conceptualized as involving nonevaluative information gathering, the same would apply to his work with the school as a social system. Though he undoubtedly did observe and listen to the way teachers behaved and talked with each other, his primary data-collection method was to administer a nonevaluative survey. Interestingly, the data he collected had little to do with the instructional program. It was focused on the emotionality of the school— "How it feels here"—and the behavioral style of the principal. As much as he was interested in the behavior and feeling tone that was present in classrooms, Ed was more generally interested in these same factors as they were present in the school.

The parallelism just noted is indicative of a consistency in Ed as a person and as a principal. Issues of authenticity, emotionality, and behavior seemed central to his existence. They not only appeared to be present when he described the ways he worked and those things he worked for, but they were also present in our interview.[2]

Ed's theory of inducing change in the instructional program and teacher behavior in his school involved, at its heart, illuminating the gaps between what currently transpires and what teachers might want to transpire. But underneath this theory is a philosophical position that highlights the element of free choice. That is, he put a lot of energy into helping his teachers become aware of the gaps with which they were confronted, but he did not mandate that they do anything to close those gaps. They must make the choice. With the faculty as a whole, the theory became actualized in the following way:

---

2. As an example of this consistency, at one point in the interview, as we were trying to understand a position he had taken, he said, "I feel like you're trying to put me in a box." Indeed, he let us know, without anger, what he perceived to be happening.

Early in the first year, I wanted to start developing the school as a community. In our before-school-starts faculty meeting, I started out by reading a statement about myself and about kids. That let them know where I was and I think it made an impact on them. Then I asked them to do two things: First, to write down what they thought was the best thing that could happen to them that year and what was the worst thing. Second, I asked them to write down what resources they had to offer our school community and what resources they wanted from our community. And that was it.

We put it all down on newsprint, examined it, and processed it all together, and then I put all the information on ditto. It's all in the teacher's room now. We have an "I want" board and an "I have" board.

Gaps are deliberately created, and people are free to choose the extent to which they want the gap to be closed. Apparently, from Ed's view, the teachers chose to help each other close some of the gaps, at least to some extent. But the issue is that they voluntarily chose to do so, because implicit in the notion of free choice in a program of change is the idea that unless those involved "own" the change, anything that occurs will leave only a superficial impact of short duration.

There is another implicit factor involved in Ed's theory of change that has to do with the change agent's view of the people with whom he/she is working. "Are these people pawns to be manipulated or are they adults who, when confronted with facts pertinent to them, can make intelligent decisions on their own?" Obviously, Ed's strategy viewed teachers as adults. And this position apparently held for things occurring in the school that he would have preferred to see change.

I think what I do is go with the strength that's already in the building. I build on that, and in the process a teacher becomes stronger. Well, the stronger that teacher becomes, the more there is a discrepancy between that teacher, and, for example, the weak teacher who may be across the hall. Then the weak person has a choice: "I see this happening across the hall. It's really going well and I want to get involved in it. Or, I see it happening, and I don't want to get involved in it."

We asked Ed if he were content to let the weak teachers make the decision not to become involved in a program that was obviously of help to youngsters. His response was in the affirmative—but there was a hedge because our follow-up question was, "For how long?" His reply was, "I don't know. I haven't set a time limit." We suspect the "how long" question got answered not by a mandate to change, but by an authentic leveling confrontation between Ed and the teacher, at which time he would share, as nonevaluatively as possible, more data about the situation. This data would include his own awareness of what is going on in him as a person as well as his perception of what is going on in the classroom. And this confrontation would be the start of building a productive relationship. The point was made by Ed, in a somewhat different context:

> I find it very difficult to force a teacher to change. What I will typically do is sit down with that teacher and point out my observations of what's happening in the classroom and sort of check out if the teacher sees the same thing happening. And then I proceed from there and ask the teacher if this is something she is comfortable with. If it's something she *isn't* comfortable with, then we begin to develop a relationship.

The style, then, is consistent, from working with the faculty as a whole to the individual teachers. Provide information, create gaps, and let people make choices, trusting all through the sequence that their sense of values about education and youngsters will lead teachers to make decisions for change they can feel good about. But there is a limit to the comfort issue.

> I always am concerned about allowing a teacher to feel comfortable with what she's doing as long as it is not detrimental in my eyes to what's happening with the children.

It was at the point of perceiving some undesirable things happening to youngsters as a result of teacher behavior that Ed departed from his general therapeutic model of working with teachers. That is, the therapeutic model to which Ed adheres suggests, by way of some repetition, "collect information, become aware of yourself and others, and examine the gaps between what you are and what you'd like to be. If you are comfortable with where you are after going through this process, well, that's okay." But it's okay only up to a point, the point being a situation where a teacher's comfort with what he/she is doing is having undesirable effects on youngsters. It's at this point that his role emphasis as a helper who happens to have responsibility for a school changes to that of a person who has responsibility for a school and who would also like to be of help. First things come first, and it is the welfare and emotional health of the youngsters in his building that takes top priority. Teachers are not allowed to place their own comfort with what they do before the well-being of students.

It is undoubtedly true that few principals would argue with Ed's position; that *every* principal's working philosophy places the welfare of the youngsters as *the* top priority in their school. For example, if every principal were asked to rank their priorities, the needs of students would come out on top. What makes Ed different is that he articulated clearly and had a well-thought-out theoretical and pragmatic model to deal with problem situations on a daily basis. The well-being of the students in his school seemed to be at the center of Ed's existence as a school principal. It took precedence over everything else, and not just at times of crisis. Ed seemed to be acutely aware of the mostly subtle, but nonetheless damaging, effects on students when, on occasion, a teacher may be comfortable doing what comes naturally—dealing with his/her anger, for example, in a way that may create undesirable, ego-deflating, and win/lose situations for students.

Obviously, then, if a situation reached the point where Ed could not allow it to continue, he had to behave in ways that caused him some conflict concerning his preferred style of doing things. His remarks illustrate the conflict he experienced at times.

> I guess I like the word assertive rather than authoritarian (ed. note: by which he means making unilateral decisions). There are instances when I have to assert myself as an individual, not as a principal, but as an individual either in speaking with parents or working with a teacher. Depending on my relationship with that teacher, I will assert myself and let her know what I find objectionable. In the eyes of many teachers I'm not void of authority, it's still there. But there's another side of me, the assertive side, but assertive in terms of being fair. And, there's the more or less sensitive, warm side of me which gets me a lot farther in terms of relating to people and helping them than does my assertive, authoritarian self.

For Ed, life in school was not one big happy helping relationship, much as he might have preferred it to be that way. For one thing, although he disliked the role of the authority figure, he recognized that he was sometimes seen that way. In his comments, the use of the word *assertive* seemed to be a semantic dodge. That is, he found it easier to see himself exercising his assertiveness rather than his authority. But the conflict is still there, and curiously, the conflict seems to have been induced by his acute sensitivity to himself that enabled him to be aware of the different sides of his makeup. Awareness, though, is not all there is to it. Most people are more or less aware of their conflicting needs and values in their relationships with others. The conflict became heightened with Ed, it seems, because of his extraordinary commitment to his "sensitive, warm side" as the most productive way to develop his school community. The problem is, of course, that life doesn't permit Ed (or anyone, for that matter) to behave in a sensitive, warm, helping way all the time. Most of us probably handle this conflict without much discomfort. The same can't be said of Ed. Missionaries, and there is clearly a missionary side to him, have never had an easy time of it.

When Ed talked about his relationships with the Central Office (personified by the superintendent) and other building administrators in his district, the impression conveyed was that they were matter-of-factly formal and distant, almost to an extreme. Part of this circumstance was influenced by the fact that his building was several miles away from the other four in the district. This separation enabled him to feel and be quite autonomous. But more important, the formality and distance of the relationships were increased by the absence of shared values and, indeed, what appeared to be little basis for communication about the substance and style of education. About his superintendent, for example, he commented:

> The relationship between me and my superintendent isn't poor and it isn't good. I don't think he would take the time to listen and understand what I'm doing. He doesn't listen well and any attempt on my part to describe our program has been completely useless. On the other hand, he's very public minded and receives a lot

of positive feedback from parents about what is going on. But it took him two years before he spoke to me as a human being. He told me he was pleased with what I had done, had a lot of confidence in me, and he talked about wanting to work with me.

Relative to the other principals in the district, Ed said:

The frequency of my relating to other administrators is not great. What I do and what is comfortable for me seems not to be comfortable for them. So, I sort of backed off and said, "Well, if they feel comfortable doing what they do, that's okay." But I don't want them telling me what I'm doing is not okay. So it's mostly just a "leave each other alone" attitude. I prefer it that way even though, if given the chance, I'd like to influence them in the direction of dealing with kids' feelings. But that's very difficult for me to do, though I'd be willing to help them if they wanted to.

The structure of the relationships between Ed and his superintendent and between Ed and the other building principals was different. But the net result seems to have been the same—the relationships were characterized by psychological distance and formality. The superintendent's poor listening was probably a result of broader concerns, the public image of the schools, for example. With regard to other principals from whom Ed might have received support and who, in turn, he might have helped, the problem was an absence of shared values. Further, the energy required to change this state of affairs would have been too great for Ed to muster.

We have to speculate that these circumstances, much as they may have their rewards, eventually have their costs. Essentially, Ed was isolated (even though it may have been a self-induced isolation) from collegial interaction and support. He may be able to continue what he is doing and find it exciting for a number of years. But this isolation may become burdensome and a source of discontent. It is even possible that Ed himself will wind down if no emotional sustenance is received from his colleagues over the long run.

The long run, though, is tomorrow, and Ed lived very much in "today." His concern with the affective side of life and with the here-and-now led him to spend a large amount of time in classrooms, not only observing, but doing, taking over a class, for example, to free the teacher for planning or inservice programs; or working directly with youngsters on the emotional side of their life, or, as Ed put it, on "the human side of education."

I'm very interested in Gestalt theory and technique. I have a group of third grade children with whom I meet twice a week to conduct a group session, using the theory and technique of Gestalt as well as the Magic Circle idea which comes from California. I also meet with a kindergarten group once a week and do a similar program with them. I am trying to work the teachers in, trying to build a community.

And on the level of the total building community:

> The whole building community—teachers, kids, cafeteria people, and maintenance people—meets every Friday morning for about twenty minutes. We say the pledge of allegiance, we sing together, we celebrate birthdays—in the gymnasium. We do a variety of things. I play my saxophone. (All my life I wanted to play the saxophone and two years ago I learned.) I also go into my kindergarten and first grades on a weekly basis and play the sax and the kids sing.

It truly seems that when Ed described himself as an unusual principal he was right. But what about the parents? How did they respond to his unusualness, particularly given the fact that the community his school served would be classified as much more conservative than progressive? From Ed's perception (and that of his superintendent, apparently) the parent community had very positive reactions to the school and what occurred in it. These reactions, however, seem not to have been a result of parents simply listening to their children describe their experiences, although that certainly must have been part of it. What seems more to the point is that Ed tried to involve parents directly in some of the educational experiences of the youngsters and in the school as a viable community institution. It's as if he took on helping parents understand the school as part of his responsibility. He described several specific activities parents were engaged in. First, an activity that was directed at the parents of children who were about to enter kindergarten:

> We have four preschool sessions for parents whose children are coming into the building. I conduct those sessions. What I do is simply to ask parents to write down what they want their children to get out of being in school. Then I read their responses out loud and put them on the board. I put those statements dealing with affect—"I want him to be able to get along with people"—on one side, and those dealing with traditional skills—"I want him to learn reading, writing, and arithmetic"—on the other side. At the last sessions, out of forty parents' statements, thirty were on the side of affect and four were on the side of traditional learning skills. Then I talked to them of what I'm trying to do in terms of helping kids with their feelings and relating to each other. The parents say, "Yeah, you know that's really important."

Early on, then, parents were given a sense of the thrust that Ed tried to develop in the school's program. They were involved and had an opportunity to react to what was going on. They also got a sense of Ed's style and his value system. However, Ed did not "put down" the learning of basic skills. To the contrary, he was vitally concerned with them, but he believed they could be learned better in an emotionally healthier environment than he perceived to be current in most schools—thus his emphasis on the affective side of life.

What about the PTA? According to Ed, the PTA was strong and also supportive. When we expressed our surprise (for our experience suggests

that most PTAs are weak, frequently becoming temporarily strong in opposing something that is occurring in a school), Ed's response was as follows:

> I think they're very interested in their children. I also feel they know they can
> come to me with ideas and know they'll be listened to. They're very active. Right
> now there are four or five things going on in which parents are involved. There's
> the library-learning center in which parents work, for example.
>
> One thing I know is that the typical turnout at PTA meetings when the kids
> aren't involved is very low. We had a "get acquainted" night. Usually this means
> the parents come in to meet the teachers. But it seemed to make a lot more sense
> to ask the kids to bring their parents, so that the kids could say, "Hey, Mom, this
> is my teacher, this is my room, this is where I sit, etc." The night we did that we
> had 600 people.

Ed also engaged with parents on school improvement projects; the playground, for example:

> I just finished working with seven parents, building a real playground. I've never
> heard of an elementary school without a playground. We went to the state fair,
> we went to dumps. We got old tires and telephone poles, anything we could lay
> our hands on that we thought would work and be important to helping kids feel
> good about being there, and teachers feel good about teaching.

It is clear, then, that Ed departed from the rather puristic helping style that
he tried to employ with his teachers when it came to working with and trying
to involve parents in the building of the school community. He initiated,
created, and engaged, and most of all he appears to have had fun. His eyes
fairly lit up, for example, when he told us about the program for parents
where a film made in and about the school was shown, and they did their
"Friday morning program."

More important, however, is the way the themes that were associated
with Ed's work with teachers and youngsters became equally vivid in his
concern with parents. School has to be a place that is enjoyed, but enjoyed
with a purpose. And even though he told us of some purely social activities
in which the parents engaged (ice cream socials, dancing, a roller skating
party, etc.), the activities that were most important were those in which
parents were participants in something that was related to their children. The
idea is to reach out to the parents, not in a ritualistic fashion, but in a way
that links them to what the school is all about. Thus, the "get acquainted"
night is not a situation where uneasy parents meet uneasy teachers because
it is something that has to be done. To the contrary, it is seen as an
opportunity to assist parents, teachers, and kids get together to share some
of their lives with each other. And the development of the program with the
movie had much more than entertainment as its goal. Most centrally, it was
another effort to reach out, to communicate the sense of the school's mission, so that parents could understand, lend support, and perhaps learn
themselves. Even building the playground had a purpose that would go

beyond merely providing a better facility for recess or other school activities. At its base, as Ed said, it was aimed at "helping kids feel good about being there and teachers feel good about teaching." But the parent involvement in the playground building project went beyond that, because it gave the parents a sense of being part of the action, of knowing that their efforts would contribute to making the school a better place for their youngsters.

The importance of Ed's involvement with parents, however, went beyond efforts to enable them to become part of the school community, although that in itself is a worthwhile aim. Underneath it all is that his energy, style, outlook on life in general and school in particular serve as a model for parents as well as for teachers and students. As Ed invested of himself, his attitudes, and his skills, with parents in this case, he also modeled for them the kinds of human relationships and attitudes toward school that best encourage productive linkages between home and school. The school, then, does not become an isolated fortress, forbidding all to enter and be part of it except those who have formal membership in it. To the contrary, the school opens itself up and reaches out to the community and says, in effect, "Be part of us. We all have a stake in what goes on here."

There is a further point of interest concerning the relationship of parents to the school. It focuses on the linking role that Ed played between parents and teachers, particularly at times when parents may have been dissatisfied or upset with a teacher's behavior in the classroom or, in a specific instance, with the behavior of teachers in general during a very tense and conflicting time in collective bargaining. In this latter situation, some of the teachers had engaged in petty, perhaps childish acts of disruption such as taking fifth grade books and putting them in the first grade classroom. Parents were understandably angry. Their children were being used as pawns. Four parents came in and confronted Ed about the situation, about which he was unaware. Ed's position in these circumstances was an unusual one. He did not become defensive and try to smoke-screen the situation by denying its occurrence, nor did he promise the parents that he, as principal, would take care of the problem—that he wouldn't let the teachers get away with that sort of behavior. He agreed with the parents that, if there had been the acts of sabotage that they had described, they had a right to be angry. Seeing that their anger had been accepted as legitimate, the emotionality that the parents felt subsided. But then, and here the departure in style and attitudes is seen, it was Ed's viewpoint that the teachers had to assume responsibility for their actions. He would not do it for them. His suggestion to the parents was that they either approach the teachers directly or make their views known to the teachers' association. The parents left "happy as they could be" according to Ed. In retrospect, he said:

> When the parents walked in the door it was my responsibility to deal with that here-and-now situation. But it is *not* my responsibility to get the teacher off the hook.

The same position holds when a parent comes in to complain about what a teacher is doing in a classroom.

> I feel the same way when a parent calls me and starts to bitch about a teacher. The first thing I suggest is that the problem be taken up with the teacher. I can't answer for twenty-five people. I can only answer for me.

As we interpret Ed's stand on his linking role between parents and teachers, it goes something like this: A central function of education is to help youngsters learn, over time, what it means to be an adult. Part of being an adult involves assuming responsibility—personal responsibility—for one's actions. If this be so, then when people are chronologically adult, they must indeed be treated as adults and they must assume responsibility for their behavior. They can't have it both ways. They can't pick and choose the times when they will assume responsibility for themselves and the times when they won't. Thus, when Ed refused to be the "protector" for teachers, when he refused to take over their problems vis-à-vis the parents, he was, in effect, placing his trust in them as adults—even though they, at times, might not like it.

The story of Ed would not be complete without a comment he made toward the close of our interview, when he was reflecting on the nature of his relationships with his teachers.

> It's just being myself with them and helping them know it's okay to be angry and it's okay to be positive. And it's okay to be warm. That didn't exist there before. To give you an example, after the negotiations were settled, eight teachers came in throughout the day, embraced me, cried, and thanked me for being so supportive of them. I had to sit back after the first one came in, a sixty-eight-year-old kindergarten teacher, and say to myself, "What the hell did I do?"—I didn't do anything. I was neutral. I was myself. And that was the measure of it all for me, right there. And how does it all come about? What the hell . . . I don't know. There isn't any recipe book for it.

And we can't add anything to that.

5

The Broker: The Low-Key Service Man Who Confronts

In his early thirties, Fred had taught in his present school system for a number of years, the team leader in an inner-city school before being selected principal for another building in the same city. The elementary school was relatively small—300 students and twelve teachers—and it served the families of a working-class, predominantly white, community. At the time we talked with Fred, he had been a principal for two years.

During our interview, Fred impressed us with his low-key, but rather persistent style. As he talked, he revealed the wide boundaries within which he was able to work, taking people as they are, working with them on their problems, and gradually trying to move them. But it was clear that he could and did take strong stands on particular issues, most of which were organizational. He seemed to have no apparent master plan for what he would like the image of his school to be in the future. Rather, his whole thrust appeared to focus on the improvement of instruction, no matter what form that might take. To this end he described himself as a "service-oriented person," the services being offered to teachers, parents, and community organizations that were proximal to his school. But Fred did not see himself as being service oriented in any community organization sense. That is, when he engaged with groups or individuals outside his school, it was all with the ultimate purpose of affecting what goes on in the school, particularly with regard to the learning of students. For example, a social worker contacted him about the possibility of conducting an Adult Basic Education program in the school, something the basic education people were loathe to do, preferring to carry out their program in their central facility.

> We got two parents to go down and beat on the door of the Adult Basic Education Center. I said, "You keep after them from your end and I'll keep after them from this end." So, it worked, because the basic education people said they would come if we could get ten people, which we did. It all just happened when I met and started to talk with the social worker from the Adams Community House. I went for it because I thought it would benefit the school. You know, a

kid might say, "Hey, Mom's going back to school tonight and that makes some difference to me."

There is more to Fred than meets the eye. When he told the parents that he would "keep after them from this end" he meant just that. There was a sense of persistence in it all, combined with a low level of tolerance for bureaucratic red tape or regulations that stood in the way of accomplishing those things that Fred felt were important. The important thing for him was to get things moving, and once they started to move, he backed off, and kept in contact only to see if he was needed.

Sometimes, though, this style of getting things going and then backing off creates problems, even failures of some programs. Fred related an example of trying to get parents more involved in the school. The teachers, rather reluctantly, it appears, agreed to go along with his idea and formed a committee to implement it. His role, as he saw it, was to let the teachers do it themselves. The idea never really bore fruit. Fred said:

> I just never pushed or followed through and I think that's why I fail when I fail. As soon as something is started, I go on to something else. I don't know why I do this, whether it's because I tell myself I have too much work, or whether I'm afraid I might fail, or it's going to bomb out and I would have difficulty accepting failure, or what.

So, we have another side emerging of Fred as principal. He seems to have been introspective, even quizzical about himself and what he did. And there appears to have been a certain amount of cautiousness in his actions, particularly where new ideas were involved, that may have headed him into acting, at times, in a self-defeating manner. In a curious way his acknowledged service orientation provided the powder keg on which he occasionally sat. These circumstances apparently occurred when the situation demanded more direction, forcefulness, and follow-through than he was willing to give, perhaps for the reasons he described above. Failure then, precisely the situation he wanted to avoid, occurred because he had not committed himself. But publicly, at least, it was not his failure. Privately, though, it appears that he internalized it as his own.

This analysis is not meant to be critical of Fred, but to indicate that he was aware of what was transpiring and that he knew people must be aware of the consequences of their own behavior before any change can take place. Another issue involved here has to do with Fred's newness in the role of principal, and the fact that the principal of the school where he taught prior to assuming his new job did not provide a satisfactory role model for him. He has had to feel his way on his own, through the entire experience. His words are best at this point:

> The nature of the job emphasizes isolation. Unless you have an assistant, which I don't, it's a pretty lonely kind of role. I really felt an overwhelming kind of loneliness.

This is a potent, if somewhat poignant, commentary by Fred about his feelings when he became a principal. Its poignancy comes, of course, from the reactions that feelings of loneliness evoke in most people. Typically they react by wanting to sympathize, recalling perhaps, times of their own loneliness and the frustration that may accompany it. But the impact of the loneliness Fred expressed goes far beyond engendering the ordinary feelings of compassion that one person might have for another. At issue is the effect that feeling lonely can have on the ability of a school principal to get stimulation, to initiate new procedures, to change things, to get feedback on ideas and behavior. It seems clear that for a principal who wants to do things with his or her school, feelings of loneliness can act only as a deterrent. There is no support system. But what about Fred's colleagues, the other elementary school principals in the system, particularly those schools in the same area as Fred's?

When we raised this question, his first response was a laugh of derision and cynicism. It was not a smile; it was a laugh. And so we talked at some length about his perception of the state of peer relations within the system, and of Central Office personnel and the effects they may have had on these relations. Perhaps that's where it all starts, at least from Fred's point of view.

> You know, there are lots of mixed messages. I think they would like, or say they would like, principals to be instructional leaders. But I have seen some appointments that really surprise me. People have been appointed as principals who neither know an awful lot about instruction, or care about it. It's not that you have to know everything, but you have to care.
>
> So, in a way, Central Office communicates that it's really a maintenance position. They feel that as long as there aren't a lot of phone calls and they don't get a lot of grievances filed by teachers, you are doing okay.

In systematic fashion, then, Fred's feelings of loneliness and lack of productive peer relations were unintended consequences of personnel decisions made at the Central Office. Public pronouncements speak to the need for instructional leaders, which is what Fred saw as the main responsibility of a principal. The subtle private communication to "keep things cool" added strength to his perception that what the system is really interested in is a "peace-keeping" operation. If, on top of that, a principal can manage to introduce some new and productive ideas into the curriculum, it's a plus. But don't worry if you don't.

In a rather direct fashion, Fred once raised the issue of the mixed messages with his superintendent.

> As I remember, what I said to him was something like this: "You say you want us to be instructional leaders. But you send out a lot of messages that are different. I get this stuff down the pike all the time. Do this; be here; do this; do that. I have to let a lot of this stuff go by the boards if I'm really going to fulfill the role of an instructional leader. So, maybe you can explain it all to me." His reply was, "Oh yeah, well you've got to do all this other stuff first so that you can then have what you want."

These comments shed some light on another side of Fred, one that is apt to be missed if focus is only on his description of himself as "service oriented." Fred is also a confronter, and a direct confronter, at that. Note that he did not hedge in his dialogue with the superintendent. He let the superintendent know that the Central Office was issuing conflicting role expectations for principals. Most principals tend not to confront authority directly, if at all. Instead they appear to be silent sufferers, performing a host of imposed routine administrative chores, complaining among themselves, but not likely to try and change things. And rarely do they tell the superintendent that he or she is running, as it were, a "leaky ship." This was not Fred's style. Rather, to continue the metaphor, his efforts were devoted to finding the leak and plugging it, if possible.

In the situation cited above, Fred's efforts to make the superintendent deal with an incongruity of the system's expectations for principals were clearly not met with a sympathetic ear. Unfortunately, the principal is then left to his own devices and without system support. In Fred's case, he appears to have done what comes naturally. He ignored the "Mickey Mouse," as he described it, let his secretary, in whom he had a great deal of confidence, deal with most of it as she saw fit, and went about doing what he saw to be his primary role—trying to improve the quality of instruction.

Recall that this discussion of Fred's confrontation with his superintendent stemmed from his feelings of loneliness which he saw, in large part, to be engendered by the role expectations that Central Office has for principals—primarily the expectation that the role is a maintenance one. If indeed this is the case,[1] then the role of principal as confronter is also a very lonely one because there is little support for this behavior from his/her peers. To confront is to risk, and if the system emphasizes maintenance, then confronting and taking risks are behaviors to be avoided. The principal who decides to confront will, for the most part, be a lonely person. This point, perhaps, accounts for Fred's laugh when we initially raised the question of his relationships with other administrators. Of all our interviewees, Fred devoted the most time to talking about the way he perceived his fellow principals. Several issues were involved.

I've never developed a good working relationship with the other three principals on the west side. They are all older; one of them is ill. I don't think I could share anything with them. They wouldn't get involved in anything, even when a decision was made to close one of the schools. This one guy's position was, "Well, it happened."

They won't become involved politically. They don't mind getting their pictures in the papers with one of their kids who won a prize, or something like that. But

---

1. We know of a few districts where the opposite holds, where the superintendents are very much instructionally oriented. Curiously, this orientation has created a great deal of superintendent-principal conflict. Perhaps the issue is that most principals, indeed, are comfortable in and desire the maintenance role.

the idea of taking a public stand on an educational issue—like picking a new school site—is something they won't do. I can't be like that.

It was a frustrating situation for Fred. Perhaps his frustration led to a bit of sarcasm and anger directed at his colleagues who were physically close to him, but it was also directed at principals as a group. He indicated, for example, that this group, which met regularly, was not powerful and gave no indication that it wanted to become powerful. There were, though, isolated individuals with whom he communicated. For example:

> There's a new guy who was just appointed at Beecher. We talk a lot on the phone because nobody can ever see anybody else. But the principals' group as a group is not a power base. We have very little to say about what happens to us in terms of professional development, for example.

This last point, the lack of any formal professional development program aimed at principals, was a bothersome thing for Fred. He saw it as an important need and one totally ignored by Central Office. The fact that the possibility of developing such a program was given no priority by the school district seemed to fit in well with his previous analysis of the district's priorities concerning the role of the principal. The situation went something like this: The messages sent by the system are that the primary role of the principal is to maintain the status quo. There is no particular educational management expertise needed by a person in order to keep things running smoothly. Principals are appointed because they are presumed to be already competent to do just that—run things. Monthly meetings, which deal mostly with "Mickey Mouse," are designed to keep things as they've always been. No directed, continued, and intensive professional development program is needed to maintain that which seems to be most desired (at least as evidenced by behavior) by the Central Office, which results in at least one talented but frustrated principal and a relatively powerless group of administrators.

An additional comment that Fred made indicated that he was not the only principal who felt frustrated in his role and who yearned for some collegial stimulation and help from the system. At one point he said:

> If we could only have a nonagenda meeting where we could talk about what are our extreme frustrations. No one has ever wanted to deal with them or even listen to them. Perhaps they just feel helpless about it. I don't think principals see themselves as really being able to solve the problems that occur daily. I think they see themselves as just being there, as not being able to change anything. I don't know how to change that perspective. Maybe it takes a few people acting together, but I don't even know how to approach it. And that's frightening 'cause I used to think it could be done.

There was a strong element of tragedy in all this, both for Fred as a person and for our educational enterprise, if what he said bears any relationship to reality—which we think it does. On the personal side, Fred's enthusiasm and energy regarding his ability to influence what happens in the larger sphere of educational endeavor, beyond the walls of his school, was waning after less than two years as principal. The system, in which there really are no villains, took its toll, and the price seems high. What Fred has described is undoubtedly an unintended consequence of the way things operate. That is, the values and procedures by which the system operates are not all designed to sap the enthusiasm principals have for trying to induce change in the system at large. Nonetheless, this appears to have happened in this one case, and probably it is not an isolated case.

Fred, however, was not completely hopeless about the situation. His perceptions were that about one-quarter of the elementary principals in his district felt the way he did and that, if they ever got together they could probably make things happen, because the other three-quarters wouldn't oppose any proposals—nor would they strongly support any. There would, of course, be some risks involved, but of an ill-defined nature. They have to do with the uncertainty attached to the consequences that might develop if people started to rebel, even softly, against the authority structure of any hierarchical system. Actually, Fred saw the risks as being very low:

> I don't think it's much of a risk because I don't think they'd know what to do if we ever made a demand on them. They'd probably faint on the spot.

So, the reasonable question is, why don't some of the principals get together, formulate a plan, and propose it to Central Office? The answer:

> We are just a weak group. And yet we have a number of strong individuals. The problem is that we have never functioned as a group, as a cohesive group, in making demands of any kind. And a good part of the reason for it is that we are by ourselves so much of the time. And the energy required to try and change things just isn't worth it.

Things are thus circular and reinforcing. The nature of the job requires principals to be lone operators most of the time, with the exception of those who have assistants (interestingly, two of the individuals that Fred mentioned as being powerful do have assistant principals working with them). They have complete responsibility for their schools and thus feel constraints against moving out into the wider system. Further, the norms of the system seem not to support reaching out in an effort to establish strong group relationships. It is not so much that anyone has said, "We discourage that kind of behavior." More simply, reaching out to establish the cohesive group Fred spoke of has not been encouraged. The message seems to be, "Stay in your school." And Fred is lonely. In addition, his assessment of the system, at least the part of it to which he was reacting, was that it is relatively immovable. As far as the energy required to change it, Fred's comment was brief and to the point, "It ain't worth it."

A certain element of sadness and frustration is in Fred's last comment. It is as though the subtleties of the system's operation were forcing him into a constricted role, one that rather effectively prevented him from getting some of the psychic sustenance he needed as a professional educator. This is no small problem. Indeed, at one point in our discussion, his frustration—not with his work in the school but with his isolation from colleagues—came out forcefully as he indicated that it was a major personal decision of his to stay on as principal for another year.

It would be incorrect to infer from the preceding discussion that Fred was down in the mouth about his work as principal. Quite the opposite. It all seemed fun, and, as he put it:

> You get your jollies at school because you know that as a result of what you do you can see something happen pretty quickly. Particularly this is true if you can help a kid or a teacher.

If the picture of Fred's relations with other administrators is a somewhat forlorn one, the same did not hold true for his behavior and relationship within his school. There were things to be done there, but, more important, he could have direct influence on the course of events. Things happen, sometimes quickly, and there was much satisfaction in it all for Fred. However, the process of getting things to happen, both structurally and procedurally, was not an easy one. Two major complicating factors were involved. The first had to do with the fact that the role of the administrator in a small school includes all the functions that would normally be performed by several people in a large school. Thus Fred was the administrator and did the work associated with that function. He was the guidance counselor, the instruction and curriculum specialist, the instructional supervisor charged with evaluation, and the school disciplinarian. He also had responsibility for school-community relations.

This set of circumstances is not unusual. There must be hundreds, if not thousands, of elementary school principals who face similar kinds of multiple role expectations. But the commonplaceness of the situation does not alter the fact that, as Fred said:

> A lot of shotgunning goes on. The whole bit is tremendously frustrating. In addition, I am supposed to help teachers and I'm also supposed to evaluate them. I'd rather have it one way or another, because the way it is now, the situation raises lots of conflicts—for me and for the teachers.

Fred's use of the term "shotgunning," as well as his concerns about the supervising-helping role conflict, provided an important clue to the source of his frustration. The implication was that he must scatter his energies, rarely having the time to devote extended thought and effort to one particular target, even though that may be what he was concerned about doing. Again, these circumstances are not unusual. Furthermore, the hypothesis that schools are organized the way Fred's is—one principal for the whole ballgame—gives subtle reinforcement to the notion advanced earlier: the system is more interested simply in keeping things running than it is in providing instructional leadership through the efforts of the principal.

The second complicating factor involved with Fred's efforts to provide leadership for the school was a bit curious, given the fact that the building was classified as "inner city." This factor was that its staff was highly stable. One of the teachers had been on the faculty for twenty-seven years and another, twenty. Patterns concerning how things happened in the school were pretty well established. Working procedures were rather firmly set. How well established and set things were is illustrated by the first major structural problem Fred faced when he became principal. It had to do with class size. More specifically, the problem had to do with the norms that had been established relative to the unevenness of class size. For years the school had operated without any deliberate organizational design to its structure. Teachers were not shifted to take student population into consideration. In the particular case in point, the two fourth grade teachers each had nineteen children in a class while the two first grade teachers each had twenty-eight. The normative attitude that teachers had learned and espoused was that different members of the faculty "lucked out" from year to year. Their attitude was, "This is our year to have fewer kids. Next year somebody else will have it easy."

As much as Fred saw himself as a broker of resources and services in his work with individual teachers, he also had clear notions about what he thought were effective organizational designs. In this case, he had a rationale that suggested that the first grades should have no more than twenty-one students, and that classes should get progressively larger, by small increments, as the youngsters proceeded through school. This was an important concept to him, and he was not about to buy into the chance pattern that had developed.

How he acted in the situation tells a lot about Fred's style when he was functioning as the *organizational* leader of the school. He took a firm and negative stand on the accepted pattern. He said, in effect, that the system as it stood would have to change, but he did not mandate the substance of the change. Instead:

> I said, "Wait a minute. Let's look at some alternatives to what we're doing." We began meeting in October. I generated four of five possible organizational structures. Well, we began to design some things so that by the end of the first year we were able to sit down and manage our structure deliberately, and in a way that I think made sense educationally.

There was a certain firmness about Fred's style, then, that was combined with flexibility and a willingness to engage collaboratively with others in problem solving. He appeared to be able to dig his heels in, not let himself be pushed around, and, at the same time, to seek out alternative ways of resolving problems. His "dug in" position in this case was:

> There is no way we are going back to our chance pattern of class size. Now let's look at this thing in a different way; see what our options are; what's good about them and what's bad about them.

There are other consequences to this way of working with teachers, and they do not appear to be a deliberate part of Fred's thought processes. Recall that Joan (Chapter 2) viewed and conceptualized most of her interaction with teachers as inservice training. And she went at it with a vengeance. Fred seems not to have conceptualized his work with teachers in this way, but the same effect seems to hold. By engaging them in an alternative-seeking process, he was also enabling them to move outside of their particular classroom concerns and view the school as more of an integrated social system. This is in juxtaposition to a school's being simply a place where what happens in one part of it bears little relationship to what happens in another part.

There is also a somewhat more abstract way of viewing this part of Fred's style. Implicitly, he was trying to get the teachers to raise questions about the "regularities" (Sarason, 1971) by which the school functioned, regularities that have no basis in sound educational practice. He said, "Now, let's look at this thing in a different way . . ." Put differently, he might have said, "Must we always do things without questioning simply because that's the way things have been done?" But what also seems clear is that, as he took the positions he did, as he raised the questions he raised, there was a sort of softly growling bulldog quality to it all. He hung on but didn't make too much noise about it.

This softness or low-key style that appears to typify Fred also became apparent in his work with teachers as individuals or in a group. For example, his goals for his first year as principal were modest, based on his view that the teachers were relative strangers to each other (they rarely communicated about school issues or solved problems together).

> The first year my expectations were that we would meet, talk about instruction, and get to know each other. It was just an opportunity to sit down and let each other know how we felt, the things that bugged us, and so forth. It was really something. For the first time they started to talk about caring what was going on in the school, not just in their own classroom.

Setting up periodic meetings where teachers can just talk with and get to know each other is certainly not a startling innovation. However, it is revealing of him, some of his basic values, and the way he conceives of himself. The values Fred held seem to have been based upon a deep faith that the majority of teachers were wholesomely motivated and had an abiding concern for youngsters. What is required to capitalize on these concerns, on a wider basis than just the classroom, is some kind of structure that enables teachers to talk with each other and to be heard and understood. The problem is to create the appropriate setting. In this case, what was appropriate had to take into consideration the nature of the school, which, as was mentioned earlier, was small and had a very stable faculty. Fred could not afford to be seen as a wild-eyed revolutionary, which he was not. He had to soft-pedal things and, in a gentle sort of way, enable things to happen as he felt they would. In no way did Fred's service orientation involve simply being "water boy" to his faculty. Rather, he seemed to know what he wanted to do, create a new setting that will enable it to happen, and stay around to assist as required.

On a somewhat different level, Fred was required to legitimize himself in the eyes of the teachers. He was younger than most of them. He could not afford to be seen as a young radical unless, of course, he wanted a rebellion on his hands. He had to move slowly, even if he felt impelled to move quickly.

The same pattern is evident as Fred described how he went about working with individual teachers on matters of instruction.

> I made a conscious effort to sit down and talk with teachers on a regular basis. Particularly in the beginning of the year, I asked them what goals they were going to set for themselves concerning their performance as a professional person. I didn't use those words. But I did want them to think about where they were going and the ways I could be of help—with getting resources, visiting other schools, getting literature. And I tried to get them to specify something, not a big global thing, but a small thing that would be helpful. Even if it was something like learning how to keep records better.

The message, then, is to go slowly, taking little steps. And speak the language they understand, lest they label you a theoretician who can't communicate—who knows the words but not the music. But there's more to it than that, as a close reading of Fred's comment reveals. One of the underlying goals of his work with individual teachers was similar to one of his goals of working with the faculty in groups—to get them to start thinking in terms that would take them outside the classroom in order to take advantage of a wider universe of resources for teaching. Thus, he offered himself as a primary resource for them, as a person who could not only bring things to them but who could also enable them to go other places to learn. In a very real sense, he was a broker of educational services and instructional resources. It seems as though he said, "I'll help you create new settings for yourself, if you'll tell me what your needs are."

It is important to take special note of one comment that Fred made concerning his work with teachers. He said, "And I tried to get them to specify something, not a big global thing." The implications of this comment for him, for his teachers, and indeed, for the whole enterprise of schooling, are very large. In the last twenty years or so the schools—administrators, teachers, students, and parents—have been deluged with massive program innovation. The history of these programs has been that few have been smashing successes, for a variety of reasons running from low teacher involvement to the notion that the changes have been too broad to be manageable. It's almost as though the schools tend to reject foreign substances (new ideas) like the human body rejects foreign tissues. Whether or not Fred sensed this predisposition, we don't know. But his focus with teachers was on something small, something they could handle, something they wanted. In a very real way, this is his theory of change, and in the process of making it work he further legitimized himself as a person who could provide helpful services. By working in this manner he also reduced the possibility of failure and frustration at not having been able to deliver on something that was too big to start with. The slogan appears to be "start slowly with little things, and test them out." Additionally, to colloquialize, "half a loaf is better than none." An example of the slogan in action was an anecdote Fred told concerning changing the role of reading aides from one where people took youngsters out of a class to work with them to one where people worked cooperatively with teachers *in* the classroom. Fred had worked in a school where aides were integrated in the classroom setting, and he thought it was a good idea. But he was also aware of the communications and role conflict problems the situation presented. His initial tactic was to visit another school that was successfully implementing a plan of teachers and aides working together; the idea of the visit was to collect information from the vantage point of a principal, not a teacher. He returned to his school and commenced talking with both teachers and aides. The reactions were mixed, from a willingness to try, to "no way." Fred's reaction was:

> Okay. Maybe that's the way it will be. But what I'd like to do is try it with the people who are willing, and set up some ways of seeing whether it's helpful or not.

Once more, then, a setting was created to test an idea. If it worked, fine. If not, well, something else would be tried. And this attitude of experimentation reinforces a point made earlier—that Fred appears to have had the kind of faith and trust in teachers that communicates that they are adults with integrity who know what's good for themselves. But they are different from each other. When this attitude is communicated to teachers via behavior and not just words, it can't help being reciprocated. And that seems to be the direction Fred was going in his interpersonal relationships with his faculty.

We would be remiss in this discussion of Fred as a principal if we did not include an issue, which, while related to what he values and how he behaves, has much wider import. The issue has to do with the quantity and quality—or more generally, the lack of it—of adult-adult interaction in the schools. It arose, in our discussion, from an anecdote concerning the integration of teacher aides into the ongoing instructional life of the classroom. Fred's analysis of what appears to be a fairly general reluctance on the part of teachers to engage in task-oriented adult-adult interaction reads like this:

> There has never been an expectation, first of all, that teachers would get along with other teachers. When I was in training to become a teacher, I never heard anything said or even intimated that a teacher has a role as an adult with other adults. Never ever. And I never came in contact with the idea until, by chance, the school I was in started a team structure. There seems to be a sacredness about what happens once you close the door to your classroom. Or, maybe it's a fear of what others will find out about you.

For principals whose goal is to maintain the system, this state of affairs, which is a fairly accurate picture of reality in most schools, presents no problem. For Fred, or any other principal who wishes to develop his/her school into an organic problem-solving system, it obviously does. On the other hand, it is both an opportunity and a challenge to his skill as a principal.

There is one other point concerning the problem of adults working with adults in a school. The fact that Fred was concerned about it is a clue to one of his major thrusts as principal. He saw his major function as improving the curriculum and the quality of instruction. But, he seems to say that the avenue to getting this done is through enabling his teachers to trust him and each other enough so that their defenses can be lowered to the point where they can be open with each other, thus permitting themselves to work together on problems that really matter. This, too, fits with Fred's sense of himself as a broker of educational services and resources—teachers themselves are a school resource that for many reasons are not used, or are at least underused.

6

The Humanist: The Name of the Game Is "People—Plus Follow Through"

At the time of our interview with John he had just changed jobs. After eight years as principal of an inner-city high school of 1500 students in a medium-sized city, he accepted a position as principal of a high school in an affluent suburb. Most people in the area agreed that his new position was one of the choice plums to be plucked by a school principal. This was the basis for selecting him to be part of this study. If he was selected from a large number of applicants to head the high school of an educationally oriented and highly demanding school district, he obviously had something that a lot of other people didn't.

To an undiscerning ear, John could sound like just another school principal who sees himself as an undifferentiated, nonconceptual "people-oriented" administrator. Indeed, he described himself as a people-person, but a people-person with a difference as shown in his unprompted use of the following metaphor to describe a school:

> I always picture a school as a moving mobile. And on that mobile, hanging out there, you have got the board of education as a group, the District Office, the parents, the faculty, subgroups of the faculty, concerns with discipline (the student), the department chairmen, and teacher union representatives. Each group mobilizes forces to put demands on you. My job is to keep the mobile in balance, and keep it moving in a direction that all these groups really want it to go.

The image is a delightful and tantalizing one, almost begging the listener to give a tug on one or another part of the mobile to see how John would act to bring it back in balance. But beyond whatever artistry may be involved, John's use of the mobile metaphor seemed to serve the purpose of providing him with a coherent concept of what he is all about. That is, what we are *not* dealing with here is a soft-hearted human relations person whose aim is simply to keep the peace in a school so that it may drone on and on. Quite the opposite. His thrust was to maintain balance while concurrently maintaining momentum and direction. And this is clearly not an easy task in any high school, let alone an inner-city one where conflicting pressures are likely to surface in more unpredictable and, at times, violent ways, than might happen in an upper-middle class suburban school.

The concept that John seemed to hold of himself as a school administrator did not appear to include in any salient fashion the classical notion of his being the "educational leader" of his school. That is, he didn't see himself, for example, as a curriculum expert or, as he put it, a "thing administrator." Rather than derogate that view of school administration, he appeared to know what he was good at, and was careful not to put himself into situations where the demands put on him would fall outside his area of competence. This realistic self-appraisal served him well in the two contrasting positions that he held—the inner-city high school and the suburban high school. In the former, the community commanded that stability be created out of a chaotic situation. In the latter, the circumstances were different. The school was stable. Its students, for the most part, would be high achievers almost irrespective of what went on in the school. What the community wanted was not a dynamic innovator (in fact, they turned down precisely that kind of an applicant for the position in favor of John). To the contrary, they were interested in someone who they thought could keep the mobile in balance and who could ". . . move in with community and parents and get things done with the student body and faculty." John fit the bill, then, precisely because he was not a dynamic innovator.[1]

But John's concept of a people administrator is not a Mr. Milquetoast, be-nice-to-everybody person. The following illustrates this point:

> I remember a teacher coming in with a student in tow and saying, "I want this student suspended." I excused the student and said to the teacher, "Look, don't ever come into my office and tell me to suspend a student. I'll make that decision as the administrator. You certainly should come and tell me you have exhausted all your avenues of dealing with the kid. But when you turn over to me, I will deal with him in my way using *my* best judgment." I don't think the teacher liked that, but we became friends afterward. Incidentally, I did not suspend the student.

To reiterate, then, John seemed not to fit the stereotype of the "peace-at-any-price" school principal. Although it is clear that the focus of his administrative effort was on the human side of his school as an organization, and not on matters of curriculum and instruction, this focus did not include being anyone's pawn. Further, although John's interpersonal manner seems to have been a pleasing one, there is no doubt that he could make hard decisions, nor did he shy away from making them. John was in charge, and people seemed to know it.

---

1. As an interesting sidelight, we know of two chief school administrators, both of whom are forceful innovators, who accepted positions in stable school communities. Both of them are facing trying problems of mistrust and communications breakdown because, it seems, the moves and demands they made upset the balance.

An interesting question arises at this point concerning the basic strategy used that enables a people-oriented principal, a so-called humanist, to exercise that orientation in a way that has the effect the principal wants it to have. The mythology that is associated with the humanistic administration, probably deriving from a misconstrual of the human relations era of industrial management, is that this type of administration is soft-headed, benevolent, accepting, all-forgiving, loving, understanding, and so forth. The myth goes further and suggests that, if the administrator simply engages in the behaviors that are associated with these descriptions, then the organization will, through some mystical process, automatically run well. In the case of the schools, this means that the teachers would be happy and productive, and the students would be happy and learn. In short, all would be right with the world.

The point is, of course, that this myth, like most myths, bears little relation to reality. Schools are organizations whose members tend to have incompatible, if not antagonistic, needs. Furthermore, the group constituting the majority in the school organizational population—the students—are there by compulsion. For most students there is simply no alternative. It is hard to imagine, then, with the conflicts that inevitably arise from these circumstances, that an effective strategy for the people-oriented school adminstrator is simply to evince caring, supportive behavior—and that's all. If that were all, depending on the relative benignness of the student population, the school might come tumbling down around the principal's ears.

It was clear that John understood the nature of the conflicts that are endemic to the schools, particularly high schools. It was also clear that he understood that (1) these conflicts are probably not resolvable in any essential way, (2) these conflicts may need to be sublimated at least for the period of the school day, and (3) in order to make his concern for people operative and effective, he needed to provide a stable structure in the school. He said:

> Southern High was just racked with chaos when I went there. In order to be successful there it seemed essential to stabilize the situation, to calm it down. Our approach was to tighten down on things in a structural way. We became more strict about student discipline in the sense of strict enforcement of already existing behavioral codes. We let students know pretty well what the limits were and then we followed through to make as sure as we could that the limits weren't violated. Of course, there were some blatant and severe violations, and the students involved had to go for a hearing with the superintendent and they were subsequently removed from school. But people knew about it and why it had happened. An example was set. The result of this is that when the faculty perceived that things were under control we were able to get their support. They put their faith, so to speak, in the administration and things settled down.

The goal of John's structural strategy was to create some stability in the situation so that, as he put it, ". . . we could anticipate things before they happened and be prepared to deal with them." But the sought-after stability was not an end in itself. Rather, it was a way station, a very necessary one, between a faculty-administrative relationship that was centrifugal—people spinning off in disparate directions—and one in which there was a coming together of people and interests.

John's analysis of the dynamics of the situation went something like this: During the latter 1960s things started to happen in the schools that had not happened before, certainly not on such a grand scale. Undoubtedly related to the trauma of the Vietnam War, to growing problems of racial inequality, to the development of the drug culture and the concurrent counterculture, and probably to the spread of what had recently been characterized by Marin (1975) as the New Narcissism—"do your own thing"—schools started to experience increasing turbulence that in many cases was severe and marked by physical violence. Both teachers and administrators, for the most part, were ill equipped to deal with these developments. On the one hand, what teachers had always assumed as a given—their control in the classroom—seemed to be eroding rapidly. On the other hand, principals, whose role was frequently a mixture of routine administration and the conveyance of a benevolent paternalistic/maternalistic image throughout a school, unexpectedly found themselves confronting incipient or outright rebellion, a situation they were unprepared to handle—and understandably so. The Blackboard Jungle, it seemed, had grown by leaps and bounds far beyond its original confines of the poverty-stricken, inner-city, black ghettos.

New administrator behaviors were obviously called for, but they weren't, from John's point of view, unilateral decisions on the part of the principal simply to tighten things up. Whatever decisions were made should have been related to the faculty expectations (demands?) of what was needed. This point may seem so elementary as not to deserve consideration, but this is not the case. The stabilization of a school's student population is not a matter of simply showing the students who's boss, although that may be a first step in some situations. What ultimately appears to be necessary is a mutually supportive administrative-faculty relationship in which each party can count on the other to meet the role expectations they have for each other. John suggested that the process of building that kind of relationship starts with the ability and willingness of the principal to listen to what the teachers are saying, even though there are times when what they say may come across in less than clear ways:

> . . . they made it obvious to me what they expected. They wanted more strict enforcement of student discipline codes. They wanted to be sure kids were not loitering in the halls. They wanted administrators around the building; they wanted you to be visible. They did not want you in your office working on schedules or other such things. As you fulfill their expectations, also taking into consideration your own priorities, you build one hell of an alliance with your faculty. You really get them in your corner, so that when the time comes for you to ask them to do something they would not normally do, they'll do it.

This is an interesting point, then, and one that should not be misconstrued. This passage could be misinterpreted to mean that John paid attention to the expectations of teachers so that he would, after fulfilling these expectations, be in position to demand some sort of reciprocation from the faculty. A better interpretation follows: The school was in chaos. Its structure of stable relationships had broken down. It was a systemic problem that required resolution by system-oriented behavior. In this situation, system-oriented behavior meant paying attention primarily, at first, to the needs and expectations of the most relevant others who had a stake in the system's stability, the teachers. But this did not mean paying attention in a manner that excluded John's own role perceptions and judgments about what action was most appropriate to the situation. For example, in the case that John described, there were some feelings among the faculty and community that what was called for was the use of higher and external authority—the police. John rejected this demand because, as he put it:

> . . . you can't go after kids head-to-head. You lose, because when you bring in the police, for example, it infuriates them. Force begets counterforce.

If you don't go head-to-head with the kids, what do you do? John's answer was that you demonstrate that you care for them by reaching out, both interpersonally and organizationally. He talked with them as people—about ballgames, for instance, or about their families. But more to the point, of the problems with the school:

> We used to have a student advisory cabinet where we would meet every two weeks. The kids would talk to me in a very down-to-earth way. We talked about the school and its problems. We would communicate very openly and try to get things worked out.

Thus, the systemic approach to resolving the school's problems seemed to work without threatening the delicate balance that exists among administrators, teachers, and students in every school. The result was the building of an alliance between principal and faculty. But the issue is that John did not engage in this system-oriented behavior for the purpose of building the alliance so that he could manipulate teachers to reciprocate on other issues. To the contrary, the alliance was to be an expected side effect of working systemically. And, not only did it enable John to make reciprocal demands on the teachers, but also it opened the door for them to make further demands on him. This is a good example of both the potential and the risks inherent in administrative behavior whose base is to view the school as an interacting social organism, or in John's words, as a mobile.

Another part of John's image of the school involved the parents. The problems he faced with the parent group seem similar to those faced by most high school principals—one of relative apathy except in times of crisis. The picture is one of frustration:

We tried to cultivate parent support. We used to send out one thousand letters a month for PTA meetings. After the issues had been resolved, after school settled down and there were no boycotts and no violence, parental concern and community concern settled down, too. We were unable to cultivate a viable group of parents. That was a failure on my part, on the school's part.

Although John was unsuccessful in dealing with the parents on an organizational level, this seems not to be the case on the interpersonal level. He would see and establish contact with them at athletic events and in his office when they came to discuss their youngsters' achievement or behavioral problems. He particularly felt good about his skills with regard to parent conferences. But, rather poignantly, he communicated his sense of sharing the frustration of parents who had problems with their late adolescent—sometimes young adult—children and who could see no way out of the situation, nor could he.

Surely this brief description of an inner-city high school principal's relationships and attempts to work with the parents of students is one with which most similarly situated principals can relate and empathize.

The feelings and perceptions John had about his relationships with the Central Office seem to typify the bureaucratic and interpersonal relationships that are associated with large systems. First, though, John was hesitant to answer questions about these relationships. And then he said:

My relationships downtown were very positive with most people. You attract more flies with honey than with vinegar. I don't like to make enemies and I don't like to get into conflict with people when I know I can't win, especially, assistant superintendents. If you alienate that group you can really harm yourself later, both in terms of your school, and possibly, of your career.

The people orientation, then, took a different turn when John had to deal with upper levels of the bureaucracy beyond his direct control. Again, we suspect these circumstances are familiar ones. When the situation was within John's administrative domain—the school—he seemed to reach out in order to "cultivate" (he used that word a number of times) relationships. When he was dealing with the administrative hierarchy beyond his school, his attempts to cultivate support seemed to be characterized by compromise and conflict avoidance. That is, when John had to deal with the Central Office, he saw himself much more in a potential win-lose situation than when he was involved with problems in his school, where he had control, or certainly more control than when he had to communicate and resolve problems with the Central Office. Given that set of circumstances, his relationships with Central Office were distinctly more "political" and not as open as they were within his own school. Although he didn't say it directly, he seemed to subscribe to rather basic managerial strategy: "The name of the game changes when you want things from others who have control of scarce resources than when you have control of those resources."

The ethics of that stance in this particular kind of situation is not the issue, or at least not the primary one. The issue in bureaucracies, particularly when the allocation of scarce resources is at stake, is to behave in ways that will get you what you want. In other words, "Keep your eye on the doughnut and not on the hole" is not a bad rule of thumb, up to a point, of course. That point being when a person cannot live with what may be required of him/her by others in order to get what he/she wants. What was required of John, in terms of his having to compromise and perhaps repress some of his feelings and ideas in order to get what he needed from the Central Office, seemed not to violate any code of ethics he held concerning his behavior. Most of his fellow administrators probably would take the same stance.

However, some school principals operate differently with upper level administrative personnel. They do not "politic," for example, but are "up front" about almost everything. And they, too, get what they want. It is not merely a matter of personal style, but one of having to develop a very strong power base among their faculty and with their parent community. The message is simple in delivery but elegantly complex at its base, "If the name of the game is power, you have three options: (1) develop counterbalancing power and use it, (2) play defensively and wait for your opening, or (3) sit on the bench." It seems John took the second one, which appears to have been a wise choice, given the circumstances of his school and its constituent parent community.

John's professional relationships with his fellow secondary school administrators seem mostly to have been related to personnel matters. These relationships, similar to those with Central Office, took on a gamelike character, but with an important difference. The game with the Central Office, although possibly sensed by all the players, was played covertly. It was like a stalking contest. By contrast, the game John played with his colleagues was overt. Everyone knew they were involved in it, and it may be likened to duplicate bridge where everyone knows the rules; whether or not you win a hand depends on your skills at bidding and playing your cards.

A substantive problem around which the Central Office game was played involved the selection and transfer of teachers:

> Teacher selection became a problem because more than the building principal was involved. Most often it was a case of when a subject matter supervisor from Central Office and a principal disagreed about transferring a teacher from school X to school Y. School X, when it has to give up a teacher, always gives up a weak one. We (the principals) all know that. We meet once a month and laugh about it. And we think when we get a chance we'll unload on someone else. But that was a source of conflict, because although we accepted the fact that we all had to take our share of problem teachers, we always felt that there were some who took less than their share. They were more successful in wheeling and dealing lemons out of their building.

It seems, then, that a sort of "clubby" atmosphere existed in the administrative peer group with which John associated. But as he indicated, it was not all "hail fellow and well met." There was conflict, and probably some hostility that became cloaked in humor. The most successful players in the games that occurred were those who were able to combine their skills at chess, where the board is open for all to see, with their ability to operate skillfully in the more covert power game of the Central Office.

Considering that this is an imperfect world, it seems that John presented a rather realistic picture of a school principal's relationships with the bureaucracy of a large city school district. The people orientation that he described in connection with his role in his school takes second or third place to the political demands on him when he moves into the larger system.

The essence of John's style can be found in his repeated use of three words, which he used in several different contexts. They were *cultivate, caring,* and *follow-through.* He used them with respect to teachers, students, parents, and, indirectly, when he described his relationships with other administrators in his building.

The concept of cultivation seems to be an appropriate metaphor to describe the focus of John's administrative efforts. As any backyard gardener knows, cultivating a garden involves more than merely putting the seeds in the ground and hoping they will germinate and the resulting plants will be healthy and bear fruit. The ground needs to be watered, fertilized, and weeded; the plants themselves have to be tended, each according to its need. But the gardener also knows that some things are beyond his/her control, such as receiving too much rain or not enough sunshine. However, if he/she has paid attention to those things over which he/she has control, he/she may get a decent crop even if the elements aren't as kind as they might be.

Metaphors, of course, tend to present oversimplified images of behavior, even if they are accurate. But this metaphor can help indicate the complexity of John's concept of himself as a school principal. The thrust of John's cultivating efforts focused mostly on his school and its immediate constituents—the teachers, students, parents, and his administrative staff. The aim of it all seems to have been the development of a stable school organization that could weather unforseen, fortuitous events and bear fruit at the end of the season.

John's primary cultivating techniques were to demonstrate that he cared about these constituent individuals and groups, and to follow through on his commitments. The ways in which he communicated his caring varied. He listened to his faculty, for example, and not only to the words they spoke but, apparently, to those that were left unspoken. It's a curious commentary, perhaps, on our complex and fast-moving organizational society, that the very act of actively listening and communicating one's understanding of others has the side effect of creating the feeling of "He/she cares." For example, on more than one occasion, each of us has dealt with students who, from their point of view, feel they have been "brushed off" by other staff members in the university. We listened to them, and by our listening, and frequently little else, conveyed the impression that we cared—and we did. This is not an unusual example, of course, and is raised here only because of the frequency that teachers refer to their principals as nonlisteners.

Sometimes, then, listening to others is sufficient to demonstrate caring. This seems often to be the case, for example, in psychotherapy and counseling. For the school administrator, though, whose job is action oriented, merely listening is an inappropriate stance in most cases. Something has to happen as a result of the listening, even if it is only to express approval or disapproval to the listener. But more often, in John's case, the listening he did was followed by an action decision. However, the cycle is still incomplete because teachers need to know that the decision was, indeed, implemented. There needs to be a following through which in itself is another demonstration of caring. John's words say it all:

> Teachers have to see you as caring, as listening to their problems. And after listening, you have to follow through so that teachers know you cared enough to do something and then communicate back to them. You may not follow through the way the teacher thought you should, but at least you did something. You heard the problem and you dealt with it in a way that you saw fit.

Caring is communicated in other ways, by involving teachers and students in decision making, for example. Again, in John's words:

> There are decisions that can be made about the whole organization in which the faculty can and should be involved. When you do that the faculty starts to feel an integral part of the school, not just a classroom teacher. It helps develop morale, and it helps bring about a sense of professionalism in the school. The faculty develops the sense that the guy running the place will listen to them and move in directions they feel appropriate.

In a way, then, John appears to reverse the thrust that Argyris (1957) has noted is characteristic of many organizations when they employ adults and treat them like children (by, among other things, denying them responsibility for planning and decision making). It is a truism that if people are treated like children they will behave like children by, for example, displaying a short time perspective, by denying responsibility for their behavior, and by refusing to take responsibility for the larger system of which they are a part.

John carried the same cultivation, caring, and follow-through notions with him in concerns with students and parents, although his sense of failure concerning the parents as a group has already been noted. Particularly with students, it seems that his efforts were aimed at helping them feel less anonymous, less a part of a nameless mass. His strategy was one of interpersonal contact:

> If you want to cultivate kids you really have to care about them and convey that caring to them. You've got to be seen as more than just the guy who suspends kids from school. I try to talk to them in the halls, at ball games, in the cafeteria, in

classrooms. I try to get to know as many of them by name as I can. In a large school that's tough, but a principal should know four or five hundred kids by name, even in a school of fifteen hundred.

As important as the ability to learn names, though, is John's comment "you really have to care about them." The point is simply this:

> If a principal really doesn't care about kids, for example, his concept of his role might be that of routinely administering the school, period—he is probably better off not trying to play the "getting to know you" game.

The youngsters will recognize the game as precisely that, a game. It will be seen as meaningless, or, worse than that, as counterproductive, as the principal becomes the butt of jokes among the student body and, probably, the faculty. For example, an elementary school principal became the object of hilarious comment because he had a perpetual grin on his face. The grin was there even when he disciplined a student.

Finally, in his relationships with his administrative staff, John cultivated and cared here, too, but his behavior took a different form.

> ... you've got to get those guys to do things the way you want them done, but they have to want to do it that way. This means you've got to be very supportive, particularly with regard to the decisions they made. I never countermanded a decision that was made by a vice principal for fear that I would have him second-guessing himself out there. If he was wrong, I would live with it, and then we would talk about it at the end of the day.

Thus, it is essential that a school principal cultivate the active support of his/her administrative staff, by caring for them, but that caring is evidenced in ways that are different from those used with teachers or students. In this case, caring takes the form, first, of conceiving of the staff in an adult manner and, second, behaving in a way that communicates this to them. So, they are allowed to make decisions (which is what they are paid to do) and to live with the consequences of those decisions. If they make an inappropriate decision the principal helps them understand why. To do otherwise is to imply that they are not adult, thus committing an act of not caring; the principal will not get nor does he/she deserve their support.

At least, this is what John, The Humanist, seemed to be saying.

7

The Catalyst: Stirring the Pot
to Create Action

Almost by definition, women high school principals are an unusual species in American education. There are very few of them to be found. Marie was one of that small number, but her unusualness went beyond that. At least, that's the impression she gave when talking about how and why she got into school administration, what she did and how she related to the people with whom she worked, and the values that seemed to guide her behavior.

Marie, about forty, could be rather salty in her conversation. If a group of men took it into their heads to tease her with "men-talk," off-color stories, and so forth, they would find themselves on the receiving end of things very quickly. Marie made no attempt to project any type of "masculine" image, but was quite aware of having been socialized into stereotypical female patterns. She said, at one point:

> I'm female and maybe I tune that out. I think it works better if I do because I don't need to jump up and down, and things like that, when the going gets sticky.

This comment strongly suggests an integral part of the problem women have if they aspire to a high school principalship. The mystique goes like this: Women as principals of elementary schools have been accepted for years. Indeed, the principal of the "grammar" school one of the authors attended some fifty years ago was a woman. The reasoning behind this acceptance—the mystique—rests in the notion of the mothering function that the public finds acceptable, perhaps necessary, in elementary schools. Elementary schools do indeed have many characteristics associated with what Levinson (1972) described as "feminine organizations." There is a major focus, for example, on nurturance, affect, warmth, and kindness in elementary situations. Secondary schools in contrast are, in Levinson's terms, much more masculine in their orientation. The focus is on work, preparing for work, learning how to be competitive, control, and so forth. This suggests that being the principal of a high school is a "man's job." Men are better fitted by temperament, by their maleness that connotes strength, to manage and control.

Marie "busted the block," so to speak, in the community in which she worked. We suspect that one reason why was she had a lot of the kind of strength that is stereotypically associated with being a man, and she was able to communicate that strength in both words and actions.[1]

Marie's motivation for becoming a principal—the very words that she used—provided key insights into her style as principal and the kinds of behavior and values she encouraged in her faculty. She started her career as an art teacher, first on the elementary level and then in a secondary school. Her teaching of art was unconventional—the whole school became the canvas for her students, or at least she wanted to make it that way, which brought her into more than occasional conflict with her administrators. She became somewhat bored with what she was doing, the boredom being strengthened by the constraints under which she had to work. In addition, and in a straightforward way, she knew that the financial prospects were limited if she remained a teacher. But more important than the economics of her situation (she dealt with that in one short sentence) were her needs for excitement, her needs for productively disrupting the system. She said:

> I was getting bored. I needed something else to do that was exciting, new, different, and interesting. I thought about guidance, but it seemed to me the hands of the guidance people were as tied as those of the teacher as far as turning the place upside down for kids. An administrator can do that.

"Turning the place upside down for kids," then, was the theme that ran through Marie's story. She expressed it in a number of different ways. She loves the taste of battle, or even the prospect of it. "I just eat that stuff up," she said, and followed her comment with:

> When it got calm and quiet in the building, one of my assistants came in and said, "It's really boring. We've got to do something to stir this place up." And I said, "You're right. What shall we do to stir it up?"

In order for Marie to feel satisfied with what she was doing, there needed to be something going on all the time. And, apparently, if there was no bubbling-up process taking place at a moment in time, she was not at all averse to lighting the fire. Critically, though, to continue the metaphor, as a teacher she was able to start numerous small fires that were always in danger of being extinguished quickly by the building fire department—the administration. In her position as principal, the fire laws became much looser. She could start big ones or little ones; confine them to particular pockets of her territory or let

---

1. In a way there is a type of tragedy in all this. The tragedy, as we see it, is related to the assumptions, based on stereotypes, that are made about what people can or cannot do. These assumptions and resulting action must lead to an enormous waste of human resources.

them engulf a major part of it. In a way, she seemed to be an organizational firebug who did indeed like to watch things burn, who got some intrinsic satisfaction, not only from watching but also from being part of the flames and their heat. But, of course, there was more to it than that. For Marie, starting fires was not just the "thing," period. Beneath it, on a level she didn't speak of easily, was a very deep concern for youngsters. The cue is in the comment noted previously, "turning the place upside down for kids." Building fires for the sake of building them was not the issue as far as Marie was concerned. There had to be something worthwhile that needed to be heated up, or, on the other side, something that had little utility that needed to be simmered down, perhaps even extinguished.

Given the history of schools as rather stable, change-resistant systems that in the past reacted mostly to pressures from the external environment, Marie's stance and value orientation as a principal has to be considered a risky one. If, to use an immunological metaphor, she may be considered a foreign body in the system—violating long-standing norms—there is always a chance of rejection. In an interesting way, she seemed to be aware of this possibility as she thought about moving into school administration. By way of illustration:

> I like running things. I think it's fun. If I'm working for somebody that I think is sharp, then I don't mind their running things. For a long time I was afraid to accept the responsibility of being out front, but I got to the point where that didn't bother me any more. You see, you can be the power behind the throne and that isn't too tough. You can get the building run the way you want it run and you can do that without anyone going after you directly. I did that as an assistant principal. But then, as I became more self-confident, I thought, "Well, you know, I can handle that out-front stuff."

Marie was clearly aware of her own needs as a person—for action, for excitement, for running things. And she was also aware of school system norms that tend to reject, or, at least, not encourage an administrator's needs to continually stir things up.

Further, although she did enjoy doing battle, the prospect of being "out front" daily, of bearing direct responsibility for her own "fire building," required that she build an image of herself as someone who could "take it." There was no question that she could do this in a subordinate administrative position or as a teacher. For a period of time, though, there was a question in her mind about how she would react in a position of top authority in a high school. For Marie the implicit question was, how would she make it as a female firebug? The answer she gave herself was that she could deal with the situation on its own terms. And this she seemed able to do. Interestingly, the "terms" of the situation—being principal of a high school—fitted nicely with Marie's earlier concerns about getting bored when she was a teacher. Further, she was very much aware of and able to articulate the difference:

Well, I just like a lot of different things going on, and that's what happens. You never know what's going to happen the next day, who's going to call up, who's going to come into the office, or what they're going to have on their mind. It's the variety and the unpredictability that make it fun.

This comment provides a great deal of insight into Marie as a person and a principal, and it is complementary to her needs to light fires, to keep the pot stirring. Marie, in a very real sense, seemed to see herself as an organizational catalyst. People rather universally strive to make their world less ambiguous and more predictable so that they have a greater sense of control over themselves and their environment; there is security in knowing what is going to happen tomorrow. But for Marie, the security attached to being able to predict events or to having her environment fairly well structured was not an issue. She enjoyed the unpredictable, the not knowing what's going to happen tomorrow. And she enjoyed the unpredictability of "lighting fires," for fires, indeed, can get out of control. Nonetheless, of course, she was human and did need to feel secure, so the natural question arises: If Marie didn't need the security that comes from being able to predict and thus structure events, from where did her security come? It seemed to come from her own confidence that she could handle unpredictable situations, bring them under control, and help create productive learning situations for teachers and for students.

Thus Marie's tolerance for ambiguity seemed to be higher than that of most principals. The needs for security were still there, but they showed up later in the chain of events. A rather long anecdote illustrates the point:

I found out that seniors didn't have to take exams. When I asked why, people said, "I don't know. It is just because they don't have to take exams." I said, "Well, you know, seniors get kind of zooey at the end of the senior year and without exams it seems to me they might get worse." The teachers said, "Yeah, they really get awful." I said, "A lot of these kids are going to college and don't you think they need the practice at taking exams, reacting to pressure, etc." The response was, "Well, it wouldn't hurt them."

Well, we told the seniors they were going to have to take exams. They got really mad and upset. They were just really furious. As a result of being so furious, they put together a student council. We hadn't been able to get them excited enough about anything before that to develop a student council, so we were able to use their anger as a vehicle to accomplish something that needed to happen. They also did some research on why you should take exams, because I told them that if they felt they shouldn't take them they would have to tell me why and they better have some data. I didn't want to hear their opinions. Well, they were very angry at the whole thing, they wanted to know what my data was. I told them my data was my education, my degree, and the fact that I had this job—"So you come up with your data."

So they did. Several of them did quite a bit of research. The Student-Faculty Senate came out of that as well as some alternatives to taking exams (community projects) but I didn't think too much of them as alternatives. They still took exams.

Well, that's what happened. We didn't know they'd get that angry, but it didn't take us long to figure out what to do with their anger.

This anecdote reveals much about Marie's view of how to induce norm-upsetting change into a school, and her style of dealing with the emotional and behavioral fall-out that may result from such action. Modern organization theory (see Likert, 1967, for example) takes the position that the management style that carries the highest potential for organization productivity is a participative one. That is, a problem is sensed, people who are involved in the problem are brought together and, because people are rational, they work out a solution to which all are committed. Overall, this notion has some utility, under certain organizational conditions. But Marie's behavior indicated that her private theory of change, particularly when long-standing normative structures were involved, didn't put too much stock in the participative model. Given the present case, for example, what might have taken place had Marie convened a group of administrators, teachers, and students to examine the problems associated with the norm of seniors not taking exams? The administrators would present the problem and give their suggested solutions, some of the teachers would support the administrators, and some would support the students, and the students would undoubtedly take the position of maintaining the status quo. After all, who *wants* to take exams? It is possible in this set of circumstances, of course, for a compromise to be worked out that would be more or (probably) less satisfactory, a watering down of each position. It is likely that the administration would mandate the change irrespective of this resistance. If the former decision resulted, things would remain the same and the possibility of a struggle for power in the school in the future would be enhanced. If the administrator's initial position carried the day, the norm would be changed, but the resistors—teachers and students—would quite correctly feel that they had "been had." That is, they had been convened to solve a problem collaboratively, but the decision had already been made. This is not an uncommon occurrence in the schools, and the long-term effect upon teacher and student attitudes is usually counterproductive. Few people like to participate in dishonest games.

Whether or not these ideas were in Marie's mind when she made the decision about senior exams is not clear. What is clear, though, is her behavior and what it tells about the problem of restructuring important school norms. It's almost as if she were saying "If you want to know what to do, do something." Marie's position was that a principal has to have confidence in his/her ability to deal with the flak that results.

Marie's style of dealing with the flak—the anger of the students—varied. On the one hand, she was prepared to do battle with them, and she did. Combined with her willingness to engage in confrontation was a corresponding willingness to turn the situation into one that had some learning attached to it (getting the students to research problems associated with taking exams), and to engage with them in building other potentially productive experiences. In addition, of course, one unexpected consequence was the development of the Student-Faculty Senate.

Perhaps the most revealing comment, in the entire story of senior exams, was the last one that Marie made, "We didn't know they'd get that angry, but it didn't take us too long to figure out what to do with their anger." The issue is what strategy and accompanying style a school principal uses when conflict and emotional upset engulfs one or another segment of the school population. There are a number of ways to meet such conditions. A principal, for example, can ignore the whole situation, using the working hypothesis that, in time, what is boiling will simmer down and things will return to normal, however that is defined. In other words, the principal can deal with the conflict by avoidance. Another strategy that might be employed under conditions of emotional conflict would be to engage in a war of attrition. That is, the principal takes a position and fends off attacks under a working hypothesis that suggests that, in time, the opposing forces will become exhausted from the battle, their energies will dissipate, and they will comply in the face of superior and immovable forces. A third strategy is to confront the conflict openly, not in a "heels dug-in" manner but in a manner that acknowledges the conflict, that stands on some basic ideas, and that opens up the system for discussion and problem solving.

Principals, of course, utilize one or another of these strategies from time to time, depending on their assessment of the situation. Sometimes they avoid, sometimes they fight, and other times they confront openly. But each appears to have his/her predominant or preferred mode of dealing with emotional conflict, which is a product of his/her own idiosyncratic socialization. Our observations of most school principals is that the preferred mode is that of benevolent avoidance, a mode that is supported and reinforced by system norms. That is, it appears that much of the conflict in schools is dealt with in a soothing manner which aims to reassure people that everything will be all right—"Just try and forget about it and go back to work."

Obviously, this was not Marie's style, although there were probably times when she used it. Conflict for her seemed to be the vehicle for change, not to be avoided but to be welcomed for the opportunity it presented to open the system. She was skilled at confronting and also at fighting. Most importantly, however, it appears that the idea of a school's being in temporary turmoil did not frighten her. In fact, she seemed somewhat exhilarated by it all. There's almost a joyous quality to it, made possible perhaps by her ability to see humor in such situations. It's easy to imagine her saying, after having thrown down the gauntlet to the students, "Wow, that was fun and even funny. Let's see what they can do."

There was a serious side for Marie involving an overall strategy to upgrade the education of youngsters and to help her make her faculty a more vibrant, realistic, thinking group. With the faculty, her primary concern focused on their insularity from the environment outside the school. She said:

> What I see in my school is a group of people who are nice and they're interesting, too. I think they have basic intelligence, but I don't think they're terribly aware of

what's going on in the world today and the implications of what's going on for the schools. For department heads to get angry because their budgets were cut struck me as very unrealistic in view of what's happening in this state, for example. If you read the news, it seems to me, you have to understand the ramifications of it all for the school. For them to sit there and blame me or the superintendent for not getting any money just struck me as naive.

It apparently was difficult for Marie to tolerate adult naiveté, particularly when she saw important issues involved. Fairly quick to anger, her tendency was to administer a quick jab. In the situations just described, she asked the department heads if they wanted her to create a school riot to convince the community to pour more money into the school. Sarcasm, of course, rarely begets a benign response, and this case was no exception; one department head actually suggested that she might well do that—i.e., create a ruckus. The situation was degenerating. It was resolved when Marie said, with counter sarcasm, that she couldn't think of a riot to create at the moment and that, in any event, "You're just going to have to function on less money."

This incident, not the most preferred way of dealing with an issue, further illustrates what Marie was all about. She could tolerate the fact that youngsters may base their attitudes and behaviors on a fairly circumscribed world view, and she was willing to work with them to help them broaden their view. That's why schools exist. On the other hand, her fuse appeared to get very short when adults, who themselves are supposed to help youngsters get an understanding of the world, exhibit a narrowness that she described as naive. Her threshold for this type of frustration was low; and her anger, at least in this situation, was reflected in sarcasm.

Once more, however, despite the fact that many people turn away from sarcasm as a preferred style, the fire was lit. Her department heads, at the least, had no doubt in their minds concerning Marie's position. There was no hedging. Rather, the position was a confrontational one. "Here's the situation. It's real. Deal with it as adults, not children. That's why you get paid."

Marie's frustrations with her department chairpeople, however, had deeper roots than their inability or unwillingness to face up to and deal with the economic facts of life that confront public education. What bothered her most were two things: (1) their apparent unwillingness to engage with her in collaborative problem solving on school problems, and (2) their inability to act as educational leaders vis-à-vis their faculty.

I'm used to working with people who will engage in give and take about important things. I think part of the problem is that they were used to having meetings with a principal who sat there and said, "Now this is what you're going to do and this is how you're going to do it." And they said, "Yes sir, no sir, aye aye sir." And if any of them dared to argue with him, they'd get their money taken away. They seem to be a little more open than they used to be. I notice they really don't sit there and just look at me anymore. They do sometimes talk and occasionally they've gotten into some fairly heated discussions. But they're not the innovators. They're not the ones who are doing things. So, when they sat there and told me that the problems they were having were how many plugs were in their rooms and the fact that the boards weren't being erased, I decided for me to get out into the staff and get staff support. I guess I'm just frustrated. I keep looking at them and wondering, you know, what are you doing here?

Marie, then, had little tolerance for dealing with minor problems, particularly when she saw people, who she expected should exercise educational leadership, consuming their time and energy with mundane issues—problems they could solve easily on their own.

Fortunately for Marie, one of her assistant principals apparently enjoyed detail work: "He just loves doing that stuff. He's there till five every day and takes work home every night. He's really into nitty-gritty details."

Basically, she saw concerns about routine maintenance as a way to avoid dealing with more fundamental issues of curriculum and learning. And *this* is what was frustrating to her, their not having a solid conceptual grasp of their program. For example:

Sometimes I just don't understand people. I try to. I spent one entire morning trying to understand an industrial arts guy and his frame of reference, because it obviously wasn't mine. He just flips around and has a good time. I don't think he knows what the hell he's doing, or why, or how. I'm not sure that our kids move out of there with any conceptual skills that are going to do anything for them.

One image that emerged for Marie as a high school principal, then, was that she found herself engaging in a number of very frustrating situations with adults in her school. But she had some insight into the situation that helped cushion, minimally, the frustration. The circumstance was, of course, an interactive one, stemming from the conflict between the needs and expectations concerning the attitudes and behaviors of department chairpeople and the way they behave as a group and as individuals:

I know me, and I know that I always want things to have happened yesterday. In addition, I have high expectations, and they know that my expectations are high, but they're not really sure what my expectations are. It isn't that I haven't told them, or that I haven't told them why. It's that they haven't hooked them all up. I guess they don't see any rhyme or reason for organization and goal setting. They never had to do it. It's almost as though a lot of people aren't sure what to do with me.

These conditions are similar to those in other school settings, on the level of both building and system-wide operation. The scenario goes something like this. A new administrator is brought into a school setting, which has been stable over a period of time during which no new or norm-upsetting demands have been made on the staff. The system had been administered with what might be called a maintenance orientation. That is, the primary thrust was to maintain, not change, what was going on. The faculty and administrative staff were contented and held perceptions of a smoothly running, productive organization. Perhaps most of all, they were let alone to work and teach in a manner to which they had become accustomed, and with which they were comfortable. The new administrator is not satisfied with what has been. The administrative orientation becomes one of change. The impact of this new orientation is two-fold: (1) It is norm-upsetting. People have to become socialized to new sets of attitudes, new goals, and new ways of doing things; and (2) by implication, subtle if not direct, the new administrator's concern with change suggests that the way the system and individuals in it have been operating is not as good as they thought it was. What seems to occur then is a sort of pulling away. A distancing effect takes place in which the people involved seek to protect themselves by avoiding confrontations with each other.

These circumstances tend not to be happy for the people involved. The well-meaning administrator becomes frustrated and angry. The staff tends to withdraw, causing the administrator to become more frustrated and angry, which in turn causes more staff withdrawal. A downward spiral of administrator-faculty relationships develops that is buttressed by a trend for one party to attribute negative motivations to the other party, regarding behaviors that may have no connection with the operation of the school. An example of such a situation, not in Marie's school, is repeated here to make the point clear.

A new school superintendent was employed in a lovely small town in Pennsylvania. What occurred in his district was pretty much what has been described in Marie's school. The district had been stable and maintenance oriented. The new superintendent wanted things to change. The same kinds of things Marie mentioned that were going on in her school were going on in that district. The staff started to withdraw and the superintendent became frustrated and angry. Part of the staff's verbalized concern was that the superintendent was using his position (thus using them) as a stepping stone toward bigger and better things. Their evidence for this perception was the fact that the superintendent had, on coming to the community, rented a house instead of buying one. The attributed motive was that he did not buy a house so that when bigger things came along he could make a quick getaway. In point of fact, he did not buy a house because he does not like to own houses.

The issue here is not the good guys versus the bad guys. At issue, is that when change-oriented administrators, particularly if they are in a hurry, are employed in stable school settings, it seems reasonable to predict that some unhappy, *but not necessarily unproductive* things will happen. And Marie appeared to be in just that kind of situation. She attempted to stir things up and the results were predictable.

But Marie was not depressed over the circumstances. To the contrary, she seemed energized by the obstacles in front of her. Her energy derived from her various support systems. One was composed of faculty and friends at the university where she received her advanced degree. She maintained continuous contact with them. A second was her network of professional colleagues in the field. She went to several workshops, for example, to sustain herself, or so it seems. A third support system was internal, composed of her two assistant principals. Although each has been briefly discussed, the focus here is on the relationship that developed between Marie and her assistants because of its effect on her day-to-day behavior.

Both of the assistant principals were men, one younger and the other older than Marie. She said that they really worked well together, but that it took quite a while to develop a good team. Marie's words best describe the situation:

> The older of the two, Charlie, he's about fifty, wanted the job. Not only didn't he get the job, he got me, a woman. As you can imagine, he really wasn't excited about seeing me come in. I knew his feelings weren't directed to me as a person, but at the situation. He's a good kind of person and I knew he'd never take his feelings out on me. In fact, he stands on his head not to take it out on me. The other assistant (Jim) and I just had instant communication. We don't even have to talk and we know what the other is thinking. We really did have to concentrate on making Charlie part of us. In the beginning it was frustrating.

What was frustrating the development of the administrative team was not the male-female issue as Marie saw it. Rather, it was Marie's action-oriented and proactive style. Charlie, on the other hand, was more traditional and conservative and, as Marie put it, "He didn't know at all where I was coming from." It would have been possible, of course, for her to brush him aside, avoid him, and simply let him pay attention to the details of running a school. Marie decided this would be dysfunctional, not only with regard to their relationship, but also with regard to the relationship of the administrators and the rest of the school, particularly the department heads. That is, if the three administrators couldn't function together, then their nonfunctioning would be obvious to the staff, and would probably split it. Marie understood this situation and decided that the only viable option was to reach out to Charlie and try to involve him in what she wanted to do.

> I knew I was going to have to spend a lot of time talking with him. He had skills and knowledge that I didn't have. So we talked a lot. I listen to him and he listens to me. I think he knows I listen to him and that's important to him. We hash stuff around, the three of us, or the two of us. By the time we're done, we're usually somewhere between the two poles from which we started. It usually works better. In department meetings, I'll say, "Charlie and I really went round and round before we presented this to you," because I trust his judgment.

So, there was another side to Marie, different from her impulsive, stir-things-up side—a concern with building a cohesive organization, not a short-term affair, and a deep concern for the value of individuals. What apparently triggered her frustration and anger was not the fact that she might differ markedly with the opinions of another person. To the contrary, she appeared to welcome a good argument. What did trigger her frustration and anger was the other person's seeming refusal to invest himself/herself in a situation in order to listen to and hear about diverse points of view. Charlie, it seems, was willing to make this investment. The result was the development of a solid administrative team from which Marie drew a lot of support.

Contrary to most of the other principals interviewed, Marie's relationship with Central Office personnel was fairly close, though not nearly as close as that with her assistant principals. If there was a problem, it was with one of the assistant superintendents who, before he went into public education, was in the priesthood. As Marie put it, "I'm not sure he really knows what to do with women." As with Charlie, rather than avoid the assistant superintendent because he, too, had important skills she wished to use, she altered her style, once more.

> I don't avoid him at all. I'm just very, very careful about how I deal with him. I try to be very calm, very logical, very rational. If I'm off on one of my wild kicks, you know, I run it through my assistant before I ever go near Frank with it.

The fact that she is female played a role in the community's reactions to her appointment as principal. There was a general curiosity, some humor, and some not unusual male doubts about a woman being the high school principal.

> I think they were startled, in the first place, to get a woman and, in the second place, to get a good looking one. Some of the kids, for example, when their parents queried them, said that I had a super pair of legs. And the parents all turned out in force for parents' night to get a look at me. Then there was the time I had to give a speech at the Rotary Club. Fortunately because it's really a funny group, I didn't get the giggles. Afterwards, I heard one of the men say to a member of the selection committee, "She must have had some set of papers to get this job. I wonder if she's going to mess around with any of her male staff?" I thought to myself, "How naive can they be?"

As we pointed out earlier in this chapter, Marie was very much aware of her femaleness in her role as principal. She also knew she had no control over the reactions of some men to women occupying positions historically in the male domain. What seemed to stand her in good stead when dealing with the problem were three parts of her make-up: (1) She is not a militant feminist. She reacted to the comments that were passed, not with anger, but with amusement; (2) She appears to have a rather firm hold on herself as a person, knows what her values are, and is not easily threatened on an interpersonal level; and (3) Her sense of humor about life itself enables her to sense life's absurdities and deal with them in a mature way. Thus, she was and is able to brush off unseemly remarks without getting upset or, if need be, play a tough game of give-and-take.

There was, however, one unverbalized issue connected with her female-ness, and Marie had to deal with it as soon as she became principal. Would this woman be able to make firm decisions, particularly with regard to discipline? Would she be able to control this school, or would the students run rampant over a female principal? Marie was unequivocal about it. She knew she had to establish herself quickly, and that discipline problems were the vehicle by which her position would become most visible.

> They had put a very heavy emphasis on discipline. The fact was that it was rotten. So, the best way to do it, for the first couple of months, was to get the police involved. There was no hesitation on my part because I was used to running a school that way. My feeling is that when the kids break school rules the school will deal with it. When they break the law (stealing, smoking pot, throwing firecrackers), the law should deal with it.

This strong stand proved helpful to Marie, not only with the community, but with her staff as well, as they gained confidence in her ability to create a more stable environment. As Marie reflected on the situation, although she was aware of issues surrounding her femaleness, she said:

> You know, the problem is not just a female one. It holds for everyone. It's like the "old hand" advice that's given to new teachers: "Don't smile until Christmas." I used the same kind of psychology as an administrator, and it worked. The cops don't have to come in as much anymore because the kids know we won't hesitate to call them. It was partly the kids testing, too, and they found out quickly.

It is true, of course, that being a good teacher is not a predictor of how one will perform as an administrator. However, depending on how one conceives one's role as a teacher, there may be some productive carryover into the administrator's role. In this connection, Marie seemed to say that, if a teacher understands and is able to enact workable principles of classroom management, there is a chance of carryover into at least some aspects of school management. "I used the same kind of psychology as an administrator, and it worked."

Reactions to Marie's femaleness arose in two other situations. The first had to do with the Board of Education. During the first year of her tenure the board voted to include two student representatives in their meetings. They were on the agenda at one meeting to report on how things were going at the school. Part of their report included a reaction to the principal, whom they characterized as cool and aloof. The reaction of the board was, "Good!" This is somewhat surprising, given current educational concern with warm personalities. Their reaction makes sense in another context, however. If one pictures a Board of Education appointing a woman high school principal, but having some doubts about its decision, particularly with regard to control and discipline, a student report of impersonality would be reassuring, even if the reassurance is misguided.

Marie was not terribly upset by being described that way, although a colleague at the Central Office was. What she did was to talk with the students in order to try to get them to understand how she conceived her role. She told them:

> I was never going to be the "Jolly Green Giant." I didn't have time to run around the building getting to know eleven hundred kids and furthermore, the building wasn't going to run if that's the way I spent my time.

Her style of direct confrontation paid off once more. The students came to learn a bit about the problems of running a school. Soon they were meeting with her before board meetings to discuss problems on the agenda.

The other situation related to Marie's femaleness concerned athletic events. She hated football and basketball, but high school principals are "supposed" to be present at all games, on the untested assumption, one suspects, that the principal's presence will be good for morale. The superintendent also thought it would be a good idea for her to attend. She did go to the football games, but not to the basketball games, and for a reason that is both comic and, from one point of view, tragic.

> I didn't go to the basketball games because I had gone to the football games with my assistant principal and a rumor started in town that I was having an affair with him. I thought it was hysterically funny, but he didn't. Anyhow, I called the superintendent and said, "Besides the fact that I hate sports this other thing has come up. Do I have to go to any more of these basketball games?" And he said, "No."

We have probably only scratched the surface of problems that arise when a woman becomes a high school principal. In Marie's case, it appears that she took things pretty much in stride, although she was aware that, like it or not, she faced role expectations from the total community different from those placed on men, particularly with respect to her personal life. These expectations, however, did not prove more than she could handle—not by a long shot!

There is another point we need to raise in order to fill in our sketch of Marie, The Catalyst. In addition to what appeared to be her ongoing tendency to stir things up, there was an enduring part of her that could best be described as "up-front openness." It seems clear that she rarely left any doubt about where she stood on issues. If she was in doubt about her position, she did not play the "certainty" game. She would tell you she's in doubt. But if she had a clear position, then there was no hedging. She did not like to play organizational games, preferring to put her cards on the table and deal with the consequences rather than engage in intricate manipulative endeavors. Such openness is refreshing. Alternatively, unless her colleagues and staff learn to deal with it, it can cause interpersonal and organizational upset. While the results are not yet all in as far as Marie and her school are concerned, she'll continue to conceive of her role as an organizational catalyst for change; she'll continue to "light fires" and "stir things up."[2]

---

2. She did continue this pattern but the politics of her school district proved too much for her. She resigned her position and is now engaged in a non-school type of work.

8

The Rationalist: A New Lady on the Hill

This chapter differs somewhat from previous ones in its overall thrust. Our discussions of the school principals interviewed tend to focus on their world view as principal and on the recurring themes in their behavior, to highlight both the stability of that behavior and its idiosyncrasies. This chapter also pays attention to behavioral themes. However, a major part of it examines the problems that develop when a woman sets her sights on becoming a high school principal, and then becomes one.

It will be recalled that Marie, discussed in the previous chapter, who is also a high school principal, tended to brush many of her initial problems aside. Not so with Fran, who ran into obstacles even in her graduate study. Thus her situation is probably more illustrative than Marie's of the barriers that stand in the way of a woman's becoming a secondary school principal.

Fran was in her early thirties. Her aura was one of openness, rationality, and verbal ability. She came across in a contemplative, but forceful, way.

When we encountered Fran she was in the second year of tenure as principal of a high school in a small town in Pennsylvania. She had enrolled in a doctoral program in a large university. She seemed excited about her job, but she had experienced some problems in it that were directly related to being a woman in what had always been, in that town, a "man's" territory. So, this chapter starts with a look at her first thoughts and efforts to move from the teaching ranks as a high school English instructor into administration. She and her husband had recently returned from overseas teaching positions. They were working in the East, a little unusual in itself as their home state was on the West Coast, and most teachers work close to their homes. Fran was unable to identify any particular person who first gave her encouragement to set her career sights on administration. There was a series of circumstances and experiences that seemed to push her along. A rather odd one, first:

> There were a few casual remarks by principals that I could have interpreted as meaning that I was too pushy concerning matters of school policy, decision

89

making, and so forth,. But if that was the intent I took it differently. That is, I interpreted the remarks to mean that I knew what was going on, that I had some ideas to contribute, and that I should just continue to do that.

Here, then, is some insight into Fran as a person. She was no pushover; she did not scare easily. Furthermore, she had a pretty clear handle on herself and was sure of her motivations. So, while women unsure of their ground and threatened by a school power structure might interpret the remarks that Fran received as advice to back off, for her it was just the opposite. The remarks served to reinforce notions she already had about herself: that she was aware of organizational function and dysfunction, could talk about her awareness in clear terms, and was assertive. "Not a bad set of skills," thought Fran. But there was more:

> In my public school teaching experience, which spanned eight years and six different principals, I worked with only one who I thought was an intelligent and dynamic educator. I thought that the batting average couldn't all be that bad and didn't need to be and that I could be better than the average. So, with a little bit of encouragement from a principal, I decided that administration might be an interesting thing to pursue on the master's level.

This anecdote smacks of one about Jimmy Carter. The story is that, during the presidential primary campaigns of 1977, Carter, then Governor of Georgia, served as host for presidential aspirants campaigning in Georgia. His reaction to his guests, the story goes, was his feeling that he was as well equipped as any of them to be president, and better than most. Why not me? The rest, of course, is history, as it is with Fran. Beneath the surface, though, is an important message about her as a person, which became evident as she commented on casual remarks passed to her by a couple of principals. The message was that she was a person of strength who viewed obstacles, not as things from which to back off, but as challenges, opportunities to be seized.

Her decision to study administration was the result of a natural progression—"I decided that administration might be an interesting thing to pursue on the master's level." Fran was not going forth to conquer the educational world. Rather, she was doing something that was quite natural, following her interests. At the time, as will become clear, she was a bit naive about the whole situation; what it would involve, and the problems to be encountered that were subtly or overtly related to her femaleness.

There was a third set of circumstances that led Fran toward thinking about administration:

> I really liked teaching. When I was teaching, I taught mostly eleventh and twelfth grades. I also had a scattered class or two at the ninth and tenth grade levels. But one summer I taught a class in photography and the kids in there went from the seventh to the twelfth grade. I was really impressed with the wide variety of experience present which led me to think about the fun of dealing with varied

aspects of education instead of being confined to teaching English, for example. I guess it really made me think that I didn't want to spend the next fifty years teaching English. So, I thought I'd like to try some other focus in education, and administration seemed an easy and compatible step.

Fran's motivation to move to administration, then, was similar to Marie's (Chapter 7), although it seems to have developed with less emotionality. Recall that Marie pulled no punches when she said she was getting bored with the teacher's role. Fran's tone was lower key. She liked what she was doing, enjoyed the variety, but took the long view, apparently feeling that a continued experience over many years would be dulling for her. Marie was already dulled, but then she was older and had been teaching longer. It's possible that Fran would have been as openly bored as Marie had she stayed in the classroom longer.

In any event, having made the decision that going into administration would be an easy and compatible step for her, Fran applied for and was admitted to a master's degree program in educational administration.

> I was the only woman there, but I hadn't thought of it too much in that light (i.e., being a woman in what was widely considered the domain of men) before I went into the program. I had an advisor who was extremely cool to me the first semester, but by the second semester we were working quite well together. Nevertheless, I had to discover a lot of things by myself that probably most men knew long ago. For instance, an internship was required in order to be certified. That's a simple thing for people who know the system, but I didn't know, and nobody told me.

It didn't take long, then, for the subtle prejudices of the system to begin to work. Fran was clearly a minority person in her degree program, and her interests in the high school principalship simply reinforced this status. It's all right for a woman to want to be an elementary school principal, because small children need to be mothered. But adolescents in secondary schools need to be managed, and this is a job for men. It makes for a quaint mythology.

The mythology, however, got played out in behavior. For example, when Fran talked with her advisor about an internship, his response was, "Well, we'll see what we can do." Fran's interpretation of his comment, which he was later willing to admit was true, was "Dammit, she had to go and bring that up!" Probably if she had not pushed the internship issue he wouldn't have either, being willing to let his "problem" graduate without being certified. For example, after the issue was raised, he suggested that most people did their internships in their own school. In Fran's case this would have created a hardship, as her home was in Oregon, 3,000 miles away from where she was doing her graduate study.

The situation did resolve itself over time. Fran did get her internship, and, in addition, it was her perception that she helped her advisor a great deal with his attitudes about women in administration. He helped her, too, but

I think he probably gave his men students more help. For sure, he was more concerned about finding jobs for his men students than he was for me. He would say things like "Maybe you can work yourself into a dean of girls position or something like that." The funny thing is it wouldn't really have mattered because I would probably have enjoyed that, too. It was just the reluctant tone of things that bothered me.

Fran finished her internship and started to look for a job, but without much assistance from her advisor. She was considering two positions in student affairs (not general school administration) when she received a phone call from a superintendent she had known previously. Was she certified and was she interested in the high school principalship? She was indeed, but the selection process wasn't easy, and the issues focused, as might be expected, on her being a woman. The primary point in her interviews was student discipline. What else!

> The school board was really concerned about discipline. They wanted to know what I would do about this, that, and the other situation. It was hard for them to envision a woman, really hard, being able to handle an eighteen- or nineteen-year-old boy. They were also concerned about how a woman would handle more serious disciplinary problems because the school had had a lot of disruptive situations—student sit-ins, student sit-downs, student strikes, teacher pickets. So, it was a real problem.

Despite the concerns of the Board (and probably others in this small community) Fran was hired, but not without conflict. The vote was four to three, and, had the superintendent not had strong support from the Board (he had been hired on a 7–0 vote), she probably would not have gotten the position. Why did she take it, in view of what she knew to be more-than-subtle opposition to her appointment? Her answer was straightforward—there were risks involved, but it was a challenge; an opportunity to do something she thought she could do and do well.

The superintendent had communicated to Fran his analysis of the types of political conflicts he saw in both the community and the school. She was forewarned, then, about what she might expect, particularly with regard to three or four members of the faculty who, it seems, had made an avocation out of making it tough for high school administrators. She was stepping into a hornet's nest, and, unwittingly it seems, she stirred it up very shortly after having arrived on the scene at the start of the school year. The school had developed a pattern that the entire student body meet at the beginning of every school day to hold, in Fran's words, a "glorified rap session." At this time, students were supposed to be able to talk about their concerns, on the theory that the talk would have a cathartic effect, thus freeing them to concentrate on their studies for the rest of the day. What seemed to be happening, though, was quite different from what was intended:

> It turned out to be a sort of sadistic arena. A lot of criticism was leveled at teachers, at individual students, and at the principal who was called a prophylactic

for the school board. Prominent students were simply playing to the larger student audience. So, instead of being cathartic for the students, it seemed to me that these daily sessions only generated more controversy.

Fran then made, in her own words, her first mistake—and it was a big one. The mistake was not in her analysis of the situation, but in her action. She decided, because the large session was dysfunctional, to stop it and substitute small group meetings composed of teachers and students with similar interests. It seemed like a rational thing to do, and Fran prided herself on her rational approach to problem solving. Rationality frequently comes in a poor second when opposing forces are mobilized mostly on the basis of emotionality, and this is precisely what occurred. The results of the decision were that "the kids hated it; the teachers hated it; and we had a student sit-in."

Fran was not unprepared. The grapevine let her know the sit-in was planned. She scheduled a meeting with the school bus drivers for the morning of the sit-in, so they would be on hand if she decided to close school. The sit-in took place and she sent the youngsters home at about 9:15 in the morning. In addition, eighteen students who could be positively identified received a three-day suspension.

Perhaps Fran's action from the beginning was ill-advised, if not a gross administrative error. Indeed, she did say it was her first mistake. One might simply suggest that she was too new in her position and should have waited until her credibility was established before making a decision that would have such a potentially disrupting effect, even though both points were undoubtedly true. But there was more to it than that. Two other factors entered the situation in a prominent way. One had to do with Fran's perspective on and analysis of the total school environment; the other with her decisiveness and ability to handle tough situations.

She saw the school as being on a downhill path. There had been a lot of disruption, and her analysis of it was that not much was happening, in any systematic fashion, that could be called good education. A crisis point had to be reached that would enable her to start turning things around, not only with students, but also with some of the faculty who, it turned out, actively encouraged student resistance, and the sit-in itself. She said:

> It seemed to me, from day one, that it would take this kind of thing to blow something out and get started again. If it hadn't been the big student meetings, it would have been something else like my reactions to too many gym classes too many days a week.

Fran's action, then, was not impulsive, even though it may have been inappropriate for the time. It was a rational, contemplative decision based on her notion that, if a program is not producing what it was designed to produce, rational people will want to change it. It was also a decision that Fran knew would shake the structure of the school and thus provide her with the opportunity to demonstrate that she was decisive, and that she could control a disruptive situation. The "New Lady on the Hill" needed to quickly be in a position to indicate to the school and the community that she was no pushover. And this is precisely what happened.

The problems that Fran encountered as a result of being the first woman high school principal in a small town were not confined to the school. In a sense she was being "double-teamed," in the school and the community. At first she was a little reluctant to talk about the situation; again, the issue was related to being female. She didn't wish to be perceived as a "whiny female." She was having enough trouble establishing her credibility as a legitimate principal so that, in order not to add fuel to the fire, she kept things to herself and tried to ignore what must have been a constant pattern of irritants. Some examples tell the story.

Six days after the student sit-in her husband, who also taught at the school, was stopped by a police officer who issued him two tickets: one for driving with invalid license plates and one for an invalid driver's license (they were from another state). When he went to court he was fined $150 when the typical fine for these offenses was $10, according to Fran. It turned out that the judge was the father of two youngsters who had been suspended as a result of the sit-in.

The small town communications and rumor networks also played their part:

> There were a lot of disparaging and condescending remarks passed around. They would come back to me and I would kind of bounce them off. Things like, Why doesn't she wear skirts more often? How come she has such long hair? Why does she want that kind of a job? Why don't we see her in the supermarket more often? Why doesn't she join the lady Elks? Who takes care of her kid after school?

Fran's strategy for dealing with the remarks and incidents, as she indicated, was simply to ignore them, to let them bounce off her. It was a deliberate strategy, her feelings being that, if she started to react, the community would take the position that she couldn't take it and that, indeed, a woman did not belong in the job of high school principal. And though Fran seemed to be successful with her strategy of ignoring, it took its toll on her. In retrospect, it was as if she were living through a state of siege, particularly in the school, but influenced by the community.

> I guess, in that first year, if I hadn't done anything different, if I hadn't started a teacher evaluation program or tried to upgrade the guidance department or focussed on rounding out kids' school experience, I wouldn't have felt near the pressure. If I'd been smart enough or dumb enough just sort of to maintain things, I wouldn't have felt that I was constantly fortifying myself and my programs against attack. The attacks didn't come from all sides, but there were a lot of people involved.

But some of that seems to have dissipated now and I think the reason is that people have become more familiar with my style. They see my behavior and decisions as consistent with me rather than as inconsistent with the guy who was there before me, or the guy who was there before him, and before him. You know, there were five principals in seven years and five superintendents in seven years.

It is easy to criticize Fran's administrative behavior. The wise old heads, on hearing of the problems that developed in the school and community, would probably shake with an "I could have told her so" attitude. It may well have been more strategically viable for her, in the long run, to just maintain things in that first year until people got used to her style and to the fact that there indeed was a "New Lady on the Hill." But that's not the point, or at least not the point of this book. The point is that Fran, her perception of herself as both a woman and a school principal, provides themes that make the situation more understandable. The theme of rationality and her sense of her own competency seem to flow throughout. Her decision to become an administrator was a rational one. What was required were knowledge, skills, a desire, and the ability to make decisions, and Fran had these qualifications.

Why the problems, then? Perhaps the answer lies in the very rationality that seems to guide her. That is, people who are guided by a forthright, empirical, rational point of view may wrongly assume that others will see the situation in a similar light. After all, the facts speak for themselves, don't they? Or do they? The facts do indeed speak, but through the perceptions of others, as well. Fran's recounting the story of the teacher evaluation program as an illustration.

Even though a program of teacher evaluation had been negotiated in the teacher's contract, for years there had, in fact, been little or no implementation. Tenured teachers, for example, had been observed on the average of once every four years, a clear violation of the contract. Fran, The Rationalist, made the assumptions that (1) the contract should be adhered to, and (2) evaluation of teachers was a healthy thing to do. So, she simply started to implement the contract. After all, if people had agreed they were going to do something, why shouldn't they do it? Predictably, problems arose as teachers resisted the process by becoming defensive about comments that Fran might make about her observations of their teaching. In addition, their resistance took the form of suggesting that she hadn't been in the school long enough to understand the total situation or the teachers themselves. Over a period of two years the situation finally worked itself out as the teachers discovered that the intent of the evaluation was to help, not to punish. As Fran said:

. . . people are probably a little more secure and accepting now. No tenured teachers were fired and I think they're coming to understand that evaluation has two purposes: to make judgments about continued employment and for professional development. Maybe it's the professional development part that they're a bit more accepting of now.

It is less important, here, to comment on the efficacy of a particular teacher evaluation program than it is to reinforce the notion that Fran's implementation of it indicated the theme of rationality that ran through her view of the principal's role. But there is another element to it. Fran not only saw herself operating in a very rational way, she also seemed to have a very deep faith in the process of rationality. It's as though she were saying, "The intelligent, reasonable thing to do in X situation is Y. People may resist Y initially because it runs counter to established norms. But if I persist they will eventually come to see that Y was the thing to do because it was simply rational, and they will see it that way." Accompanying her view of herself, then, is an implicit position on a technology for integrating the individual's needs with the organization's objectives. That is, her behavior suggests the technology—or mechanism—of socialization. It says, in effect, that "I will present a model, and as you learn to live and work with that model, you will find it is a productive one. It will become part of you."

An additional clue to this part of Fran's make-up was provided earlier. She had spoke of the faculty's need to learn something about their relationship with her. That is, good relations depended less on her being inconsistent with previous principals and more on her behavior being consistent with her values and beliefs. Again, the picture is one of rationality, persistent rationality, which communicates a great deal of faith in the reasonable intelligence of others and ignores the political consequences of behavior that may be deviant from the accepted normative structure of a school or community. As a matter of fact, Fran seemed almost to be apolitical in the way she worked. At one point she said, with reference to the mayor whose son broke a window in the school during the sit-in:

> I haven't catered to the power structure and, because that was a working policy before I got here, it's created some uncomfortable situations.

It seems clear that her refusal to cater to the community power structure was reflected in the way she worked in the school. Recall, for example, that Fran didn't mention any consultation efforts on her part when she instituted the evaluation program. She just did it because "what was right, was right." Unfortunately, as she found out, what is right may have little to do with the political or socioemotional realities of a situation. This point is raised, not in criticism of the way Fran operated, but to point out that every behavioral style has its costs as well as its benefits. A clear benefit, among others, is that what she did and the way she did it enabled her to maintain her integrity and her view of herself as a person who dealt with facts and objective reality. One of the costs, also a clear one, was that she felt herself under siege.

When it came to curriculum, it seems that Fran's strategy, her reliance on reason, remained the same, but her tactics changed. With regard to those matters that she felt were within her administrative prerogatives, she had little hesitation about making a decision and living with the consequences. However, in matters that were essentially faculty prerogatives, she altered her ways of working. Her first concerns with curriculum problems were met in an informal way by attending department meetings, asking a few questions, or making a suggestion or two. She also, and again her rationality emerges, provided suggestions for new materials.

> . . . because I'm really becoming more and more convinced that the quickest way to incorporate movement in the curriculum is via materials. You get materials into the teacher's hands and you can work at changing methodologies. For example, if you get a math teacher some materials that have differentiated assignments built in, you can start to work more on grouping with that teacher. To me that's the easiest way, it really is.

Of course, this position can be debated. But that really isn't the point. At issue here is that Fran's emphasis on materials reflected, in addition to her rational perspective, her overriding concern with the use of language—the right language—that would enable her to reach and communicate with people in *their* frame of reference. The use of words, the deliberate phrasing of ideas, then, was Fran's stock in trade as she worked with teachers. She came by this stance naturally:

> It was one of those things about growing up. The people around me were always concerned about their language. My dad, for example, was in the newspaper business. So it's always been a real natural thing for me to be concerned about what words I choose and how I use them.

Fran elaborated further on her concern with language.

> The reason I think it's so extremely important is that, through language, you create reality as well as describe it. For example, I've seen people create problems for themselves by the way they describe those problems. Perhaps it gets to be a fine line between seeking the right words and manipulation. But I do think you can change or improve situations by describing them in ways that are different. The point is not to sweep things under the rug, but to help people see things differently through the language they use. So I try to figure out a way to talk about a problem or a situation in a way so that the other person's understanding and mine are congruent with each other.

Interestingly, the focus Fran put on language and its use fit neatly with the way she spent the bulk of her time on the job. Not surprisingly, she said that the main part of the job had to do with communication; with processing communications, relaying communications, or getting other people to communicate.

> It's sort of putting it all together. If you ask me what I spent most of my day doing, it would be that, in one form or another. Talking to people, incorporating data, and giving out data.

In a sense, then, Fran articulated her primary role as principal as an information processor and communicator. She didn't see herself as an innovator in terms of altering the structure of the school (into modular form, for example) or of introducing other innovations (such as management by objectives or team teaching). Overall, she thought the system was a reasonable one, but that the people involved had to make it work better. Her strategy to get it to happen was to collect data and then deal with people on the basis of what the data said, not on any preconceived notion about what ought to be. Again, this is a reasonable and rational position, on the face of it, and should not lead to any particular problems. But reality is frequently different from what appears to be reasonable; this problem resurfaced as Fran talked about the ways she saw the demands on a principal whose philosophy and modus operandi resemble hers:

> You have to be a person who doesn't need a whole lot of positive reinforcement, because as I see it, the position is at the vortex of a lot of political activity in the school and in the community. You just don't get a lot of positive reinforcement. So, you have to be pretty sure you're collecting the data accurately and that you don't have tunnel vision or tunnel hearing. And you have to be pretty confident in your own decisions because a lot of other people won't be.

In a way, it seemed that what Fran was saying was that, if a principal acts to make a school do a better job and to get teachers to improve the way they work with youngsters and each other, the school becomes politicized, and a battle ensues with the principal on one side and most of the teachers on the other. The principal, in these situations, has to "go it" pretty much alone, according to Fran, and has to be able to move through the day without much positive feedback. This position can be argued, of course. But that's the way she perceived the situation.

The thrust of this chapter is somewhat different from that of the others, in order to consider problems that may face a female high school principal, particularly in a small, conservative community. The emphasis on these problems should not hide the fact that Fran's concept of the principal's role—above all to be clear and rational in her thought and language—helped her change things. Perhaps she, more than any of the others discussed, tried to insure that her role and her expectations of others would not be ambiguous.

The epilogue to this story of Fran The Rationalist is not one of success. The conflict in the school and the community apparently worsened as historical factions grew stronger. The superintendent, her main support, was suspended on what appeared to be trumped-up charges motivated by political conflict in the community and the school board. Fran clearly saw the handwriting on the wall and knew her survival was closely tied to the superintendent's. Fran and her husband decided they had had enough and left the community with few regrets, having learned a lot.

9

The Politician: "It Really Is a Political Game, You Know?"

Paul is black. He was principal of an inner-city elementary school with a primarily black student body. There was also a sizeable group of children whose parents were attracted to the school because of some special programs. Listening to Paul talk about his experiences as principal, how he went about learning to survive in the system, and how he clarified his role, was a fascinating experience. It was fascinating for many reasons, but two stand out. First, was his political sensitivity to his faculty, parent community, and Central Office. He projected an image similar to that of a floor manager at a political convention whose primary role was to be aware of where the power rested and whom to contact to get a crucial vote on his side. Second, Paul conveyed a real sense of having fun through it all. Indeed, his role was like a game to him but the precise nature of the game was elusive. Mostly it seemed like chess, although the object was not always to win. For example, there were times that Paul made his moves just to "tweak" Central Office personnel, and he would sit back and chuckle about it. In fact, there was a good bit of chuckling among the three of us. Clearly, the games Paul saw himself involved in as principal were fun for him, and though he appeared to win most of the time, others don't necessarily end up losing.

At the time of the interview, Paul had been principal of his school for five years. Prior to that he had been assistant principal in the same school for two years. There were unusual circumstances attached to Paul's becoming assistant principal, and then being promoted to principal, which are necessary to understand in order to appreciate his view of himself and his role relations with the various individuals and groups with whom he interacted. First, Paul did not arrive at the principalship through the typical route. That is, he had not been a teacher who, after having taught for a few years, decided on an administrative career, took courses toward certification, waited for an opening, and so forth. Rather, he had been a psychology major in college and had obtained a position with a community mental health organization in a western state. He had applied for the job of assistant principal because he was attracted to the idea of trying to influence the education of black children in an inner-city environment.

Second, the fact that he was made assistant principal without the necessary credentials is testimony not only to his skills but, more importantly, to the fact that the principal of the school at the time was a rather unusual sort himself. He was a white college professor who became a principal in order to "go where the action was" and test out some of his ideas about developing a community-oriented inner-city school. He was highly charismatic, loved to make speeches and stir people up, and enjoyed a great deal of community support. Thus he was able to get a noncertified person appointed as assistant principal, in spite of establishment objections.

Third, the school was organized in a manner that structured and encouraged a high degree of faculty and community participation in problem solving and policy making. This point is important because, when the principal resigned to return to university life, both faculty and parents became pressure groups for Paul's appointment as principal even though he was still without credentials. Thus, in no uncertain way, Paul owes his position to the efforts of those two groups, a fact that he was reminded of from time to time, albeit in subtle ways.

These facts, then—that Paul was promoted to the principalship in his own school, that he was without credentials when he became principal, that he followed in the footsteps of a very dynamic, charismatic person, and that both the faculty, and, critically, the parent community played an important part in having his appointment accepted—all had a crucial influence on Paul's view of his priorities and of his role and on the way he developed it. These influences assumed primary importance during his first year as principal, when his main concern appeared to be job security and survival. He said:

> During the first year, you know, my survival was basically out of my hands. I think the feeling of the staff was, "We're going to support this person because he was our choice, we put him in there." But this was not the same with the parents. Whatever I wanted to do I had to bear in mind the reactions of certain key people who had let me know in no uncertain terms that they had hired me. Two, in particular, were the chairperson of our Community Cabinet and the secretary of the Cabinet. They were two very powerful people.

Two points in Paul's comments need further consideration. First, is his concern with survival. Second, and related to the matter of survival, it is of interest to note the way Paul viewed the two groups—the faculty and the parents—without whose support the board quite probably would not have appointed him. His comments suggest that by lending him their support the faculty had, in a way, limited its ability to reject him or his policies, at least over the short run. That is, once having gone out on a limb to influence his appointment, the faculty indeed had a stake in promoting his success. To reject him after having supported him would cause a severe loss of face in the educational community, and possibly a detrimental effect on the potential of school faculties to influence administrative appointments in that system. This is a particular possibility inasmuch as the school board was not enthusiastic about Paul's appointment to start with. The faculty apparently did not constitute much of a threat to Paul's survival, as he saw it.

The parents were a different matter. Their freedom was greater than the faculty's, and they were not under the same kinds of constraints as were the faculty and, seemingly, felt few compunctions concerning letting Paul know that, in a sense, he held his job at their pleasure. While they might not be able to "make" him, quite possibly they could "break" him.

It was also interesting that Paul's comments about survival as a principal, and his focus on the parents and faculty, occurred at the very start of the interview. These comments provided a theme that ran throughout the interview. They indicated an essential clue to his personal style and his style as an administrator—his deep down politicalness. That is, Paul—what he did, his successes and his failures—must be understood from the point of view that he was a most political person whose first impulse, when confronted with a problematic situation, seemed to be to analyze it in political terms. In a sense, for Paul, being a principal was a juggling act that took place as he stood on a teeter board. Not only must he keep things moving in relation to each other, but he must also watch that he doesn't lose his own balance.

Paul's concern with survival was the most forthright we encountered in all our interviews. This point is congruent with his being highly politically oriented, particularly in view of the fact that he owed much to a nonestablishment constituency. It has been said many times, for example, that the primary job of the politician is to get re-elected—to survive in office. There seem to be two primary strategies by which elected representatives manage to do this. One is to maintain a low profile, keep things running, avoid irritating people, and "don't rock the boat." The other, particularly for those who want to create a high profile, is to develop a strong power base that will lend support in times of stress, thus insuring, as much as possible, re-election. The history of our representative democracy is replete with examples of both strategies. A similar history can be found for school administrators. There are hosts of school principals whose major operational—thus, survival—strategy is, indeed, to maintain things, to try to make sure that no one gets upset, not to "rock the boat." These principals tend to last a long time. There are also a few whose goals are movement and change and who survive, but seemingly not as long as their maintenance-oriented colleagues, by establishing a strong power base in the educational and lay community. Paul seems to belong to this latter group, and the power base he chose to cultivate was a boundary-line one relative to the system—the parents. His thoughts about the group as a power base were analytical and predictive, and also based on hard-nosed political pragmatism. He said, relative to the future:

> I think more and more principals are going to have to recognize parent groups as a source of power, and one that they are going to have to deal with. This is

already true in many cases. Take Brownsville, for example, where community people, parents and school people, combine to make some decisions or effect some change. It's all coming and principals better believe it.

And, as concerns the day-to-day realities of a principal's life and tenure in this job:

> You might see your first line of security as being downtown—the Central Office. These are the people who hired you and whom you might expect to support you. Or you might look at your teachers as your primary support group. But I think that anybody who is really aware of what's happening to them on the job as a principal will recognize very quickly that even having your hand in the pocket of somebody downtown will never save you if a parent group comes down there. They can raise so much hell that any superintendent would rather let you go or move you than fight them.

It's important to note that Paul did not speak of the quality of education being enhanced by the power and involvement of parents in school matters. Rather, his concerns were almost totally political. He viewed school systems as sociopolitical and seemed to base both his interpersonal and group interactions on that concept. Indeed, as noted earlier, seeing Paul as a politician is the key to understanding him as a principal.

Paul's appointment as principal—promoted to that position from his previous one as assistant principal in the same school—is not common practice. These circumstances presented him with problems of role clarification and development that were both political and interpersonal in nature. Somewhat surprisingly, in view of his rather acute political awareness, Paul seemed to approach this role change relative to the faculty and staff in a rather naive manner, almost with the view that nothing else would change. But change it did:

> When I first started I felt I still wanted to maintain peer status and buddy status, with the faculty. I wanted to be a nonauthoritarian principal, but I think I misunderstood what that meant. What I tried to convey to the staff was: let me be, let me grow, don't push me, leave me alone, and you know you can do whatever the hell you want to do.
> This couldn't last because pressures started to mount, particularly from the parents. It was after Christmas and I started to get messages that it was time for me to start producing. But the group I changed with first was with the teachers. The change was in me in that I accepted the fact that I was their leader, whether I liked it or not.

A fascinating process was occurring. Here was a person who wanted to be appointed to a position for which, in terms of credentials, he was not eligible. Nonetheless, because of the support and pressure of two district constituent groups, he was appointed. He brought with him the interpersonal baggage from his previous position, and thus the need not to have relationships change; they were comfortable. Paul thought to himself, "If I can swing this, I'll have it made. If they will 'let me be, let me grow, etc.,' I'll be able to be principal, which I really want, and not disturb the relationships I previously had." The naiveté of this thinking is obvious but understandable. Paul wanted his cake and he also wanted to eat it, a difficult task under the best conditions.

That these were not the best conditions for "having and eating" was a result of the previous principal's attempts to build both a powerful faculty group and a powerful parent group. The expectations of both of these groups were that Paul would not simply let things remain status quo. If he was going to grow, he would grow in the process of doing something, a reasonable expectation that escaped Paul, but understandably so. The first crunch came from the parents whose messages communicated "It's time for you to produce." And the first change came, not in action, but in Paul's thinking as he started to reconceptualize his role and accept the fact that he was the leader of the faculty.

Accepting the idea that he was, indeed, the leader of the faculty, was a crucial first step in Paul's development as a principal, but it was only a step and, by itself, implied no leadership. Action had to follow, and this point led to the second crunch in Paul's development—how to deal with the ambiguity of the role of the principal. What is it that he/she is supposed to do? The ambiguity started with the Central Office.

> This is a fairly good sized city. There is one person who is ultimately in charge of more than forty elementary schools, and he communicates that he doesn't particularly want to know what's going on in those schools. When I was interviewed with five other people, it was made clear that he assumed I knew what the role of the principal was, and his only task was to help me get staffed for August.

For a person like Paul, then, particularly given the circumstances of his appointment, the messages he received from his immediate superior were not helpful. His superior assumed he would know what to do. But, implicit in his message was that Paul should be careful concerning the extent to which he asked for help. Requests to Central Office for help in role clarification might easily be interpreted as a confession of inadequacy for the job. Common wisdom suggested, "Keep your problems to yourself." Adopting this tactic did protect Paul, but it did not help clear up the role ambiguity of the principalship. In retrospect, he had several rather illuminating comments to make concerning the role of the principal, particularly when one is new at the job.

> I think that the role is always ambiguous. The only time you can clarify it is when you take control of it and define it for yourself, or let the most powerful reference group around you define it for you. I haven't talked with a first year principal yet who hasn't said, "Hey, what the hell am I supposed to do?" And this goes even for those who've had an internship as an assistant principal.
> When you get to be principal, into the big time, you sit down and wait for

someone to tell you what your job is. Nobody from below is going to tell you. And from the people on the top, everything they want from you, you can do by the end of September.

Because of the ambiguity of the role, one thing that I think can happen to a person is that you can produce very little and not get fired. In other words, I think if you ever did a job analysis of what most principals do they would be out of a job. I mean in terms of what they really productively do. You know, you check attendance, you check in at the office to make sure all the teachers are there, you make sure the substitute is in the room to cover the class that needs to be covered, you make sure the janitor is running the boilers. And at ten o'clock you don't have a damn thing to do until lunch time.

The only way you are really going to know what to do, is to do something. And it has to be something outside of routine administration. In effect, you have to step on people's toes, and they will let you know how much it hurts, which means, of course, you'll start to learn your role, what its boundary lines are and whether or not you want to enlarge them. Even if you don't step on their toes, even if you initiate some kind of action that doesn't affect anybody's territory, they'll respond to it. So again I say, "If you want to know what to do, do something."

In a nutshell, these paragraphs speak to school principals and would-be principals in a way they rarely get spoken to, either in university training programs or once they get the job. There is a certain amount of laughing at the system and the demands it puts on principals, as well as some rather astute advice for the person who may not be satisfied simply with being a routine administrator. Paul reaffirms the notion that the principal's role is an ambiguous one, and there are two general strategies a person can use to clarify it. The principal can step into the situation and control it by asserting and inserting himself/herself into the system, or he/she can become more political and try to decipher the messages that are transmitted by the most powerful reference group with which the principal has to deal. Typically, in elementary schools, this would be either the teachers or the parents.

But Paul said that, as a rule, the teachers won't tell you anything, and then a sort of cat-and-mouse waiting game starts. The teachers wait for the principal to initiate something, and the principal waits for cues from the teachers. When cues are eventually given, if at all, they are very subtle. How to break the game open? Paul's answer has much wisdom in it, "If you want to know what to do, do something." The simplicity of this statement is elegant. In order to reduce role ambiguity and the tension that accompanies it (Kahn et al., 1964), some action needs to take place so that role boundaries can be established. Conceivably there are two general action thrusts. The first is to test out the boundary lines by pressing against established norms, or by initiating action that may not press the norms but, nevertheless, conveys movement. When a principal engages in either of these behaviors, the teachers will respond to what is essentially a testing of power. The messages will probably not be long in coming. The principal will find out whether or not toes have been stepped on, and how much it has hurt. Depending on the amount of pain that is felt, and by whom, the principal will start to learn about the role expectations that the faculty has for him/her. Judgments will then have to be made. Did the testing clarify things sufficiently? Is it time to lick his/her wounds? Was the action too fast or too slow? What was learned about the faculty as a group as a result of the principal having "done something"? Are they powerful or are they patsies? Other similar questions can certainly be raised, but the essential point remains the same: "If you want to know what to do, do something."

The second action thrust that a principal can engage in to reduce ambiguity, according to Paul, is to play the system's game by focusing his/her action on the Central Office, rather than on the teachers or the parents, as his/her primary reference group. Undoubtedly there will be many—perhaps most—principals who will disagree with Paul when he says "you can do very little and not get fired"; and, probably with some exaggeration, "everything they want from you can be done by the end of September." And certainly there are school districts that expect principals to do no more than fill their days with routine administration. This notwithstanding, far too many principals do precisely that; they make a career out of "being busy" and "keeping the peace" (Blumberg, 1974). As they do this, of course, they do reduce their role ambiguity. But, as Paul suggests, most of the routine work in a school can be done by 10 o'clock in the morning—and then what?

So much for Paul's analysis. On another level, his comments reinforce the earlier interpretation of his view of himself and of the principalship as, at root, political. In addition, Paul saw the gamelike quality of the situation and the various "game plans" that a principal may adopt. His comments are laced, at times, with a certain humorous cynicism directed less at principals who are overloaded (or overload themselves) with the busywork of school administration and more at the system for permitting, if not encouraging, that style of school management to prevail. But then, back to an earlier theme, it's necessary to survive; and the route to survival is a matter of personal choice.

Paul's choice of "doing something" was influenced by the parent group's demands for production coupled with his survival needs, as well as his mission to develop a higher quality program for black youngsters. His action took the form of developing a program for the school that emphasized a concern with black culture in the context of a predominantly white society. In a curious way this program reflected his own concerns with survival, the thought being that if blacks are to be able to enter and produce in this society they need to have a strong sense of who they are and from whence they came. But the focus here is less on the content of his plan than on his action: he developed the plan, presented it, and in the process assumed a leadership role in the school and the community—all of this not without consequences. The consequences took the nature of radically changed relationships with individuals and groups. For example, with the assistant principal:

> My role with my assistant principal changed first. He was the person I had really keyed in on when we were assistant principals together. When I finally decided

that "here's a program" it was the first awakening that there was a difference between the two of us. The difference was accepted but I don't think we ever got good at relating to each other—with me as boss, that is. It wasn't nearly as open as it had been. I got support, but mostly on the basis of my need for it rather than for the ideas.

And with the staff:

Once I took leadership, after that first year, I never relinquished the fact that I was their principal. I accepted the fact that I wasn't going to be their buddy. I accepted the idea that I was going to take some flak for things I had not done; I accepted the idea that if there were screw-ups I'd take the responsibility for them but that I would also take the role of making final decisions when necessary. And things changed from that point on.

And with the parents:

Once I had a program in mind which was going to last for two years, I went to the parents. I felt like I was principal of their school, I was a member of their community to whom they could look to make some changes they wanted. It was the kind of role where I was champion of educational causes in their community.

And with a subgroup of the staff:

The black members of the staff had been an important group for me. We had become very close. We socialized together, had lunch together, and so on. Once I pulled the staff together and told them what I thought we should be doing, that I wasn't happy with some things, that it was time to get on the stick, the relationship changed. When I walked into the lunchroom the conversation stopped. It wasn't disrespectful or that I was being responded to negatively. It was just all of a sudden I was "the man," you know?

The lesson is a clear one, then. If a principal chooses, as Paul did, to define and clarify that role as "running the school," that principal marks out and then crosses a self-made Rubicon. Things will never be the same. The comment above, that "all of a sudden I was 'the man,' " tells it all, for it speaks specifically to the issue of power. Responding to the pressure of the parents by asserting himself and his prerogatives, Paul implicitly raised issues of power in his school where none had been raised previously. The effect was to differentiate functions and relationships in the school and parent community. But as a person gains something he/she loses something; and he/she risks losing many things. In this case, as Paul gained a clearer sense of his role and the power he could exercise by initiating action, he lost some of the warmth that went with previous relationships. He also risked losing a lot more, in that once he raised people's expectations, he faced the possibility of not meeting those expectations, thus failing and, perhaps, not surviving.

Recall the teeter-totter, juggling act metaphor earlier. To continue the metaphor, as long as Paul refrained from "doing something" (reducing his role ambiguity through routine administration), he remained on the ground, refusing to mount the teeter-totter. Once he assumed a different role by directly proposing a program, the balancing and juggling began. Further, for people who are interested primarily in movement and change, not simply maintaining the status quo, there is probably no easy turning back once the process has begun, though there may be occasional rest periods. For Paul, one of these times was a sabbatical leave, but even then:

> Despite the fact that I am on sabbatical I will never miss a Cabinet meeting. I recognized that that can always be a focal point for change, and I'm not willing to let the change go on without my being there.

A person in power who wants to create change stakes out territory that's important to him/her and which he/she needs to control. Other people or groups seem to be motivated to chip away at the territory, thus to loosen control. So, although he appeared to have much fun playing the game he started, Paul's life seemed not to be a restful one, as all parts of the territory needed to be continually watched for possible encroachment. The roles that Paul staked out and clarified for himself—leader of the faculty and educational champion of the parent community—had to be maintained and enhanced.

Paul also had to confront the problem of how to link the role he chose for himself with his faculty with the one he developed with the parent community. In most school situations this link-up presents a minimal problem for the principal, because the parent community is not well organized, nor does it become a powerful pressure group except, perhaps, in times of trouble or disruption in the school. In addition, most parent community groups are organized by parents and are treated, for the most part, as a necessary evil by principals, though they make public utterances to the contrary. The situation in Paul's school was radically different. The parent group was very powerful. It had been initially developed by Paul's predecessor, and Paul had deliberately moved in directions that enabled it to exert a lot of decision-making power relative to school programs and policies. It was not a necessary evil, but an integral part of the school's policy-making structure, thus making the linking problem one that demanded attention.

What occurred was the creation of a relationship not unlike that between a superintendent of schools and a board of education. An elected representative group of the parent body became the accepted, if not legal, policy-making board of the school. The principal was the chief operating executive. But policy makers cannot make policy in a vacuum. They must have problems or proposals to consider. Here it was that the link-up occurred. That is, Paul worked with the faculty to develop program proposals, which were then taken to the parents to be enacted, hopefully, into official policy. But it was no rubber-stamp operation. The parents could, indeed, block proposals if they wished. As well, had there been no development of Paul's role as leader of the faculty, there would have been no program proposals forth-coming so that the parents would have some policy decisions to make. As Paul said, "I needed the support of my staff so I could take on a viable role with the parents."

One thing feeds into another, then. But more importantly, this process of reciprocity indicates the character of the school that developed under Paul's principalship, and the demands that the school, in turn, made on him. The political juggling act continued. It was not enough for Paul to deal only with complex faculty relationships, or with equally complex (perhaps more so) parent-school relationships. The two had to interact and contribute to each other. In the process, Paul found that (1) his power to act unilaterally was constrained and (2) his power to induce change was enhanced. This seeming contradiction is not really one at all. What it meant, in this case, was that while Paul became somewhat limited in his personal powers, his organizational power base, and thus his ability to influence a wider range of issues, was enlarged.

Although he had a few close friends who became principals at about the same time he did, Paul's early relationships with the large group of elementary school principals in the system were limited to monthly meetings. In addition, these relationships were colored by the fact that he was new in his role and, as was noted, somewhat insecure. First he described the meetings, and then his feelings and role in them:

> You have, at least once a month, a principals' meeting where the assistant superintendent stands up and talks for half an hour about nothing. Then there's time for coffee and doughnuts which is followed by some announcement from the personnel department. After that it's talk about the teachers' union and the latest nasty thing they're trying to get away with. And then there's a report from our own union about all the things we're trying not to let the teachers get away with. And that's it.
>
> When I went to my first principals' meeting, I felt like a kid. The first time I walked into that group I thought it was awesome because they all looked to me like principals ought to look. They were old, they were quiet, they wore ties. I sat there very subdued for the first couple of meetings. Then when they started to talk I found out they didn't know anything. And they never should have let me find that out, because after that, oh man, my whole life's happiness would be to go in and disrupt a principals' meeting. I lived for those days. After awhile, though, I stopped going to the meetings. That's when the pressure came on from Central Office. I got some nasty letters telling me that I was a principal and I had to go to the principals' meetings. So, I buckled under and decided to go, even though they were worthless. I sent a letter saying I thought they were worthless, and that I would like to go to a principals' meeting where they talked about kids.
>
> So, anyhow, I'd go to the meetings and when they were in the middle of some nonsense I'd raise a point of order and ask if it would be possible now to talk about kids. Or, when they were talking about how they couldn't give in to teachers on some issue, I'd stand up and say that I thought we ought to do it. It was just anything to keep me from going to sleep.

This is a rather sad commentary, albeit one person's, about how school principals in one system spend their time once or twice a month. More importantly, though, is the additional insight into Paul, and his growing security in his role. His comments lend added weight to earlier ones about his concerns for survival when he spoke about the necessity of building support in the parent community. That is, the more powerful his home base became, the less attention he felt he had to pay to the norms of the larger system. There were boundary lines, however, that he could not cross. The norm that principals had to attend meetings was one that he could not violate with impunity. He gave in to pressure from Central Office. The role he chose for himself in those meetings, however—apparently one of a gadfly or devil's advocate—was permissible, if not encouraged. What was required was that he be present, almost regardless of how he behaved, as long as his behavior was civil; another sad commentary.

Other facets of Paul as a principal and as a person came to light as he described his reactions to the principals' meetings. It may seem, for example, that for a political person he was behaving in an unpolitic way. The principals' group, as far as Paul was concerned, offered no power base through which he could achieve any goals for this school. He could almost ignore it—but not quite. Other forces entered the situation that clearly signalled the extent of deviance the system would tolerate, and Paul understood these forces well. The penalty for his deviance, as would be expected, was that he became an isolate among his fellow principals. However, this turned out to be not much of a penalty because, as we have seen, Paul devalued the group.

This situation remained stable through the first year of Paul's principalship. Then:

> A year later a lot of new principals were hired and membership in the group became a very different thing. Then I felt I didn't want to be all alone. I wanted to stop playing games, and I wanted to form a reference group of principals that I could relate to and maybe change things.

The situation had changed, and the change meant a potential shift in the power base. Paul's attitudes changed. Perhaps with this new potential for exercising influence the principals' group could shift and deal with issues which, in Paul's eyes, would have impact on what happened to youngsters in the schools. It didn't turn out that way. Paul's efforts failed. Briefly, this is what happened: At a day-and-a-half meeting held early in Paul's second year as principal the school district presented a proposal for evaluating principals. Paul was very upset, not with the idea of evaluation, but with the fact that the proposal contained no reference to problems of urban schools and black children. He cited experiences he had had with other administrators concerning problems they encountered with black children, but he received very little response either from Central Office personnel or the other principals. This lack of response only added to his anger.

At lunch time, Paul gathered the group of new principals together, plus some older ones. They caucused, refused to go to the afternoon session, and instead drew up a proposal countering the one that had been presented earlier in the day. As can be imagined, the group's actions, particularly when they asked for recognition to present their proposal, were not greeted with enthusiasm by the people running the meeting. A good bit of turmoil ensued, but the counterproposal was finally presented. The upshot of all this was that the group was asked to take responsibility for planning a program for the next Superintendent's Day (system-wide inservice) that would focus on the problems of black education.

The group accepted this responsibility and planned a full day's activities with a black emphasis. The results of the program were both exciting and upsetting. The principals' group, however, became fractionalized. Another result was that the group that had planned the meeting, composed mostly of newer principals, apparently became frightened at the disturbance that had been created, disbanded, and refused to take further responsibility to follow through on the implications of the program for principal evaluation.

What had happened? Paul is not sure, but he had a hypothesis that provided a *raison d'être* for the story being told here.

> I was really excited by the group, but I didn't realize how insecure they were in the system. I wasn't concerned because my support and security was at my school. I could be deviant because back there was the school, the parents, and the teachers.
>
> Just meeting my school's (i.e., parents and teachers) wishes had caused me to get my bell rung enough times so that I was no longer afraid of having it rung again. I began to learn about the impotency of the system.
>
> You know, the only big stick they hold against you is firing you. Well, after a couple of years as principal, you realize they just don't do that. They have to catch you on a morals charge or something like that. Once you've recognized that, if you are willing to risk being alienated, all that can happen is that you get your bell rung.

Things come full circle. Three sets of circumstances seem to have inter-acted to produce Paul's reactions. First, he had deliberately set out to build a base of support and power among the parent community in his school. As his support and power grew, he was enabled to take positions and behave in ways that were quite deviant, even though these positions and behaviors apparently caused some of his superiors to react with a great deal of anger and distress because he had violated his role as they saw it. Second, tempo-rarily and as it turned out, mistakenly, he thought he had developed another base of support within the principals' group. He was mistaken about his cohorts for the obverse reason he was sure about himself. That is, he assumed that they were as secure as he and had a support base as strong as his, which was not the case. The politician had made a political error. The votes were not there. Third, Paul had diagnosed the system in political terms. Recall that he characterized it as impotent, i.e., powerless insofar as imposing severe sanctions on the administrators was concerned. Thus his characterization provided yet another clue to his action predispositions and style. He could have described the system in any number of ways. He chose the adjective "impotent," reflecting his concern with power.

It should be said that an effort was made to remobilize the group of principals that had taken part in the earlier action. This, too, failed, and for the same reason—the failure of its members to assume shared responsibility for dealing with and confronting the system on issues that were separate from their own particularistic school needs.

Paul was left a little sadder but wiser for it all. The sadness came from the fact that he still felt very much alone in his position. The wisdom came from his realization of the basic inertia of the total system and his own impotence with regard to changing it.

In an interesting way, the image presented of Paul as an administrator has changed, but it doesn't change when the focus shifts to his relationships with the youngsters in his school:

> When I became principal I decided I didn't want to become removed from my students. We had developed a close relationship. I was now the "stick," though, and I wanted to break through that. I never relinquished my behavior of touching the kids. But it's a conflict. You are an image for them; the kids will psyche you out. They will know if you're a person they can respect and depend on. They'll know whether or not you're a "bad ass" principal, which is good, or whether you are just a principal to play with. And you can get involved in their lives, which really blows their minds.
>
> When I had lunch duty I used to get a group of kids during lunch time, because I was not about to walk up and down the halls, and go outside and play with them. The older kids, as soon as they knew I was going to play, like in a snowball fight, would gang up on me to see if I would get mad. I figured that one out, but I got mad anyway. The younger kids,—well, you're like a Messiah to them. If you come out and touch them they just think this is the most wonderful thing in the world. Here is the person who comes out from the loud speaker, which is right next to God because the loud speaker is "up there." That's really the way they treat you.

The beginning of this discussion of Paul mentioned the funlike quality that he communicated, as well as his gamelike style, and the balancing and juggling acts he performed. All of this came through clearly as he talked about his relationships with "the kids." The fun was there; it was easy to visualize him in a snowball fight. But the political game was there, too, particularly with the youngsters who were older. They tested him "in combat," so to speak, and he was aware of their testing. "Is he really one of us, or, when the chips are down, when we challenge his authority, is he 'the Man'?"

Once more, then, the question is how to keep the power balance, a question that becomes difficult to answer, given what appear to be Paul's needs to be close to the students in his school. In a sense he created his own problem, but he probably wouldn't have had it any other way. Relative to the students, if he chose his role as "principal," there would be no issue. He could do what principals tend to do, maintain his distance and no one would question his stance. His needs for warmth seemed to lead him down other paths, thus creating situations that he must balance. It got untidy, at times, but the untidiness also contained some beauty and elegance.

10

Complementary Perspectives on the Principalship: The Job and Relations with Others

As was mentioned in the introduction, the aim in interviewing these eight principals was to develop some basic understanding of the manner in which these men and women described and dealt with the problems they confronted in the principalship. This chapter thus begins an integration and analysis of some of the observations collected in the eight preceding sketches. The first portion of the chapter draws on some of the interview excerpts mentioned in previous chapters, for two reasons: (1) to provide a brief review of the different perspectives these men and women had toward the principalship, and (2) to illustrate phenomena other than their individualistic approaches to the job.

As expected from the outset, these principals reported both similarities and differences vis-à-vis their work world. The description and discussion that follow here are offered as a framework for understanding some of the similarities and differences in their lives. They were not, for example, as functionally idiosyncratic as they might seem from the thumbnail sketches.

The chapter is organized in the following way: First, the general viewpoints of each of the principals will be briefly reiterated, focusing on several of their most distinguishing characteristics. Second, their relations with peers, superiors, teachers, students, and parents will be described. This chapter concludes with some general observations and speculations regarding some of the factors that have influenced, and continue to affect, the daily on-the-job behavior of these eight elementary and secondary school principals.

VIEWS OF THE PRINCIPALSHIP

Although we began this study with a number of preconceptions regarding the responses we would get to our rather simple invitation to some principals to talk with us, we were nevertheless surprised to find that our hunches were not as accurate as we had anticipated. Perhaps the most startling discovery was that, while we had expected some common approach to the problems encountered, they held rather idiosyncratic perspectives regarding their work worlds. While the general types of problems they reported were fairly similar from one school situation to another, their reference points for action were individualistic. Each of the principals interviewed held a particular view of himself/herself in his/her role which served to guide his/her day-to-day behavior on the job. Paul, the Politician, suggests his viewpoint in the following comments:

> I think the role is always ambiguous. I think that the only time you can clarify it is when you take control of it and define it yourself, or you let the most powerful reference group around you define it for you . . . you can produce very little and stay in the role. In other words, I think that if they ever did a time job analysis of a principal, we would be out of a job. You know, in terms of what (principals) productively do . . . check attendance, you check in at the office to make sure that all the teachers are there . . . that the substitute is in the room to cover the class . . . make sure the janitor is running the boilers. And at 10:00, you don't have a damn thing to do until lunch time . . . we don't really know what people expect of us . . . there's nobody below you who is going to tell you. And everybody above you is going to tell you what they want from you, you can do in September . . . it was clearly understood that you know the role of principal and that the only task for him (assistant superintendent) was to help you get staffed in August . . . and then give you a list of reports that he was going to need from you—most of which I could do in September. . . . Once that's done you will not hear from downtown again. . . .
>
> The only way you are really going to know what to do, is to do something. And it has to be something outside of routine administration. In effect, you have to step on people's toes and they will let you know how much it hurts, which means, of course, you'll start to learn your role, what its boundary lines are, and whether or not you want to enlarge them. Even if you don't step on their toes, even if you initiate some kind of action that doesn't affect anybody's territory, they'll respond to it. So again I say, "If you want to know what to do, do something."

The sort of limits-testing behavior implicit in these remarks characterizes Paul's approach to problems of the elementary principalship. George, whom we've call The Value-Based Juggler, takes a somewhat different approach to the demands of his high school work world. For example, he stated:

> If I get an idea in my head, right or wrong, I tend to pursue it and convince other people or groups regardless of whether or not it's the faculty, parents, kids, central administration, or what have you. Let me give you an example. It's been my worst experience ever as a principal. Graduation has traditionally been held outside on the football field which is a beautiful setting. (The school is nestled in a beautiful valley.) Four out of the last seven years it has been rained out. A year ago I attempted to switch graduation indoors. The students said "NO!" and against my better judgment I gave in. Not only were we rained out, we were flooded out! We regrouped two hours later in the gymnasium and that area of the building was hit by lightning. It was a bad scene.

My judgment on it was that *that* was not the way to conclude thirteen years of education. If graduation was at all meaningful—then let's do it right. The following year I made a dictum—come hell or high water it's going to be inside. I told the superintendent and the president of the Board of Education, "Next year you are going to have to get another principal if you want to hold it outside. It's going to be indoors." And they both concurred.

One of the things that was so striking, as the interview with George progressed, was the continual and strong reference he made to his value system when it came to making decisions affecting both the substantive education of youngsters, the quality of their life in the school, and the quality of his relationships with the faculty. The problem that concerned George in the foregoing example is not that the weather fouled up the outdoor graduation and necessitated a move inside to the gymnasium, but rather that graduating under these less than idyllic conditions was just "not the way to conclude thirteen years of education." In other words, it was disturbing to George's personal sense of values to have it end this way. As he said, "if graduation is at all meaningful, let's do it right."

In contrast to, although not incompatible with, the preceding perspective, is that of John, another high school principal, whom we referred to as The Humanist:

I always picture school as a moving mobile. And on that mobile, hanging out there, you have got the Board of Education as a group, the District Office, the parents, the faculty, subgroups of the faculty, concerns with discipline (the student), the department chairmen, and teacher union representatives. Each group mobilizes forces to put demands on you. My job is to keep the mobile in balance and keep it moving in a direction that all these groups really want it to go.

John's sense of himself as balancing the competing demands of individuals and groups implies a view of the high school work world that is quite different from George's. John's frame of reference doesn't suggest that he was guided in his work by a strong sense of values about education *per se,* or that he was a change-agent bent on making his impact in the schools. Rather, John saw himself as a "people man" concerned that all the school machinery is well oiled and that nothing gets in the way of his staff's efforts to be successful at their work. He knows he's best at working with and through people; that he's not a "thing administrator," as he put it.

A more proactive view is taken by Joan, an elementary school principal, whom we called The Organizer. Joan's approach seemed to be to keep "the big picture" continuously before all the participants in her school:

. . . I see myself as an organizer; a person who puts ideas together and presents them . . . because I don't think teachers are organizing their classrooms and their instructional program, and they don't have time to see the huge scope of everybody's involvement . . . so I see me putting all those ideas together. I gather information from them and I put the ideas together . . .

And again:

> See, for me personally, we are going awfully slowly. In fact, I would like to go ten
> times faster, but I knew I had to control myself . . . I knew when I talked that the
> first words out of my mouth, for instance, people didn't even understand the
> difference between "cognitive" and "affective." It was just appalling to me when
> I first talked with the staff and used the words and I looked across a whole room
> of blank faces and I understood that I had to back up twenty paces . . . and so, I
> think, while the change has been very slow for me, for some people the pace has
> still been pretty rapid.

In a very real sense, Joan was more of a promulgator of change and
innovation then any of the others interviewed. She recognized that she was
aggressive, always on the initiative, and that she had to guard against becoming too frustrated over her staff's not getting "the habit," not getting
hooked on her ideas as hard and as fast as she'd like. She clearly assumed
an openly proactive style as her approach to the day-to-day problems evolving out of the elementary school work world.

The viewpoint of another elementary principal contrasted sharply with
the rather aggressive, change-oriented perspective just mentioned. Fred's
view of himself as delivering necessary services to school participants, as
being at the center of many of the exchanges and bargains which occur in
school, led us to call him The Broker:

> . . . I spend probably the greatest portion of my time with teachers, in a couple of
> different roles, one in a direct supervisory role and another in a less formal
> but . . . still sort of quasi-supervisory role just talking about directions in the school
> and things like that, where we are going, how we are going to get there, and
> trying to get them to commit themselves more to the organization . . .
>
> I see myself as giving direct service to the teachers in a sense of getting them
> involved and helping them in areas that I have expertise in, or finding resources
> for them, trying to work with them in solving problems, again, just seeing myself
> as a service person.

Fred's service orientation extended not only to his faculty and the children in his school, but to the parents and other members of the school
community as well. For example, he stated:

> I guess that a lot of my work with parents has been in terms of problem solving. It
> is often in a negative situation, although we have gotten down to the point where
> we did a little needs survey in the community and said, you know, "What are the
> things parents need and want?" One of the things that came out was they wanted
> an adult basic education class and we got them to set it up in the school; and they
> also got some recreation services going for kids in the evenings, again, branching
> out into the community. I have gotten involved with groups like the Rescue
> Mission and some of the local neighborhood groups . . .

While some of the other principals interviewed touched upon the "bro-
kerage" and service aspects of their role and of the school, none seemed to
make it as much of an anchor for their behavior as Fred did.

Ed, another elementary principal, may most vividly be referred to as The Authentic Helper. It was clear in our discussions with Ed that helping teachers help themselves was his major reference point in his role as principal. Above all else, Ed saw himself as a human being first, a principal second. Ed had a desire to help improve the quality of life in his building, and he clearly wanted his staff and the children in his charge to view him as more than merely an authority figure. He reflected on his orientation.

> I'm interested in instruction and curriculum as well as developing a climate where children feel good about being here and teachers feel good about working here . . . I'm very much interested in human relations, in helping relationships, not only between teachers and children, but also teacher-teacher, administrator-teacher, and more specifically, administrator-child.

Marie, whom we refer to as The Catalyst, noted early in her discussion that she liked to get things going in her school. As was mentioned earlier, Marie's prime orientation to her work world environment was to "stir things up." It was important to her that things were happening, that people were alive, in her school. Part of the basis for Marie's orientation as a "catalyst" seemed to stem from the difference between her personal perspective on school and society, and that held by her staff:

> What I see in my school is a group of people who are nice people, and they're interesting people, and I think they have basic intelligence, but I don't think they're terribly aware of what's going on today . . . they're isolated; here is the building and this is what I do all day; this is the community and this is what I do at night; and here's the world—and it doesn't really have too much to do with me.

The Catalyst spent much of her time as principal stirring up people's awareness of what they were doing, why it was important (or silly), and the relation between what was occurring in their school and the larger society.

Another high school principal, Fran, The Rationalist, seems to be distinguished from others primarily by her deliberate and calculated approach to the problems of the principalship. Fran was a stickler for clarity of language, and went to great lengths to reduce ambiguity in terms of her role relations with others. She was viewed with suspicion as the "New Lady on the Hill"—in light of this she took great pains to insure that others did not misunderstand her actions, her intentions, or her motivations. Fran observed:

> The reason I think it's so extremely important is that, through language, you create reality as well as describe it. For example, I've seen people create problems for themselves by the way they describe those problems. Perhaps it gets to be a fine line between seeking the right words and manipulation. But I do think you can change or improve situations by describing them in ways that are different. The point is not to sweep things under the rug but to help people to see things differently through the language they use. So I try to figure out a way to talk

about a problem or a situation in a way so that the other person's understanding and mine are congruent with each other.

For The Rationalist, then, it was critical to introduce change and encourage diversity, but to do it in a careful and deliberately calculated manner. As Fran noted toward the end of her interview, one of the biggest problems she confronted was "misinformation or misinterpretation of actions."

PEERS AND SUPERIORS

These principals reported that they spent little time with their administrative peers. With some exceptions, these men and women didn't talk to, observe, consult, or otherwise interact with their fellow administrators except to the extent required by their presence at meetings called by superiors. When asked directly about how principals related to principals, a typical response was "They don't." While their assessment of the situation is not surprising, their comments on the consequences of this relative isolation from one another shed important light on understanding the principal's work environment. Fred noted that "the nature of the job certainly almost emphasizes isolation . . . it's a pretty lonely kind of role." He continued and pointed out the source of the problem as he saw it:

> . . . I don't know how you break down the isolation and develop . . . relationships with other principals. . . . It is a lot easier for me to have a good relationship with a teacher than it is with another principal. . . . I mean, just the time that you expend with other principals is minimal. You see them for meetings, and generally what happens at a meeting is there is an agenda . . . and we have never planned to sit down and just, you know, have a nonagenda meeting where we could talk about what our extreme frustrations are at this point. No one has ever wanted to deal with our frustrations. . . .

Fred went on to say that:

> . . . principals don't see themselves as being able to solve any of the problems they face on a daily basis. . . . They have existed all their lives and they don't see themselves as being any kind of agent that could ever change the situation.

In Fred's school district a special effort had apparently been made to facilitate interaction. "Intervisitation teams" of principals had been established but, in Fred's view, he "never developed a working relationship with the other three principals. One guy used to be the principal in the building I am in, and another guy is physically ill. . . . They are all older principals . . . I don't think I could share anything with them."

Joan, The Organizer, in commenting on her situation, suggested other factors that may be related to the lack of interaction and support among principals. She said:

Maybe it's because they feel that they are not skilled in it, or maybe they feel they don't have enough time to assess you, or maybe it's because they are frightened, or maybe it's because you haven't built a relationship.

Joan was even more emphatic when she confided that she thought:

> . . . there isn't much of a relationship. . . . I think administrators are really frightened to tell other administrators about their behavior. . . .

Paul, The Politician, when asked how principals related to each other matter-of-factly stated "They don't!" he went on to comment about his first year on the job:

> I felt so all alone my first year. The first time I walked into the principals' group I thought it was awesome because they all looked to me like principals ought to look. They were old, they were quiet, they had on ties, and I would sit there very subdued for the first couple of meetings. Then when they opened their mouths, I found out they didn't know anything. And they should have never let me find that out, because after that, oh man, my whole life's happiness would be to disrupt a principals' meeting.

The Helper also seemed to see himself as rather distant from other principals. Ed commented that the frequency of his relations with other principals was "not great." He stated that he:

> . . . never really looked at his relationship with other principals. What I do and what is comfortable for me may not be what they do or is comfortable for them . . . so I sort of backed off. . . .

He continued to talk about his situation.

> The school district that I'm in has only four buildings, so there are only four administrators plus a vice principal in the high school . . . three of the buildings are close to each other in proximity . . . my building is six miles away from the rest. So in a sense, I feel very autonomous. The frequency of my relating to other building administrators is not great . . . what I do and what is comfortable for me may not be what they do or what is comfortable for them . . . so I sort of backed off and said "Well, if they feel comfortable doing what they do, then that's okay." On the other hand, I don't want them saying to me "What you're doing within your building is not okay." So it's almost like a just "leave each other alone" type attitude.

While this is representative of the general thrust of how these eight principals perceived their relations with other principals, several of them were more pointed in their remarks. The Humanist noted:

> . . . a lot of infighting among building principals, but we all learn to accept it. . . . a school having to give up a teacher always gives up a weak teacher. We know that

and when you are—there are thirteen or fourteen other colleagues—all principals . . . you meet once a month and you laugh about it and think about it, and when you get your chance you unload a lot onto somebody else. That was the source of conflict.

The Juggler observed:

> . . . in groups, I find it very difficult to relate to other administrators on how they act or behave, or the way they feel. . . . I don't respect the way they operate. . . . They are different than I am . . . dull, dumb, noncreative, authoritarian, not open. . . . I view myself as . . . a unique school administrator—in terms of experience and background. I feel I'm different from most school administrators. I got into it at a very early age and so I don't have the background of classroom experience and the classroom teacher feelings that other administrators have. In groups I find it very difficult to relate to other administrators on how they act or behave, or the way they feel. I don't respect the way they operate.

When Fran was asked about her relationships with other principals, she said, "There are none." The Rationalist went on to clarify her comment by adding: "Well, there are two but . . . there are no other junior-senior high schools in town. There is no one, sort of, that would be a colleague." When pressed to consider the possibility of relating to assistants within her school, she said: "Somewhat. They've been there for years, and there they are, all settled in and mostly they're just—you know—nothing too exciting, nothing too terribly wrong either, but they're just kind of there."

Marie's circumstance was similar to Fran's in terms of other principals, but she did seem to have established a somewhat more productive relationship with the two assistant administrators in her building. In speaking of her relationship with them, The Catalyst stated:

> The older assistant, he's fifty, wanted the job—so he not only didn't get the job but he got a woman. But, I'm finding that older men have sort of made their peace with men and women and the difference in sexes. And even though they may be raving, screaming chauvinists, they still accept you for what you are and never mind what sex you are. But he wasn't really excited about seeing me come in; and it wasn't directed at me—it was just directed at the situation. But he's the kind of person who would never take it out on me; he stands on his head not to take it out on me, which he accomplished. The other assistant and I had just "instant" communication—and we don't even have to talk and we know what the other's thinking about; and so we really did have to concentrate on bringing the older assistant in as part of the group. . . . We bat stuff around, the three of us or the two of us, and by the time we get done, we're somewhere between the two ends of the poles, and it usually works better. . . . It isn't a fighting kind of situation—I present my side and he presents his.

While a variety of views are expressed in these remarks by principals regarding their relations with other administrators, they appeared as a group to be somewhat dissatisfied with this situation. Although some were clearly more emphatic than others in detailing the inadequacies they perceived in the quality of their relationship to other principals, each of them directly, or indirectly observed that there was just not sufficient opportunity for them to interact with other principals. In those cases where opportunity was not a problem, these principals suggested that they did not view the peers with whom they could interact as particularly worthy of their attention—they were not seen as good models, or as having special skills or insights. Clearly, they did not seem to value or rely upon other administrators for help or advice regarding job-related problems.

Although these principals didn't interact much with their administrative peers, they did seem to have more frequent contact with their superiors. It should be noted that in most cases the quality of the interactions reported seemed to be of a relatively low level. In other words, the inadequacies in peer relations were in no way made up for or compensated for by relations with superiors. Usually those contacts reported were a function of either a specific problem, which the principal felt the superintendent could help solve, or an initiative on the part of the superintendent. Again, while interaction between principal and superintendent seemed to occur more often than between principal and principal, it was not frequent.

The excerpts noted below suggest the character of these principals' encounters with their respective superintendent and Central Office staffs. Marie observed:

> They're in and out of our building quite a bit, which is fine. The superintendent— I like very much; and we have an assistant superintendent . . . and he's not real sure what to do with women. . . . I don't avoid him at all, I'm just very very careful about how I deal with him. I try to be very calm, very logical, very rational. . . .

Marie interacted relatively frequently with her district superintendent and seemed to pride herself on the fact that he and members of his Central Office staff felt free to come and go as they pleased at her high school. She saw them as resources she could use, and she mentioned that, even though they were her evaluators, she would go and sit down with one or another of them and discuss what she had in mind for her school.

> I go do that and then they know what's going on in the building and how I'm thinking—so they don't perceive me as pulling a fast one—the superintendent said the only thing he cares about is "no fast ones". . . . No one is going to tell you you can't do it—or that you can do it. That's not the issue, the issue is no surprises!

In fact, in her circumstance, the superintendent was one of the few people she felt she could rely upon for expert advice:

> I like the superintendent. . . . He has skills . . . on perceiving groups, and he's about the only one in there I can call on and say "Okay, give me a reading on that group." And we'll go back and forth on it, and so, he's of extreme value. . . .

She went on to point out that the assistant superintendent in charge of special services had been a big help to her with developing her guidance department. Marie concluded her comments on the superintendent and his two assistants by noting that "all three of them feel a lot more comfortable about coming into the building now that I'm there—rather than the former principal—like then they were fighting."

In a similar vein, Fran also made a point of commenting on her relationship with her superintendent. In fact, the historical relation of the former high school principal to the superintendent had been somewhat problematic, so that she now prided herself on the positive character of that relationship. The Rationalist elaborated:

> . . . there's some historical business here, too. The superintendent and principal have never been able to work together . . . and it's distracting, I think, for the faculty, because they know that fifty people aren't going to agree on everything—and these fifty people always had an audience somewhere. They've always either had a school board audience . . . or superintendent, or the principal. The superintendent and I have no public disagreements, and that's worked to my benefit, to his benefit, and the school district's benefit.

Part of the basis for her good relations with the superintendent seemed to stem from the general political environment of the small community in which she worked. In discussing the general base of her support in the face of criticism, Fran commented that:

> . . . support comes forth in critical times with people, but I don't think it's strong enough that if the superintendent were fired, that support for a local person wouldn't be overpowering . . . to be really realistic about the situation, politically, I'm very much aligned with the superintendent, and that's inescapable in this town . . .

However, in addition to this reason for interacting with and maintaining good relations with her superior, Fran also viewed him as the one fellow professional in town with whom she could talk in a nitty-gritty way about problems on the job:

> . . . we're able to sit down at the table and bang our fists, and say "You stupid fool—you shouldn't be doing this" and "This is why." You know—that kind of thing. I mean it's, who else—you know, on a day-to-day basis—would I have to do that with? There isn't anybody. . . .

For Fran, then, her relationship with the superintendent was both politically necessary and a source of professional feedback and criticism that she valued and felt was otherwise unavailable from her administrative peers. While she was aware of the disadvantages of her alignment with the superintendent, she placed a high premium on having someone she could really talk to about job-related problems.

In contrast to the situations of Fran and Marie, John's relationship with his superintendent and Central Office staff was much more distant and infrequent. The Humanist's high school was one of four in a large city school district. His remarks contrast somewhat with those of Fran and Marie:

> . . . in dealings with Central Office . . . my relationships with most of the people down there were very positive. I'm of the opinion that you attract more flies to honey—I don't like to make enemies. I don't like to get into real kinds of conflict situations with guys I can't beat, particularly with assistant superintendents. And in alienating that group you could really harm yourself later, in terms of the school and even in terms of your own career, if you're thinking of that. So, if you get into situations with those folks you just try to work them out as best you can. I always realize that I cannot win them all and I accept that.

John recognized his need to maintain good rapport with the Central Office staff, but he did not view the superintendent or any of his assistants as a real source of political support or as any sort of professional confidant. Further, he did not interact very often with either the superintendent or members of his staff.

George's relation with his superior seemed to be somewhat of a blend of the situations of Marie, Fran, and John. Although George's high school was smaller than John's but larger than either Fran's or Marie's, The Juggler's situation seemed similar to theirs in at least two respects. One is that the town in which his school was located was fairly small—the high school was a visible entity in the town's social and political life. In this respect his situation was more like Fran's and Marie's than John's. Another is that his relations with the superintendent and the Central Office staff were relatively infrequent and fairly distant. Unlike Fran and Marie, George did not have a very close relationship to the superintendent, so in this respect his situation was similar to John's. When asked about the superintendent, George stated "The new superintendent—I don't know him. The old one—I ignored him." We asked George to explain why he ignored the former superintendent:

> . . . the only reason I was beginning to go to him . . . was because another building, another principal was beginning to really interfere with our act and I couldn't fight that battle—two principals, two schools.

George was unable to work out his difficulty with the other principal and thus went to the superintendent, even though George viewed him as relatively unimportant. He explained that he did this largely because of his relation with the "interfering" principal:

> . . . as two equals we had gone through all discussion. "Let's look at the problem and talk things out." We had gone through all of that and it came down to either the situation remaining the same or one of us shouting the other dead. And so I was going to the superintendent to get power.

Even though George viewed the superintendent as a relatively powerless individual, he believed he'd be able to gain some leverage as one principal in relation to another, if he were able to gain the superintendent's support. He explained a bit further that "It was the only place to find it—except if I wanted to go to the Board. But at that point I wanted to try the superintendent first . . . there wasn't any harm in it."

While George viewed himself as a fairly independent operator, vis-à-vis the old superintendent, he was somewhat unsure of his standing with the new one:

> I'm not clear about how this new fellow is going to operate. One of the first things I'm going to do is sit down and explain some things about myself, and let him explain some things about himself. In fact, when I wrote up my year-end report, almost the whole thing was aimed at the new superintendent. . . . It was to serve him as recommendations as to what I saw as necessary.

Even though George had not had much to do with his former superintendent, he seemed pleased at the prospect that things might be different with his new boss. When we asked him to talk about what sort of relationship he'd like to have with the new superintendent, George said:

> I'd like it to be very open. I'd like him to have a sharing type of relationship with me as the high school principal. I view that as a great opportunity to learn from a guy who ran a two-thousand student school. And I feel I might have some things to offer him in how to work with groups of people.

What he seemed to be saying, then, is that working with his superintendent hadn't been very fulfilling or helpful in the past, but that he saw the possibility of much better things in the future. George clearly wanted more out of his superintendent than he'd been able to get previously. He evidently attached great value to establishing contact with someone with whom he could interact and have a dialogue regarding the problems of administering a large high school serving a rural community.

These four high school principals' relations with their respective superintendents and Central Office staffs were not particularly extensive or fulfilling. However, when compared with the elementary principals, the high school principals seemed to have closer and more continuous contact with their superintendents and Central Office staffs. The elementary principals reported having very little to do, either directly or indirecly, with either their superintendent or the Central Office staff.

For example, Ed, reflecting on his relationship with his superintendent, observed:

> I don't feel I have a poor relationship with my superintendent, but I don't feel I have a good relationship either. I don't think he would take the time to listen and understand what I'm doing. He is, in my estimation, a very poor listener, and any

attempt on my part to describe for him a program that I have going on in my building has been completely useless. On the other hand, he's a very public-minded person, and I'm sure he's received a lot of feedback from parents, because I get letters from parents all the time about things that are happening in the building, and I know he received phone calls about this also. It took him two years, and the end of last year was the first time he ever spoke to me, I think, as a human being. He said to me that he was very pleased with what I had done, that he had a lot of confidence in my ability as an administrator, and talked about working with me.

While Ed, The Helper, seemed reasonably sure that his superintendent thought highly of him and of the programs in his school, there seemed to be a certain pleading in his comments for more frequent and more meaningful contact with him. Ed felt it was important that the superintendent be sincerely interested in and actually understand the focus and the substance of the programs Ed had developed with his teachers and students—but that this really was not the case, and was unlikely to occur given the low level of interaction and understanding between the two of them.

Paul, The Politician, seemed somewhat more jaundiced than Ed in speaking of his relation to the superintendent and Central Office staff. Paul's elementary school was in a larger system and because of this his formal contact was with the assistant superintendent in charge of elementary education. Paul suggested the nature of this relationship in the remarks below:

> When he interviewed me . . . it was clear that the only task for him was to help you get staffed in August—to help you in the selection process . . . and then to give you a list of reports that he was going to need from you, most of which I could do in September. These have to do with attendance . . . with supplies . . . and with finalizing the staffing ratio. Once that's done, you will not hear from downtown again.

Paul went on to explain the other sort of contact he had with the Central Office staff:

> . . . the other thing they had you do from downtown was to come to meetings. You have, at least once a month, a principals' meeting where the assistant superintendent stands up and talks for a half-hour about nothing. Then they allow time in there for the chairman or the person who held the meeting to give you doughnuts and cookies, and then you have a few minutes when you hear from the personnel department about whatever is new in terms of monitoring attendance . . . teacher contracts, and all the nasty things they are trying to get away with. Then you will hear from your own union about all the things we are trying not to let them get away with . . . and that's it.

Paul viewed the Central Office staff as more of a necessary evil than a resource for him or his school staff. Indeed, if Paul had his way entirely he would not even go the monthly principals' meetings. The only other occasions for Paul to interact with the assistant superintendent and the Central

Office staff were either the need to account for or explain the basis of a parent complaint, to discuss a severe discipline problem, or to take care of certain routine matters such as a mandated state-wide immunization plan. All in all, then, Paul, The Politician, seemed not to place much stock in trade with either the assistant superintendent or his Central Office staff.

Joan expressed laments similar to Paul's. The Organizer had virtually no contact with the superintendent, and her interaction with the assistant superintendent and Central Office staff was minimal:

> . . . we have no contact. We meet once a month . . . and we get lecture 902 from somebody—or the assistant superintendent lecturing about something ridiculous—we get lectured to instead of becoming a problem-solving interacting group . . . A policy decision will come out and, you know, it will be something that is just absolutely ridiculous. We have to decide—do we ignore the policy and go on?—because probably nine chances out of ten they are not going to know you are ignoring it anyway. . . .

Joan and Paul were both in charge of large elementary schools in different sections of a large school district. While they both faced fairly similar sets of problems, and while they both seemed to have equally limited contact with superiors in the Central Office, Joan seemed to think there was some possibility that principals and the Central Office staff could in fact work together and develop into a viable problem-solving team. Paul clearly differed from Joan in this respect.

Fred, the most recently appointed among the eight principals, had the following commentary to offer regarding his superiors:

> . . . they feel that as long as there are not a lot of phone calls . . . and they don't get a lot of grievances filed by teachers, you're doing okay.

Fred, The Broker, had been on the job only two years, and while he indicated that he read a lot on his own, he felt it was unfortunate that he hadn't really had much of a chance to bounce ideas around with his peers or his superiors, or to reflect on his situation. He noted that:

> For the first time, this year, the difference between this year and last year, is that the assistant superintendent and the director of elementary schools came into my building twice—which was a whole different pattern of behavior. Once to sit down and say "Hey, how's it going, what's happening?" You know, "What are some goals you want to set for yourself? What are some problems?" You know, they did ask if there was any way they could help. I didn't have confidence that they could, but the fact that they asked was at least something.

For us, Fred seemed to represent the epitome of the character of the typical relation between principals and their superiors—there just wasn't much of a relationship. The extent of interpersonal interaction between principals and superiors at all levels was infrequent, and practically nonexistent at the elementary level. While there did seem to be somewhat more productive relations between superiors and principals in the smaller school systems, in larger systems the interaction was sporadic and usually impersonal at best.

While Fran and Marie seemed to come closer than the other principals to having what might be termed a healthy, productive, and mutual-benefit relation with their superiors, all of these men and women seemed to put a high value on the possibilities extant in a relationship with administrative peers which permitted reflection, feedback, criticism, and exchange. Their message was clearly that they sorely missed what might best be termed a "sounding board" for their ideas and problems. They all seemed troubled somewhat by the risk and the burden of performing their administrative and leadership functions with so little contact with other members of the administrative reference group. While most seemed able to cope adequately with this circumstance, they all seemed to feel that it detracted from their productivity and general feeling of belongingness, and that in many instances it resulted in frustration and stress that might otherwise have been energy devoted to developing themselves, their peers, or aspects of their school program.

PARENTS

As a group, parents seemed more involved in school affairs at the elementary level than in the high school. All four elementary principals viewed parents and, indeed, subgroups within the larger parent community, as having an important influence upon their behavior in the principalship. For example, The Politician stated:

> ... the parent groups influence me in the sense that any time I like to make a major decision, I have to find a way to present it to parent groups. It is not one group; it is not one concise group, but it is several groups ... and there are several ways of presentation; there are several different key words that each of these groups are going to respond to, which usually causes a hassle. For instance, if you are talking about report cards, there is going to be one segment of the population that wants to see skills reported. . . . There is going to be another group that is going to be very much into traditional reporting, in terms of grades, so that they have some references to where the child is and how they should react and respond to the child. So, if I wanted a new plan in reporting, somehow I would have to endear myself in that program to both sets of parents. And, of course, if they are both in the audience at the same time, we really have a juggling act. . . .

And again:

> ... anybody who is really aware of what happens to them on the job as a principal will recognize very quickly that even having your hand in the pocket of

somebody downtown will never save you if a parent group goes down there. . . . If you want to make some changes, you have got to have somebody to support you, and you can't count on the teacher group to support you because the change you want to make may be exactly what they are fighting against. They may be the group you want to change or motivate. You can't count on the district to support you because, again, they are affected by a greater body—maybe politically or by other factions of parent groups that may be stronger or have their ear. So, in a sense, if you want to make a change, it seems to me that (parents) have to be your key group to get together; and once you have cohesiveness with them, they reflect some kinds of power that you don't.

While Paul clearly viewed parents as a power source relative to the principalship, Joan, The Organizer, held a somewhat different perspective. For her, parents were viewed more as an ingredient in the education of children than in the survival of the principal. For example, in explaining a special Monday morning program she and her staff inaugurated to help students make the transition from a weekend at home to the demands of school, she said:

> . . . we realized that a lot of things happened on weekends that we did not know anything about, and that the kids brought problems to school on Monday—whether they were family versus family or just kid and kid, something that happened on the playground at their apartment building, or whatever. . . . We instituted what we called "Drop-In" to try to get feedback from parents; and that happens two days a week at different times, where parents can just drop in and talk about anybody, doesn't necessarily have to be the kids that go to our school, but any kinds of problems. . . . We asked the parents if there were problems over the weekend, if they would communicate to us problems that might have occurred that would affect their kid's behavior in school on Monday morning, or at least cause them some frustrations during the day. . . . So the first hour of every Monday morning, what we do is we check down those things. . . . If we didn't take care of those problems, the teacher would have to keep taking care of the individual problems and disrupt the whole instructional atmosphere.

For Joan, then, the parent reference group was viewed not as a direct influence on the behavior of the principal *per se,* but was instead seen as a possible source of help about problems affecting the instructional environment of the school.

The Broker viewed parents in a manner similar to the Organizer's, although Fred had not been as successful as Joan at developing a way to involve parents in the education of their children. In relation to an adult education program he helped start, Fred stated:

> . . . I saw that as benefiting the school because our kids saw their parents going to school at night in our school . . . motivations for a lot of kids, then, to say "Hey, Mom's going back to school tonight and that makes some difference for me." So I saw it in that light . . . what effect it would have on the kids.

While he viewed parent involvement in school affairs as a positive influence upon the education of their children, Fred lamented that he had not been as successful in gaining their participation as he would have liked:

> . . . this year in particular I had said I am going to set aside some time, we are going to sit down with some parents and try to get some input from parents about what they see as problems in the school and, you know, how we could possibly improve any kind of parental commitment, or whatever. Just, you know, even the numbers of parents coming through that door to sit in on classrooms, to do a number of things in the building and possibly even leading to some types of educational programs—if they so wanted. Other than the adult education thing that we talked about . . . we began this fall with a goal-setting workshop where we took the time to call the parents, we had like ten participants in our school of three hundred kids; that's, you know, ten parents is a fairly insignificant number. . . .

Fred was clearly disappointed that he had not been able to secure more input from parents, particularly so because of the added influence such involvement might have on the educational program.

As was mentioned earlier, Ed's major orientation to his work world was his authentic "helper" thrust. He said that his PTA was extremely strong. We asked him to account for what we viewed as an uncommon view for a principal—to have a strong PTA:

> I think they're very much interested in their children. I also feel that they feel that they can come to me with ideas and will be listened to. . . .

Ed was as concerned about helping parents as he was in helping children and teachers.

While these elementary principals appeared to expend considerable time and energy working with or trying to involve parents in school affairs, the four high school principals seemed less inclined to involve themselves directly in such activities, although all acknowledged that parents could have considerable impact on what occurs in schools. The Humanist indicated:

> We tried cultivating parent support. We used to send out one thousand letters a month for PTA meetings. . . . We were unable to cultivate a viable group of parents that represented our school. That was really a failure, I guess, on my part, the school's part. I was just unable to do that. As a result our PTA group fell away and was not viable any longer. The only contact with parents I would have after that would be at ball games, or in parent conferences when parents would come to school to discuss their student's achievement or any problems we are having. Most of the parents, I felt, were very nice people, were concerned about what was going on with their child, were frequently so caught up in the economics of making a living that they didn't know what to do. And frequently the child was eighteen, nineteen, even twenty years old, and they felt that their child was an adult at this point and there was nothing further they could do as parents; and if the school couldn't do anything they didn't know where to go. Frustrating sometimes! But most of the people were good people and did care about their kids;

and were positive in their dealings with the school. I wouldn't have very many parents at all come in angry. . . . If we did have parents come in angry, I was always able to turn them around so that when they left they felt good.

The Juggler expressed similar sentiments:

I want them involved and I can't get them involved. We started two years ago what we called a PTSA-Parent, Teacher, Student Association; and our hope was to . . . form a PTSA which was outside the formal organization of the school, which would meet to discuss the same things that involve parents, teachers, and students, and it was used as a sounding board for faculty meetings, department chairmen; . . . so I think parents can be a great help.

When George was asked to explain why he wanted parents involved, he indicated ". . . we can then use the parent group as a sign of approval. . . ." When pressed to explain their reason for not becoming more involved, he said "They are satisfied."

The Catalyst's relations with parents did not consume much of her attention, although Marie did note that some were "curious" about a female high school principal. She said:

. . . one of the first things I did was pull together a philosophy committee, and I included parents on it, and they were really pleased to be included—I had no problem in getting parents and they all turned out in force for the parents' night, because they wanted to see what the new female principal looked like, but they're getting kind of used to the fact that they've got one of those.

For Marie, then, parents did not seem to be as critical a reference group for her as they were for some of the other principals.

The Rationalist's relations with parents were, again, somewhat limited, and mediated more by parent special interests than by deliberate initiatives on the part of the principal. Fran indicated that, as a group, parents did not have much direct influence on the high school:

. . . although individual parents and their concerns certainly have an influence—but not as a particular advisory group. There is a pressure group in town . . . and I would say they do exert some influence in political kinds of ways, maybe more at the superintendent's level than at my level.

While parents were involved as participants on various committees, and while Fran did indicate that she dealt occasionally with individual parents concerned over particular child-related issues, she did not interact with or relate to parents as a group in any systematic or frequent way. They were not, for example, viewed as a potential power source that the principal could draw upon, as was the case with Paul, The Politician.

All eight of the principals were involved in varying degrees with parents: While two viewed the parent group as a power source relative to influencing policy decisions in the school, four felt that parent involvement in school affairs would contribute to the educational program for children. Of the eight, only The Politician and The Organizer were able to turn this desire for parent input into operational programs.

STUDENTS

Students, like parents, also had some impact on the daily lives of those principals. In contrast to their relations with parents, the high school principals seemed more involved with student affairs than were the elementary principals. Further, while all eight seemed concerned with the behavior of students, the magnitude of concern was greatest among the four high school principals. Conversely, the magnitude of principal concern over academic achievement of students appeared strongest among the four elementary principals.

The Humanist spoke of his relations with students in the following way:

> My relationships with students, I think, were very good. I think kids saw me as not an authority figure. I am speaking now for those kids in the inner city and I suspect that those kids in the suburbs are going to behave quite the same way. Might begets might. In other words, you can't go after kids head to head, you lose—an authority figure just infuriates them, police, and things like that, and so do school principals for the most part. So, I think in cultivating kids, I think you really have got to care about kids and you have got to somehow convey this to kids—that you do care and that you are more than just a guy who suspends kids from school. If you get a chance, meet them in the hallways and talk to them about the ball game the night before; or in the cafeteria or in the classroom. You try to get around as much as you can, to get to know the kids by name. Now that's a big thing. A principal should know as many kids by name as he can possibly get to know. Now, in large schools, that's tough. But he should know four or five hundred kids by name, even in a school of fifteen hundred kids or more. It is so much better when you can walk down the hall, or in the cafeteria and you say, "Hi, John; Hi, Bill; Hi, Tom;" and they know that you know them. That means a lot to them.
>
> And another thing I have noticed particularly, is after kids have graduated—two, three, or four years—and they are now young adults and you are walking down Main Street, or you are in a store and they bump into you, you call them by name, they are delighted that you still remember them and they convey a lot of happiness that, you know, that they are happy that you remember them. And I think that means a lot to the kids. You know, they are from large families; they are still living in the neighborhoods. They talk to their brothers and sisters and that came to be a help in years to come because I have worked in the inner city around fourteen years. I got to know families, and brothers and sisters, and I could ask the younger brother how's the older brother doing, and where is he working, and how is he doing in school. And they saw me as someone not transitory, not passing through, but someone who had been on the scene quite awhile and who knew their family. And this helped. It helped with their parents, it helped with the kids. But I think, too, there are certain groups you can set up. We used to have a principal's cabinet, or a student advisory cabinet, where we would

meet every two weeks and the kids would talk to me on a very down to earth plane and discuss the school, the problems in the school. And we would communicate very openly and we would try to get things worked out, and I think this helped.

It seems from the comments of The Humanist that he spent a good deal of time with students; indeed, *cultivating* a good, healthy relationship that carried beyond the immediate work environ of the school. It was important for students to know that John really "cared" about them, and that he was more than ". . . just a guy who suspends kids from school."

The Juggler, in contrast to The Humanist, was much less intimately involved with the students in his high school. George stated that he paid most attention to students, as a group, ". . . when organized. When they have power. When they are going to be sitting up on that hill across from that school if you don't do something." He seemed to view students less as individuals and more as members of an intermittently influential group within the school. For example, George says:

. . . one of the things I do is, you know, put the knife in the ground and see which way the herd is running, and either build a stone wall or a bridge depending on which way I want them to go. . . . It seems as though it comes from all around you. You try to find out from what direction it is coming and then you begin to deal with it before it gets to that stage. And I think it is a more effective way too—it gives you a little more time to plan and look rather than reacting.

This tendency of George's to think of school participants as members of groups becomes even more evident in the following remarks:

If you stay on that knife edge, it is an extremely difficult job—where the students don't view you as being wishy-washy. And so you find that—and I think it is very narrow—the zone of acceptance between the view that the students tolerate and think is necessary and the one which the faculty tolerates and thinks is necessary. That's just in discipline.

The Catalyst, on the other hand, did not seem to have close contact with her students as individuals, although as a group they were important to her. In addition to her concern for their academic development, Marie made it clear what the standards for their behavior were going to be:

. . . my feeling is that when the kids break school rules, the school will deal with it; and when the kids break the law, the law will deal with it. . . . The cops don't have to come up so much anymore because the kids know we'll call them—it was partly the kids testing, too, and it made the staff feel comfortable that the halls are clear and things are quiet . . .

Marie's contact with kids, then, was sporadic, and usually occurred in relation to some discipline issue. In her view she was "never gonna be the

Jolly Green Giant . . . and didn't have time to run around the building and get to know eleven hundred kids." As she saw it, "the building wasn't gonna run if that's where I spent my time."

The Rationalist's relations with students were similar to those of other high school principals. While students were indirectly of concern as the eventual focus of particular curriculum development efforts by the principal, they did not get directly attended to as a group, or as individuals, except as particular discipline problems arose. Again, as was the case with other high school principals, the issue for Fran was one of control and maintaining school behavior standards that would facilitate, not impede, the educational program she was trying to build.

While their styles differed somewhat, two of the high school principals felt it was especially important to know students. It was important for George to "know" the "zone of acceptance" of what students would tolerate in terms of controls imposed by teachers and administrators. The Humanist felt it was important for the students to know that the principal really cared about them as individuals, that he was more than "just a guy who suspends students from school." The Catalyst and The Rationalist were both somewhat more removed from students than The Humanist, but like George, The Juggler, Fran and Marie felt it was important to "know" what was happening vis-à-vis the education and behavior of students in their schools. They were not "close" to students, but certainly did make a deliberate effort to keep themselves informed. In each case it seemed clear that these four high school principals viewed students as a group of important school participants whom they needed to understand and be attuned to if they were to be effective on the job.

The four elementary principals, in contrast to the high school principals, seemed to us to be able to exercise much more choice over the nature and extent of their involvement with students. Unlike the high school situation, where there seemed to be a tendency to exercise control over student behavior in terms of their adherence to school-wide norms, the focus of the elementary principal seemed more concerned with the behavior of individual students in relation to their academic performance, and the quality of their relations with the teacher and the students in their classroom. While there was *some* concern with adherence to school-wide behavior norms at the elementary level, this group seemed to be primarily interested in assuring that students experienced success in school-related activities, particularly in academic aspects of the curriculum.

The focus upon school-wide behavior norms is evident in these comments by Joan, The Organizer, about the results of a three-year effort by her staff to socialize students in a particular direction:

> . . . we have really helped kids learn . . . that there are acceptable ways in school to solve a problem, and we have told them "We can't control your behavior

outside on the street—that is like swearing or fighting. If that's what you do when you are home, and that's acceptable to your parents and it is acceptable to you, then we can't do anything about that. But it is unacceptable in the school situation and really stops you from learning, and so what we'll ask you to do, is instead of engaging in some physical battle, to see if we can work out the problem, and problem-solve."

Even here, however, in contrast to the situation described by the high school principals, there is an implicit attempt to integrate these norms within the school curricula—in a word, to teach students how to behave in an acceptable way, and not merely to sanction them negatively for misbehaving. The Organizer in describing how this was accomplished, stated:

> We listed all kinds of problems that stopped kids from working in a really acceptable learning environment. After that we brainstormed all the different kinds of ways that we could alleviate those kinds of problems . . . and decided that problem solving was a really important part of the instructional program. If we didn't help kids learn that, there were lots of things they couldn't do.

In a similar vein, Fred, The Broker, reported that:

> I spend some time with kids in class meetings, and direct contact with kids. I don't know if that is for my own ego or just for fun and relaxation. But my purpose there is more or less to get kids involved in problem solving with teachers and with themselves. And we do role playing and things like that. . . .

Although Joan was not as explicit as Fred, her sentiments about the relation between principals and students were similar to his comment that he "will make a fuss over kids . . . being an advocate for kids." In further clarification, The Broker stated:

> I sometimes get into that role (advocacy) dealing with some teachers in our building. In other words, if teachers are, for instance, demeaning a kid in any kind of way, you get into that. I find myself advocating for kids a lot of times, and I have been accused of being on the side of kids at times. I don't feel uncomfortable doing that. But I also talk with teachers from the point of view of "Hey, look, there are other alternatives in dealing with kids' behavior. Let's explore what they are . . ."

In his role as student advocate, Fred chose to extend his service orientation. In a sense, he "served" students as as arbiter with teachers. That the elementary principal seems to have more degrees of freedom in choosing the nature of his/her relations with students contrasts sharply with the almost "given" expectation in the high school that the principal is the disciplinarian. The high school principals did not appear to have as much "choice" over the character of their relations with students. This is probably in part due to the increased size and complexity of the high school situation, as well as a function of the organizational culture extant in schools regarding "appropriate" student behavior.

Ed saw himself as very involved with the children in his elementary school. For example, in addition to becoming involved in a large group activity with all of the children each morning, The Helper held special "therapy" sessions with smaller groups. All of these efforts were, in Ed's view, part of his goal of making schools more humane and helping children develop their emotional and feeling capabilities along with their cognitive development.

The Politician described a wide range of possible student-principal relations in elementary schools. When asked what students did that required the principal to attend to them, Paul replied "Not much, not much; I think that's by choice." He elaborated:

> I think it's the choice of the principal as to whether, for instance, if you get bored with the two hours worth of work that you do in an eight-hour day, you know, some people could then expect you would take over the problems and discipline with kids. Therefore, you might get to know the kids as a disciplinarian, which could keep you busy all day if you did it right, you know? If you had people sent to your office, six or seven of them in a row, and you talked to each one of them for fifteen minutes, and took a cigarette between them and the next group that came in, you could keep yourself busy all day with kids.

Paul then went on to suggest the nature of his relationship with the students in his school:

> You are an image for them. You can set yourself up as a person they respect and look for, and they really always know who their principal is. And they always are going to decide whether you are a bad-ass principal, which is good, or whether you are just a principal to play with—you know, you are a principal who will give a kid a piece of candy if he cries long enough or kicks you in the shins long enough and often. Or, you can get involved in their—really—in their lives, which then blows their mind. They are just like teachers. When you go out on the playground and play with them, the kids who are fifth and sixth graders, who have been involved with principals before you, that blows their minds. You know, I used to do that. I'd go out; if I had lunch-time duty I was not about to walk up and down the halls. I got me a group of kids to do that and I went outside and played with the kids, you know. Then, you know, the older kids kind of look at you like "What's your plan, sucker?" You know, or "How much will you take?" For instance, when we had snow I would go out and have snowball fights with them. Well, as soon as they would see I was really going to come out and play, their first thing was to gang up on me and see whether I was going to get mad and use my authority role. Well, I kind of figured that out so I, you know, I got mad anyway. You know, I could tell what their game was. The younger kids, you know, you can be a Messiah to them. If you come out and touch them, they just think this is the most wonderful thing in the world, because for the most thing, you will never see them discipline-wise, the little kids, and here is a person who comes on the loudspeaker, which is really next to God, because the loudspeaker is up there and you see, now,

that's really the way they treat you—"Oh, wow, and this person will touch me?" Then you can, really, a few years later it'll pay off. But the older kids look at you—"What are you, some kind of kid?"

From Paul's perspective, then, elementary principals have many alternatives regarding the sort of relationship they establish with students in their school. In his own case he distinguished between the views that older and younger students have of the principal, and noted that fostering a little "hero worship" among the younger students will have positive results relative to the relationship they have with the principal as they grow older and become more experienced in the ways of schools and principals. We felt that, in some respects, Paul's view was similar to Ed's in his belief that principals need to be seen as more than just disciplinarians if they are to be effective with students; they must be seen as human, caring, credible, and trustworthy individuals. Beyond this, and establishing oneself as a good model for children is certainly not the easiest task to accomplish, Paul, The Politician, felt that principals really don't have much to do with kids as a group. He contrasted sharply with Ed on this point.

In summary, it seemed from our interviews with these principals that at the elementary level two conditions appeared to obtain: (1) the principal had a great deal of choice in defining the character of his/her relations with students, and (2) there seemed to be a tendency for principals to conceive of their relationship with students more as an extension of the school's instructional program than as an organizational phenomenon related to issues of control and coordination of school participants. The nature of the principal-student relationship in the high school seemed to be more a consequence of the structure of the school situation than of the principal's personality. However, even in the high school, as The Humanist maintained, some felt it was important for the students to know the principals as more than "just a guy who suspends kids from school."

TEACHERS

Unlike their relations with parents and students, all of the principals seemed to have much more in common relative to their relationship with teachers. As will become evident from the excerpts to follow, they put a high premium on the necessity to establish and maintain an open and trusting relationship with their faculty toward the ends of securing commitment to school programs, and involving participants in the decisions affecting the teachers' work world.

These principals tended to speak of their relationship with teachers in terms of either organizational maintenance activities or program change. For example, relative to faculty expectations, The Juggler observed that:

An awful lot of people look at the school as a maintenance type function. You know—being sure the supplies are there on time, the machines are operable, master schedule isn't screwed up, the change of schedule done neatly so everybody knows where the hell they are going, and that duty rosters are balanced out with fairness and equality for all, and that teachers' time isn't impinged upon to any great extent, too, you might balance, you know, teacher's time versus the job, the administrative jobs to be done. And you find that we can't get everything we want done but we can get this much done, and we better get secretarial help for the rosters. . . . I think in the area of leadership, real leadership, the principal has a free hand and makes his own decisions—nobody's pushing the principal to a new curriculum, nobody's pushing somebody to make a new schedule or new program for students. There is no push for that, there is no push for new budgeting techniques . . . you take the school budget and just let it be and nobody would care about it. Even though one department had 50 percent of the budget, and could be that way for ten years, and there would be very little pressure to change it from other departments because it is too big a task for them. . . .

In clarifying the different relations he had with teachers, George indicated that on issues of change "you have to be a salesman," and that "on issues of maintenance . . . there is more debate on how it's divided up or how it's done rather than what is done." In trying to clarify these differences in his relations with teachers, George said, regarding changes:

. . . you trade. You know, like, "All right, if I do that, what do I get for it?" You might get an extra period of planning time to get this thing set up, you might get four weeks' summer work for it. You don't do that for the maintenance.

For The Juggler, then, his relations with the faculty group varied according to the types of issues at hand. Maintenance issues required a sort of "balancing act" on his part to insure that these activities, the demands on teachers, were fairly and equitably distributed. On the change-related issues he assumed a "salesman" orientation wherein his relations with teachers assumed more of a "bargain/exchange" quality.

The Catalyst related more directly with the department chairmen in her school, and Marie was especially sensitive to the historical pattern of poor relations between the faculty and past principals. She commented:

. . . a lot of people aren't sure what to do with me. I don't think people perceive me as threatening as they used to, and usually when I sense that, that's where they're coming from, I back off. And I'm very cautious with them because that isn't going to accomplish a whole lot if they're scared to death. Sometimes it's appropriate for them to be scared to death, but not these people in this situation.

In contrast to Marie, Fran interacted more directly with her faculty. While her faculty was organized by departments, there were no department chairpeople. Fran indicated that she worked most closely with faculty on curriculum matters, usually effecting change by making new materials available and helping faculty learn how to use them. In terms of department meetings, Fran, The Rationalist, would call the meetings and sometimes attend—sometimes not attend. She was generally perceived by the faculty, in her view at least, as competent relative to instructional matters. While they were generally supportive of her as a principal, she did not view them as particularly helpful, given her needs for feedback and reinforcement:

> ... you have to be a person who doesn't need a whole lot of positive reinforcement. ... You have to be pretty sure in your own mind that you're collecting data accurately and, you know, not having tunnel vision or tunnel hearing. ... You have to have a lot of confidence in yourself because you just don't have a whole lot of support from a large group of people.

There was contact with teachers, then, but it seemed more of a crisis intervention or initiation of change variety than the sort associated with a collegial or collaborative relationship.

Another high school principal, The Humanist, raised similar issues, but couched them in different terms. On the issues of maintaining an orderly environment and good student discipline, John reported:

> ... teachers made it obvious to me that ... they wanted more strict enforcement of student dicipline codes, they wanted to be sure that kids were not in hallways loitering. They wanted administrators around the building and not working on scheduling things or, you know, they did not want you in the office; they wanted you around and visible. So that teachers made their needs known in various ways. In faculty meetings in the halls, issues would come up. I think as an administrator, you have to sense what they are saying to you. You know, you do think through what they are saying, where are your priorities, how should you be behaving, what should you be doing, and then you try to fulfill those expectations that that group of people had for you. ... Now, in fulfilling their expectations you build one hell of an alliance and, with those people, they really get in your corner, so that when the time comes for you to ask them to do things that they normally would not do, they will do it for you—plus it establishes tremendous morale. An administrator always has to cultivate faculty support. If you lose faculty, you have lost—you can't exist without that faculty. ... Teachers have to see you are caring; teachers have to see you as listening to their problems and really caring about their problems. If teachers bring problems to you, I think it demands follow-through. ... You involve faculty, too, in decisions in the organization that affect them, like "Should we go to computer report cards or do you like the hand grading system?" Now that should be a faculty decision and they do appreciate a guy who will involve them in the decision. And then, as an administrator, it is always your task to get people, if you can, to do the things that you would have done anyway. If you can. Now sometimes, that will backfire, but I think here is where you sharpen your skills a little bit in forms of dealing with people, and see if you can maneuver a group into doing what you really wanted to have them do. And there are decisions that can be made about the organization that you can involve the faculty in so that they really feel an integral part of the school. And it helps. It helps in morale; it helps them in feeling that they are professionals and that they have something to say, and that there is a guy running the place that will listen to them and move in the directions that they feel appropriate. ...

John went on to elaborate on how he cultivated the faculty support he felt was so necessary, and what some of the results of his relations with faculty yielded:

. . . we used to meet once a month with representatives from the teachers' union, and this would be to go over mutual concerns. And when the teachers would lay their concerns out, you know, I would respond to them and we would follow through. We would take action if the concerns were legitimate—and they usually were legitimate concerns. And this helped cultivate that kind of faculty support. It even got so that some of the teacher representatives would come in and see me confidentially and say, you know, "So and so's bitching today about something and I was not going to bring it to you, but, you know, I am a teacher rep; but I am just telling you and what they are saying is—I'm telling you, but I don't expect you to do anything about it." I say "Okay, fellow; gee, thanks." And you would get that kind of report. And it's not that teachers would come in and be stool pigeons; they didn't do that. But when they did get complaints from different people in the organization, a lot of times they would slough them off, which helped me. And it even came to a point . . . where we didn't have these monthly meetings anymore, which I was grateful for.

Thus the bulk of The Humanist's activities with teachers was concerned with organizational maintenance issues, although at times it was clear that change, some new direction, was at stake. John more specifically addressed his style as a change-agent in suggesting his part in curriculum development:

. . . I can develop curriculum if what I do is . . . do it from the grass roots level, and they will come to me with situations, and I will perceive whether or not it is a direction we want to go, or that it is educationally sound. I can make those kinds of decisions, but I see myself as facilitating the kinds of directions they want to go. That's my function as an administrator—to pull everything together and make it go. And that's the way I see myself. I am not a curriculum leader. I think I can get people to do things I want them to do. And it might be a function of personality; I think it is. I like people, I'm very sensitive to facial expressions, I can tell, I can usually read people pretty well as I'm talking to them. But, what they may be thinking about—I can detect if somebody's nervous. Very suddenly you can usually tell if somebody's got a hidden agenda. I think this ability to read people and to be able to work with them is probably my forte.

Although John was perhaps a bit more indirect regarding the focus on his relations with faculty, he and the other high school principals seemed to us to put a high premium upon establishing and keeping a healthy and supportive relationship with teachers. While most of the issues at the base of their relations seemed maintenance oriented, each of them felt it was very important to be a sensitive listener and observer and to involve his/her faculty in making and implementing decisions. None of the four high school principals indicated that there was any strong teacher pressure for change. When demands were made, they usually were related to maintenance issues, which faculty perceived to fall primarily within the principal's domain of responsibility.

The four elementary principals' observations of their relations with teachers were similar to those of the high school principals, although the focus was more diffuse in some areas. The Politician was the clearest of the three regarding his relations with teachers. Paul stated:

> If I wanted to maintain the status quo, I think I would deal with my staff first. I think teachers, your staff, would be your cohesive group that would maintain; that's what keeps the machinery going. . . . I guess I don't see myself as a principal as having the answers to a lot of the ongoing machinery type things. I think that I can sit down on Sunday mornings, before the football games, and analyze what it is that needs to maintain the school without ever having to do it, you know, in such a sense. The key thing for me would be to pick out four or five people whom I could count on, who are upwardly mobile or for some other reason are very much attached to the same idea of maintaining the school; maintaining whatever it is—short-sighted but very consistent every day. You know, and pick them out in different areas, for instance, and make sure that these kinds of maintenance things are going on. . . . I would have another reference group in terms of people who would make changes, or who would be looking for improvement. In other words, an improvement committee would be very different from your maintenance people.

He differentiated, though, his use of upwardly mobile teachers:

> I would look for some people who are upwardly mobile, within the organization, that I could count on. You can depend on them. . . . You know—"I'll make you a unit leader" or "I will train you to be an assistant principal." Or, "You are an administrative intern and you want to get into administration. Here are some tasks—and they are really 'Mickey Mouse' everyday tasks that have to be done. . . . They have to be done, but if you delegate them, you are the one whose head will roll if they don't get done." So, it is very important to you to know that this person's going to take almost as strong a look at it as you would, and probably do a better job.

For The Politician, then, it was important for him to identify dependable teachers who could be counted upon to carry out many of the organizational maintenance tasks that the principal does not want to do himself. Regarding the clarity of his role relations with the faculty, Paul made it clear that the quickest way to reduce ambiguity was for him to do something:

> . . . if you don't do anything, you remain ambiguous . . . as soon as you begin to initiate some structures, as soon as you begin to make some decisions, the effect of that is going to be to reduce the ambiguity because you sure as hell are going to have a clear understanding where your problems lie, where people are coming from, which reference group you should have paid attention to. . . . Even if you don't step on their toes, even if you just initiate some kind of action that doesn't step on their toes, they will let you know—they will respond to it.

The Organizer, in describing her relations with teachers, echoed many of the observations made by other principals. Joan elaborated on her feelings about the importance of touching base with her staff before making decisions affecting them:

> ... I always do it, because if they don't support the idea, then it does not get going no matter what I do. If they don't believe in it, they're the people that for the most part have to implement it; and I can't do that by myself. ...

In analyzing their involvement in the decision process, she stated:

> I don't think they do any of the organization. The ideas don't usually originate with any one person, meaning classroom teachers, but they are clarifiers, they are—they have their input ... they feel very much a part of the decision.

The Organizer described her relations with teachers as:

> Positive. Trusting. It's a pretty warm relationship. They still—I'm sure—see me as their administrator. There is no way you can take that away, because I do make judgments, I do make evaluations, I do make recommendations to them, so they still have to see me in that light somewhat. But they are a lot freer now to bring their—not personal problems, we don't even deal with that, there is no way I even want to deal with people's personal problems unless it is affecting what they are doing in the classroom—but they are very free to say, come in and say, "Hey, I tried something today and it didn't work. Do you have any ideas?"

It was clear that Joan's work to establish an open and trusting relationship with her faculty had paid off.

It is also important to note here that each of the principals interviewed made it clear that it is a misconception to think of teachers as a *single* group sharing sentiments. Rather, these principals' perspectives indicated that teaching staffs are composed of various factions and special-interest groups adhering to different and sometimes conflicting views and priorities. As The Organizer indicated when commenting upon the introduction of a change at her school:

> ... you never put anything out unless you go to each group and find out how they feel about it. ... I never take anything to a large staff meeting. It would be ridiculous of me to go to a staff meeting with a brand new idea and try to sell it to everybody at one time. I just never do it.

Joan, like the four high school principals and her elementary peers, felt that if changes were to be made, they would likely be directly or indirectly initiated by the principal. In either case, the principals perceived that it was important to test their ideas with a few teachers before attempting to convince the entire faculty. Of the principals interviewed, the one with the least experience commented repeatedly upon the difficulty of introducing change in his school. In trying to explain the difficulty as he perceived it, Fred, The Broker, stated:

Adults don't spend very much time together—there has never been an expectation first of all, that teachers would ever get along with other teachers. Never ever. That was never raised, until we began to get into some teaming. I think there is a whole area of sacredness here about, you know, discussing really what goes on once your door closes; that's some of it. I don't know whether that's because there is some fear that somebody may be doing something that may not be in agreement with someone else, or nobody ever thinks to share what's going on in a classroom. I think time pressures are some of it—that keep people from communicating. I think people may be afraid to communicate with other people; I don't know. I don't know why. I think sometimes they think it is easier just to close the door and get away from me—take this number of kids and just deal with them and maybe the problems will go away.

Indeed, The Organizer reflected a similar frustration when she made it a point to mention that, after three years, her staff had finally grown comfortable enough in their interactions that they could begin to rely upon and consult each other: "They are very quick to say (to other teachers) 'Look, I have a really tough home visit today. I don't think I can make it alone. Is there anybody who can go with me?' "

The foregoing is not to suggest, however, that everything is "peaches 'n cream" in terms of principal relations with teachers. The Organizer, for example, made it clear that one of her most persistent problems was getting individual teachers to solve their own problems rather than bringing them to her:

> . . . one thing that I have instituted is "I will not do it for you, but I will help you learn it." And that's when I got in a bind. When I started doing things for people, then I became dissatisfied with me as a person. . . . Every time a teacher had a problem—and you know just before vacations teachers have a lot of problems, okay—they're tired, they're exhausted and they—see the trend coming?—they start sending kids down, one right after the other. And I kept doing that—I kept taking the kids instead of doing what I normally do. I fell back into the trap. And I knew the reason for it. But instead of trying to help the teacher by relieving her for ten minutes, or taking her out of the classroom to help her solve the problem with the kid, I was taking on the problem again and trying to solve the problem. I was not liking myself. I wasn't helping the teacher because the problems kept recurring.

Nice Comment

Joan indicated that she'd been working on this problem for three years, since first coming to that school, and that it had affected her relations with teachers:

> I would sit and confront a teacher about a problem, for instance, and say "Could it possibly be your problem?" and watch the teacher get very offended; and instead of dealing with me on a factual level, deal on an emotional level and say things that were very cutting and hurt. I would sit there and I would grind my teeth so as not to, say, play the same game which I tried to help them learn that they were always losing with kids, if you play it on that kind of level. And so I would sit there and grind my teeth. But it still hurt. And you know, when they went out, the door closed, and I cried a lot, and I got it out of my system, and I

started over again. And it took a long time. It just didn't take overnight. And, I'm sure, I'm sure I can safely say that there are probably two or three people that I probably don't have a good relationship with right now. I'm sure there are.

In commenting on his relations with teachers, The Broker echoed The Organizer's feelings and also suggested that interpersonal relations among teachers themselves were at times problematic:

> . . . in a small school, you can't let people get upset; there is a real need to keep a balance of personalities. I mean, you get two people going at each other in a small building, it seems that it can really raise hell as far as staff relations can be. I have one person that cannot get along with anybody and it's raising hell, you know, everybody is all upset all of the time because of the one person.

The Helper's relations with teachers reflected his response to the general condition noted by The Broker, and were aimed primarily at setting a climate conducive to growth—establishing a trustworthy relationship with teachers was a major priority for Ed. He observed:

> . . . as far as teachers—it's just being myself with them and developing a sense in them—that it's okay for them to be themselves. It's okay to be angry, and it's okay to be positive; it's okay to be warm. That just didn't exist before.

Good relations with their teaching staffs was a primary concern of all these principals. While the focus of their interactions could roughly be categorized into issues related to maintenance or change, they all felt that success in both spheres was necessary if they were to be effective principals.

CONCLUSION

While The Juggler, Rationalist, Catalyst, Humanist, Politician, Organizer, Broker, and Helper each brought a different perspective to bear upon the daily work world demands of the principalship, they each felt they were perceived as effective principals by relevant others. Even though they did not have extensive relations with either other administrators or their immediate superiors, all of them were actively involved, on an interpersonal level, with parents, students, and teachers. While the demands of these three reference groups varied somewhat across different school and community circumstances, and the strategies and behavior of the eight principals differed according to the particular viewpoints they held toward the principalship, their responses to the demands of the school work world had many elements in common, probably, in part, because of similarities in the conditions of their work environment.

The principalship portrayed in the observations reported here is of a highly ambiguous and normative character, mediated primarily through face-to-face interpersonal interaction between the principal and other participants in the school situation. These principals were "people administrators" in the sense that effective interpersonal skills were a critical ingredient of successful on-the-job behavior. They also were inquiring individuals in the sense that, although their perspectives were different, it was crucial to their effectiveness to keep themselves informed of and responsive to the work world demands characterizing their particular school situation. Also, they may have felt isolated from other principals and supervisors, but they were certainly not alone in terms of the amount of time and energy they expended in interpersonal interaction with students, parents, and teachers. The quality of their relations with members of these three groups was perceived by them to be closely tied to their success as principals.

One of the most striking observations is that while each appeared to have evolved a rather individualistic and idiosyncratic ideology toward his/her job, the types of problems he/she experienced were similar from one school to another. The "commonality" of problems encountered generally reflects the evidence reported in other studies of school organizations. However, the strikingly different yet similarly effective conceptions guiding these principals' orientations toward their work world run counter to what seems an implicit, if not explicit, notion abounding in the literature that effective administrators hold some common viewpoint regarding their role and the nature of their work situation. While it is true that these principals experienced a number of similar problems in their relations with others (individual and organizational change, and "keeping the peace" in their respective school systems), each held a rather unique perspective toward his/her role. Some of the behavioral results of these seemingly idiosyncratic viewpoints have been highlighted by reporting a few of the more obvious differences in their role orientations and administrative style characteristics. Although the distinctions that have been drawn may at times seem fuzzy, such gross categories do begin to capture much of the essence of these individuals and the nature of their on-the-job behavior.

While these principals definitely have a "framework" for understanding their work world, it only remotely resembles the sort of highly abstract and rational conceptual frame one would find in the usual textbook on school administration. It is, instead, highly idiosyncratic to the needs and dispositions of the particular principal and the context of the particular work situation. This individualized view of the role serves as a reference point for action for these people—problems and solutions are shaped by the nature of the individual's personal perspective.

All of these principals spent a great deal of their work day in direct interpersonal interaction with students, teachers, and parents. While each of them perceived few opportunities for interaction and dialogue with their administrative peers, all felt that this would be highly beneficial. Students appeared to be a more potent reference group for the high school principals than for the elementary principals. In each case, success seemed to depend largely on their ability to listen to and dialogue with members of these reference groups. The degree of the principal's interpersonal competence, particularly those skills related to establishing and maintaining desired identities, both for the principal and for others, serves to mediate much of the principal's work world activity, and as a consequence is probably pivotal in differentiating the more effective from the less effective principal. These principals reflected a low conceptual/technical, high human relations orientation to their work world.

The principal's general work situation is ambiguous and as such is likely to produce much psychological stress for the individual and, in some instances, may severely impair the principal's ability to perform to the level of his/her expectations. The performance/expectations discrepancy created by these circumstances seemed to be managed effectively by these eight principals—they seemed to be able to cope well with their circumstances.

The particular coping strategy adopted by each of them seemed to be a critical variable intervening between the potentially impairing aspects of their situation and the actual level of their on-the-job performance. Each believed he/she could influence the situation. In this regard, it appears that they maintained a *proactive confrontation*, rather than a *reactive avoidance* strategy toward the problems they encountered.

Further, the proactive coping strategy employed also seems related, in part, to the character of the organizational situation and, additionally, to the level of interpersonal competence of these principals. It is reasonable to speculate that proactive coping strategies are most likely to be used if a principal has a high degree of interpersonal competence and if the character of the organizational situation is sufficiently ambiguous to permit reinterpretation and channeling of role demands. Principals who are able to employ such a strategy will probably experience a lower performance/ expectations discrepancy in their on-the-job behavior than will principals using an avoidance or reactive strategy. These data suggest that principals who cope in a proactive manner will be perceived as more effective than those employing an avoidance strategy. The character of the coping behavior of these eight principals had much to do with their success on the job.

Two themes underlying this discussion need to be emphasized. First, while each principal held a tacit and almost unconscious understanding of factors related to his/her on-the-job behavior (Polanyi, 1967), each had an extremely difficult time explaining specifically why they did what they did on the job. In other words, they could perform, but could not clearly explain or otherwise systematically articulate the why and wherefore of their behavior; they just knew that it "worked." Their theories of action (Argyris and Schön, 1974) were effective, yet they were unable to explain them. Second, the socializing influence of the school situation itself appeared to have an informal and unobtrusive impact on the development of the interpersonal skills, the work-world perspectives, and the coping strategies guiding these principals. While the data are unclear on these two issues, research currently being conducted by one of the present authors (Blumberg) seems to confirm the pervasiveness of these themes.

11

All That Glitters Is Not . . .

Part of the design for this study of some out-of-the-ordinary school principals called for their reactions to what we had written about them. We wanted to know how they would feel about how they were seen by others, and how accurate we were in our portrayal of them. In addition, and more important for our purposes, we wanted to know what this group of intelligent and skillful administrators would talk about together. What would be their concerns? How did they feel about their jobs? What was the job doing to them as people? How did they perceive their futures?

Six of the eight people interviewed and written about were able to meet with us for about a four-hour, rather free-floating, discussion. Some of them knew each other, others were strangers to the group. Each had been provided with a copy of our sketch of him/her so that they were not coming in cold to the situation. The meeting started with our asking the individuals to talk about the reactions they had as they read about themselves. We sat back and listened.

For the most part, what had been written, the descriptions of their behavior and the interpretations we had made, was seen to be accurate. The reactions they had ranged from one person's being somewhat uncomfortable and embarrassed at being pictured in too heroic a fashion (his interpretation), to another's being frankly pleased and flattered. Mostly though, each individual said, in effect, "Yes, that's the way I am. The picure you painted tells the story." More important for our purposes, however, was that sharing their perceptions and reactions to our sketches of them led to a wide-ranging discussion of what life in general was like for a school principal. The discussion was problem oriented in the sense that it focused on some issues that these people had to live with, on a day-to-day basis, that were emotionally and intellectually draining. It was also problem oriented in that the principals were saying, in effect, "Here are some things that stand in the way of our doing the job better, of creating a better setting for the education of youngsters."

Our interest in this discussion was not a casual one. Indeed, the case was quite the opposite. While we were not interested in conducting a "bitch" session, we were most attracted to the idea of engaging the principals in a thoughtful analysis of some of the factors in their work life that had the effect of inducing a long-term negative emotional impact on them. Our attraction to this type of discussion stemmed from several sources. It first started conceptually, with our reading and discussing between ourselves and with several of our students the notion of "emotional toxicity" (Levinson, 1972) of work environments. Levinson is a clinical psychologist who has devoted much of his career to inquiring into the psychology of person-work dynamics. He suggests that there are four major feelings with which every individual has to deal throughout his/her life: ". . . love, hate, feelings about dependency, and feelings about one's self image" (p. 36). The work situation—the problems that arise, the pressures that exist, the interactions that take place—create conditions that confront an individual with the necessity of dealing with these feelings as they arise. To the extent that a person is able to cope successfully with these feelings on the job, work and the demands of work become less emotionally toxic for the person and he/she can devote optimum energy to the tasks at hand. By contrast, if the individual is unaware of these feelings or aware but unable to cope well with them, the work environment becomes more emotionally toxic, with results that may be observed in psychosomatic illness, lessened ability or desire to do the job well, or a physical disengagement from the job, perhaps through resignation.

Second, it had become increasingly apparent that the conflict occurring in the field of public education was inducing larger and larger amounts of stress into the lives of practicing school administrators. The data came from a number of sources. For example, we had only to talk with some of our students who were principals to note their weariness and frustration, not merely from working long hours, but from continually confronting situations—with parents, teachers, students—that were charged with high emotionality and, thus, extremely draining. It was almost a relief for many of these students to come to the University for conferences or classes so that they could, for a brief span of time, withdraw from the action they encountered all day long. In close connection with this point, we held numerous talks with chief school officers concerning problems they faced, and how we at the University could bring our resources to bear to help resolve those problems. Their suggestions have unanimously and consistently been, "Help us learn better how to cope with the increasing stress that is attached to our job." The pressures from the community and teachers' unions are putting these people squarely in the middle of a no-win situation. They are damned if they do, and damned if they don't.

The phenomenon of emotional toxicity that accompanies the work of school people is not confined to isolated pockets around the country. That it is a widespread concern is evidenced in the announcement of the 1977 Suburban Superintendents Conference, organized by the American Association of School Administrators. A featured highlight in the conference was an all-day program entitled "Learning to Deal with Stress: How to Cope." The program was conducted by The Menninger Foundation, the same organization that sponsored Levinson's (1962) early research concerning problems surrounding individual-organizational relationships. The present study, of course, deals with school principals and not superintendents. The substance of the problem, however, remains the same.

The third source of our interest in getting our group of principals to talk about the emotional toxicity of their job stemmed from a seminar we conducted with several of our graduate students in the fall of 1976. The seminar focused on a phenomenon we called "administrative impairment," a term that was difficult to define precisely. Despite its imprecision, and thanks to some informal data that our students collected in the field, it appeared that things were indeed happening to school principals that were having deleterious effects on their morale, their energy, their motivation, and their perspectives on the future. What was occurring seemed to have little to do with the technical competence of the individual to do the job. Rather, and probably symptomatic of our society in the last quarter of this century, school administrators like other public officials seem to be becoming "emotionally battered" adults. Indeed, as the tremendous turnover of school superintendents shows, and as more and more school administrators apply for early retirement, there is a strong suggestion that they are "burning out," and that they want relief from a difficult situation. It appears for many that the only relief in sight is to get out of it as quickly as they can. "Getting out" is probably the extreme example of burning out, according to the findings of Maslach (1976). In her study of people involved in social services of a broad nature, Maslach reported that the primary symptom of being "burned out" was the tendency of people to distance themselves, psychologically, from those they were serving. For example, a nurse, instead of referring to "Mrs. Jones, in 419, the person with the heart condition" might say "the coronary in 419." By objectifying, by removing the humanity from the problem, the nurse is able to insulate herself from the human trauma that accompanies the job. Our concerns, of course, are not as dramatic, but when a school administrator is "burning out," that person is putting both physical and psychological distance between himself/herself and a situation that is at least emotionally, if not physically, debilitating.

The stories in this book indicate clearly that these eight principals are vital people and that they had or were in the process of making an impact on their schools. Nevertheless, it was important to learn—indeed, it was striking—that all but one of these principals had either left the school in which they were working at the time of our interview, or was thinking about leaving, despite what appeared to be the ever tightening job market in public education. Their reasons differed, of course, but behind most there was some factor which had, once more, to do with the frustration that accompanied the negative emotionality that is part of their everyday work life. Thus our interest in inquiring into these situations that drained them and caused them to distance themselves, at times, from people and situations that were ultimately important to them.

THREE MAJOR PROBLEMS

Three major problems seemed to emerge from the discussion our principals had that seemed to have a negative emotional impact on them relative to their jobs. They were:

1. The problem of the exceeding difficulty and accompanying frustration that is attached to the process of terminating a tenured teacher.
2. The problem of power and/or powerlessness that they felt relative to their prerogatives inside and outside the school.
3. The problem of the behavioral constraints that are put on the person of the principal by reason of the role expectations that are held for him/her by others.

The Problem of Tenure

While problems that school principals encounter with tenure ultimately involve issues of power, they seem to be in a class by themselves and so are here considered separately from a more generalized discussion of power, which will follow. Concern with the effects and complexities of school tenure laws in the various states is not a new phenomenon. In recent years, however, particularly in the light of the economic difficulties schools find themselves in, declining enrollments, and increasingly concerned and vocal parent groups, tenure as a global construct and as a specific fact of life in the schools has come under heightened criticism from a variety of sources. Parents ask, "How come, if a teacher is not doing a competent job, that teacher can't be released?" It is a good question. The answer is that a teacher can be released, but the problems associated with the legal procedures involved frequently become overwhelming for the school principal and the superintendent who, of necessity, become central figures. There must be an iron-clad, well-documented case that has been built over a period of time before school administrators will risk the trauma associated with bringing action to terminate a tenured teacher's contract. Evidence for this statement can be easily had by querying any school superintendent about the number of tenured teachers who have been released while he/she was in office. The chances are excellent that there will have been very few, and that the superintendent will be able to recall vividly the circumstances surrounding specific cases—inferential testimony that when these situations occur they are most unusual. Even so, superintendents and principals will talk freely of teachers they feel are less than adequate—but not so inadequate that a solid case could be built, one that would "stand up in court," figuratively, but sometimes literally.

On a level somewhat removed from the building principals who are the concern in this book, but important nevertheless in any discussion of tenure, is the problem faced by school boards as they try to balance budgets. Their question is, "How come, if we think a particular teaching job is unnecessary in order to accomplish our system's goals, we can't release a tenured person?" Again, this is a good question, and again the answer is that it can be done. The outcomes of the decision to take such action, however, may be even more in doubt than in the case of the incompetent teacher, because the school board must then deal with the power of the teachers' union and their concern with job security. Just such a set of circumstances developed in a nearby school district. The case involved a board decision to eliminate the position of nurse teachers in an effort to cut costs. The union reacted strongly, and the case ended up in binding arbitration where a decision was rendered in favor of the teachers. The board was not permitted to terminate them. The long-term result of this situation was that the board decided its management power had been eroded and, in its next bargaining round with the teachers, it endeavored to develop a major revision of the contract. What eventuated was a damaging teacher strike. The cycle seems to degenerate.

The message that comes from teachers, then, loud and clear, is "Don't tamper with tenure!" This view seems to be silently reinforced by school boards, under the notion that the cost of revising tenure regulations is too high compared to whatever benefits might be gained. The maintenance of the system is a clear priority for teachers, taking precedence, or so it seems, over the potential positive effects that such changes might make in the quality of teaching in the schools.

Our task here, though, is not to make a brief for the abolishment of tenure laws. Rather, we are concerned about what happens to these eight principals as they confront the constraints that these laws impose on them. Several comments that were made during the meeting illustrate the problem.

Ed, an elementary school principal, had an overriding concern for the emotional health of youngsters while they were in his school. Perhaps more than the others, because of his therapeutic training, he was more acutely aware of some of the behaviors of teachers that are punishing to children, and that these behaviors may cause children to see school as an environment not to be enjoyed, but to be psychologically, and perhaps physically, avoided. He said:

> I've had lots of confrontations with teachers when I saw children being harmed to a degree that is uncomfortable to me. I used to think that I could help any teacher but I've learned that I can't. I've learned that positive relationships don't necessarily develop no matter what. Teachers do not always change. And that's the frustration that I have to deal with.
>
> Legally, I really am not sure what recourse I have. We're talking about ten-

ured teachers, some of whom have been in the district for twenty-eight years. And I'm stuck.

It's not hard to imagine Ed's concern about the situation. Two factors seem to stand out that had emotionally debilitating effects on him. The first has to do with his frustration at not being able to apply his skills—and he was skillful. The school situation is clearly light years away from the therapeutic situation when it comes to intervening in teachers' lives. In the latter, a person recognizes a problem and seeks out help voluntarily. In the former, the need for help and change is seen by the intervener, the principal, while the teacher may, probably is, perfectly satisfied with his/her performance. Understanding this, of course, does not at all relieve the frustration. Indeed, it may not only increase it but also transfer it—the second factor—to the system. For what Ed is really saying in his comment about having little recourse, is that the system unintentionally supports mediocrity and practically gives an implicit license for school people to damage youngsters. For a person like Ed, whose aim is to combine authenticity in the classroom with effective subject matter, confronting this circumstance became, at times, extremely aggravating.

Ed went on to say that the problem doesn't rest at the point of his being nonconfrontive, for he saw himself being quite the opposite. Nor is the issue that of there being only one teacher in his school who creates a problem for him. Rather:

> I'm not just talking about one teacher. I'm talking about a staff of twenty of whom 25 percent I could easily be rid of tomorrow and be very comfortable with not having them there.

The fact, then, that there was a sizable percentage of his faculty who Ed judged were incompetent teachers—teachers who harm children—and about whom he could do nothing, created a situation that bordered on being hopeless as far as he was concerned. If it were only one teacher, Ed might have been able to collect the necessary data to institute termination proceedings, or simply to ignore that person as best as he could. But to collect data and institute dismissal proceedings against five teachers out of a staff of twenty would be too disruptive for the system and, in all likelihood, for the community to take. The political fall-out would be intolerable. And Ed was left essentially in a situation in which he was helpless to do what he saw to be necessary.

The result of feeling helpless in these situations had a powerful impact on Ed, more so perhaps than on others because of one part of his make-up that was not shared by the other principals. It is that he saw clearly that there was a part of him that could be described only as missionary:

> I'm trying to understand the missionary side of me. I'm beginning to see that my wanting to rescue teachers, ultimately rescue children, is coming from my own needs to rescue myself.

These are powerful words, and there are people who might take the position that this type of motivation is inappropriate for a school administrator. But a principal's reasons for wanting to develop a healthy learning climate in a school should be unimportant. What is important is that the effort be made. Where motivations and needs do become important is when consideration is given to the consequences of failure. In Ed's case, unless he was able to downplay, perhaps soften or put in perspective, the missionary self-rescue side of himself, his failures would probably tend to increase the toxicity of the school environment for him, to the extent that he might have been no longer able to function as he wished. If this happened, he would probably seek another position, quite possibly outside the field of education. In fact, when another principal asked him how long he'd been at the school, Ed said, "Four years, but this one could be my last."

As George joined in the discussion, he seemed concerned about the manner in which the tenure laws limited his prerogatives, but he was not emotionally tied up in the situation. This is understandable both from the point of view of personality differences and differences in school environments. Although there seemed to be a bit of the missionary in George, it was of a much lower key than in Ed. He appeared better able to say "the hell with it—I can't take care of everyone" and not let it eat at him, as it did with Ed. But perhaps the nature of their respective schools made a bigger difference, at least as far as the emotionality of the situation was concerned. Ed was principal of a relatively small elementary school. Everyone, teachers and principal, was visible most of the time, particularly for a person like Ed who spent a great deal of time outside his office. The problems were there for him to see daily. George, on the other hand, was principal of a high school which, while not huge, was spread out physically, and had a faculty of about fifty. It is somewhat easier to put things aside in this situation, or at least not have to confront them on a daily basis, thus lessening the tension the principal might feel. Nonetheless, George did have a concern, and a deep one. He first reacted to Ed's situation by agreeing that it was a difficult one, and then by talking about some things that had occurred in his school.

> When I first took over the school, we got rid of one teacher through a superintendent's hearing. And that was a bad scene. One left last year as a result of a job change. He was forty years old, had seniority and everything else, but he left. We put him in a different position and he left.
>
> I'm not really strong at the kind of conflict and confrontation that Ed faces, I was fortunate to hire an assistant principal who just loves that kind of eyeball-to-eyeball conflict. I hired him, not deliberately for that purpose, but to balance me. He is keeping tabs on one or two teachers that we think are at the point where they're harming kids. Either they're going to change or they're going to be out. It's a long process.

The terms "got rid of" or wishing to "get rid of" characterized much of the talk about problems associated with inadequate teachers who are tenured. It is strong wording connoting being relieved of something rather noxious, not merely a passing annoyance. And that may, indeed, characterize the tenure problem. It is noxious for school principals both to have to confront the problem and to have to go through the long and arduous task of preparing a case for termination. George recognized both of these issues. He referred to the "bad scene" that developed as they were finally able to terminate a teacher, and to the "long process" that would be involved in present and future cases, to say nothing of the interpersonal and organizational trauma that accompanies the process. No wonder principals will avoid, if they can, starting down the road to termination. It is wearying and painful for all parties concerned.

Yet George seemed rather confident of his ability to do what he thought might have to be done. He also seemed happy that he had an assistant principal who did not shy away from the kinds of interpersonal confrontations that inevitably take place if and when the prescribed procedures are started. As he said, "I'm not strong on that kind of conflict and confrontation."

Marie, another high school principal, agreed with George concerning the trauma that would accompany the whole process:

> We're coming up on a teacher now about whom we know something needs to happen. He's bad for kids. He only changes when we exert enormous pressure, which means we're constantly in his classroom, and constantly doing conferences with him. It takes a tremendous amount of time and energy. I don't mind confronting him and telling him, "I think you're a crappy teacher. What are you doing here?" But when you talk about firing him—Wow! I sat down with our lawyer the other day and talked about what I would have to deal with. The lawyer talked about the fall-out, the ramifications, the Board meetings—about keeping the thing under control so it doesn't disrupt the whole community. As you know, I like action in my school. I do stir it up, but it's controllable. This other thing is uncontrollable, and I don't know whether or not I want to go to bat on that issue. There's got to be another way. I don't want that kind of conflict. I'm getting tired, really tired. And I'm not sure that if that's part of being a principal I want it. I'm strong enough and I know my assistant is, too, to deal with it. But you almost have to destroy the community.

It's interesting that Ed, George, and Marie all echoed similar themes. They were not talking about teachers who were merely not the best of all possible teachers. They used the words "children being harmed," "harming kids," "bad for kids." Obviously, they were not dealing with situations that could be ameliorated by a good inservice program. To the contrary, they were involved with people who, according to their best judgment, ought not to be, perhaps never should have been, in the classroom in the first place. So the circumstances were serious, at least from their perspective. Further, each of them talked about the emotional trauma, for them and others, that would inevitably be a partner to any legal proceedings they might institute. This inevitability was seconded by other members of the group. Thus they saw themselves caught between "a rock and a hard place," feeling damned by others if they do, and damning themselves if they don't.

Recall that the aim of this discussion was not to debate the issue of tenure, but to inquire into some of the circumstances in the lives of school principals that had the effect of making their environment emotionally toxic for them. Having to confront the prospect of a tenured teacher who is damaging to youngsters, and who ought to be removed, is one of those circumstances. Conflicting values are involved. How does a principal balance the benefits that might accrue to a school by terminating a tenured teacher against the possibility of severe disruptions of the school community? What does he/she do with his/her feelings of guilt if he/she does nothing in the face of a situation that is obviously wrong, that should never have existed? How does a principal weigh the costs in time and energy that would be needed to institute termination proceedings, against the way that same time and energy might be spent in working with other teachers and other parts of the school program? Further, and more specific to Levinson's points about emotional toxicity, what does the principal do with his/her frustration and anger at not being able to remedy a bad situation quickly when the answer is obvious—get rid of the teacher?

Clearly, the circumstances described put an emotional burden on some school principals, but not necessarily on all of them. For those principals whose concept of running a school keeps them mostly in their office, and there are many of them, probably the burden is light. For those like the people who were part of this study, who are activists, who are of the school as well as in it, the burden was probably much heavier.

Conditions of Powerlessness

The concerns and frustrations that these principals felt, their relative helplessness to deal quickly and effectively with tenured teachers whom they judged to be incompetent, can be subsumed under a more general heading of feelings of growing powerlessness, an increasing loss of potency. However, in addition to the problems associated with tenure, they spoke most directly of their concerns about loss of power in general, and their frustrations at not having as much as they wished in a variety of situations. They were concerned with both personal and group power.

Fred, who was an elementary school principal when we first interviewed him but was since promoted to the Central Office, started the discussion:

> As you know, I had a strong feeling that there was very little power in the elementary principals' group, and there was very little of a support system other than with isolated individuals. But with these individuals, it was a random kind of thing, not a planned support system in any kind of way. We've just come through a period when the superintendent has talked about decentralization and giving more power to the principal. I got into a confrontation with him about the role of

the principal as an instructional leader. I said, "We've got to talk about what it means to be an instructional leader." He said, "Okay." I said, "If you're telling me that in buildings where we've got more than 500 kids, we've got breakfast programs, we've got kids with a lot of problems, with learning disabilities, and we're also giving all sorts of messages out to principals that they're not king of the castle but we're not giving them more resources, then why bother? We're cutting supervision back to nothing."

I got to the point where I called some principals and said, "I think you've got to get a proposal together and make some demands. You need additional building personnel if they're cutting back on supervisors." I got some receptivity and the superintendent was at least willing to listen. But nothing happened and I still feel that elementary principals are powerless. And I don't know how to help them be more powerful.

It is an interesting and conflicting scene. Not only are double messages being sent—"Be more powerful, but we are not giving you any help"—but they are being sent during a time of financial crunch, when administrative positions and salaries are facing closer scrutiny than ever before. Principals seem to be increasingly insecure about their jobs. It is not surprising, though still aggravating for some, that as a group they wish to maintain a low profile. Paul, an elementary principal in the same district as Fred, provided a specific case in point:

I think Fred is right about principals being powerless in the sense that they see themselves as being powerless. I know that, in reaction to the superintendent's reorganization plan, about four or five of us tried to get together. We picked a few key people and said, "We're going to come together and we're going to make some demands. We're going to tell them they're not going to reorganize the district without involving the people who are supposed to pull it off." I spent two days going around to half the principals—about fifteen buildings. At least seven of those fifteen principals were actually afraid for us to come together and demand of the superintendent that we be listened to, even though we were going to have to carry it out. And of these seven a couple of them are definitely going to be cut. They have no idea what their job is going to be next year.

Another illustration of the same phenomenon—school principals being a frightened group, leery of asserting themselves—was provided by George. When the right to bargain collectively was granted to school personnel in New York in 1966, he took the lead in organizing the thirteen administrators in his district. But George realized that, though they negotiated a strong contract, the group itself was not strong. As he said, "I got tired of holding the ball. A lot of administrators would just sit there and then I'd have to do it myself." The problem was compounded when a new superintendent arrived on the scene, took a dim view of the administrators' bargaining unit, and wished to dissolve it. The principals were upset and there was talk about going to court. George responded with:

And who's going to take him to court? Me? For you? Not on your life! The problem is that principals are scared. I just sit there now and when an issue comes up I'll tell them I have my own problems in my building.

If these anecdotes are at all representative of the wider picture in education today, and our casual observations and discussions indicate that they are, an interesting and vexing development seems to be in process. First, individual principals are becoming frustrated as they see themselves unable to revitalize the power of their peers who are frightened. Their energy becomes sapped and they start to withdraw to the confines of their school, where they are relatively insulated. In the process, of course, their morale becomes lower as they survey the futility of their situation. But the problem, ultimately, will not be confined to them and their feeling of discontent at having no basis of power. Eventually, it would seem, the system will become infected with its own virus. That is, as school principals fail to mobilize and assert themselves, the implicit message they will communicate is that they will remain compliant and open to coercion by higher authority. Perhaps the message even includes their willingness to be coerced, as long as their job security in some form is maintained. The most vital principals, those who provide a spark for the system, will find it difficult to work productively under these conditions and, as was indicated earlier, this was occurring to some extent with several of the people in our group. They were discontent and wanted to get out. If they did indeed leave, the system succeeded in depriving itself of the very people who can supply the negative entropy on which it depends for its vitality.

There is no inference in all this, of course, that this potential cycle of events is part of some master strategy to get people to resign. But then, there doesn't have to be. In an unplanned-for way, and in the name of economy and "tightening things up," the situation will simply become too emotionally toxic for many people.

When the scene shifts to the individual school buildings where our principals held sway, their reactions were different with two exceptions. The majority sensed that their position was a powerful one and that they enjoyed feeling that they had strong influence over their day-to-day work lives. A fascinating insight, about the impact that achieving a sense of power in a school has, was provided by John as he contrasted his position in an inner-city high school with the change that occurred when he accepted his current position in a suburban school. Reacting to Paul's frustration over his loss of power, John said:

I felt very much like you do when I was principal at Southern. I felt I didn't have any power. I had no viable parent group that would go down and pound the door down for things we needed at school. I had no board members' children in my school. I really became discouraged. Anything I wanted was always put off with, "Well, we're only going to keep that building open for another year or two." In the meantime, things were dying. They told me what teachers I had to take. I had very little say in hiring and firing or transfers. Supervisors would come in and say that this was the way it has to be. I could rant and rave but I never seemed to be successful at that.

In my new school I sense a lot of power. In fact, I don't know how to use it.

That's one of the things I'm going to have to learn. I've got a large parent group and they're extremely vocal and concerned about educational issues. This concept of power—I'm just beginning to appreciate it. I enjoy, now, the feeling of running my school much more than I did at Southern because I feel I'm more in command. I'm really the guy that makes the decisions. At Southern, I never had it, I just never had it!

It's almost as though moving from a situation where he felt like a functionary to one over which he had mastery had given John a new lease on his professional life. It's also interesting to note his insight as he talked about needing to learn how to use power now that he had it. There is a certain humility to that point that is attractive, because it suggests clearly that the issue is not power for the sake of power. Rather, it's a sense of having control and influence over one's life—or an essential part of it. And perhaps this is the central issue. Levinson (1968) calls it the need for mastery, the need to feel that one has control over one's environment, and that it's not the other way around. When this need is not fulfilled, particularly for the kind of principals studied here, the effects are debilitating, draining and lead to discontent. For example, listen to Ed as he reacted to John's story of having been powerless at Southern:

> That's amazing to me because I live in autonomy. I feel what happens in my building is my responsibility—instructional programs, staff, budget, transportation—you name it. I function autonomously and I have a great deal of power. I can't envision a situation without it. I don't think I could stand it.

And Marie chimed in:

> Yeah, I could envision myself that way but I couldn't handle it.

And then George, who saw himself having more and more of his power taken away by his new superintendent:

> If I could retire tomorrow, I would.

And then Paul who, though he didn't want to retire, was seriously considering another career for himself because he saw his prerogatives so reduced that the excitement of the job had diminished greatly:

> I think a good deal of my discontent is over loss of power. I mean a loss of power in the sense that I don't have anywhere to fight. The population's changing, the neighborhood's changing, and the school system's changing and I have no control over any of it. What I have to do now is try to eke out enough supplies for the kids. That's not very exciting.
> A few years ago everything was creative. Everybody was trying to do something and there was power in the sense that you had to deal with conflicting groups to see if you could bring something off. That's gone now and it seems like we're just trying to exist.

The concern that these principals had about power and the lack of it, then, is very clear. It is not as if they were "jungle fighters," a type of organizational manager whose goal is power for the sake of power (Maccoby, 1976). They do not experience ". . . life and work as a jungle . . . where it is eat or be eaten, and the winners destroy the losers" (p. 47). To the contrary, none of them seemed concerned at all with self-aggrandizement, or that their organizational life was one big win-lose game, although they certainly won and lost their share of battles. What really was at the heart of things seemed to be two factors. First, they had a notion of the kind of school they wanted to develop and, second, they needed to have the power to do it, relatively unfettered by external constraints. They are activists and as such, quite simply, had to have the freedom to act. Without that kind of freedom it seemed as though they would wilt. Power was, indeed, an energizer for them, and if they didn't have as much of it as they needed, they lost part of their sense of being.

Constraints on Emotionality

In one sense, people who are school principals operate under constraints on their behavior that are similar to those that the executive of any enterprise must confront. That is, the managerial role carries with it a mythology that suggests that managers are supposed to be rational at all times, be able to separate their feelings from their thoughts, and to keep themselves under control at all times.

The same set of constraints does not hold, in the case of industry, for production workers or their immediate supervisors. It is not forbidden for them to show their anger, for example. They can swear at each other and it is permissible. The phrase "got chewed out" by the boss is a common one, illustrating as it does the freedom that people who "work" have to deal with their emotionality, particularly when it is negative. Similar circumstances hold in schools. Though it certainly isn't encouraged, it is not considered a major role aberration for a teacher, on becoming angry with a class or a student, to release his/her anger by yelling from time to time. It is only when the frequency or intensity of such behavior exceeds whatever informal norms have been established that other teachers or the principal might become upset.

The same freedom, however, does not hold for principals. If anything, they operate under more constraints than do managers in the private sector. For one thing, public officials, which principals are, are expected to behave with more decorum than their private sector counterparts. This is, perhaps, an unreasonable expectation, but it is the case. Second, they are "professionals" and so must behave in a "professional" manner. It's not clear, of course, what that means precisely but, for sure, it excludes the free expression of emotions, whatever they happen to be. Third, although schools are complex organizations, they are not highly compartmentalized.

Thus, if a principal explodes at a teacher in his/her office, that principal can be assured that the incident will not remain in the office. It will be all over the school shortly, and the chances are good that at least some of the students will also have learned of its occurrence. The principal's seeming indiscretion will soon, then, become public property as the youngsters tell the tale at home.

When we introduced this general condition of work to our group of principals, it seemed to strike a resonant chord. They talked first about their anger, then their needs for warmth, and concluded with their feelings of not being able to display their own humanity, in general terms, while they were at school. The following is some of the discussion as it occurred:

Marie:

Every now and then my hostility seeps out because it's not appropriate for me to have a temper tantrum, much as I would like to have one at times.

Ed:

Bullshit!

Marie:

(*laughing*) You know, it's loss of control.

Paul:

I respond to that. It's frustrating just not being yourself. And Ed, I hear you saying, "Well, why not be yourself?" For me the answer is that, as an administrator, you take on a certain responsibility. What you do affects a wider variety of people than yourself. There's many a day that I envy a teacher, who has run into a frustrating situation, who can come into my office and throw a temper tantrum. And I know full well that when I have thrown temper tantrums the clean-up afterwards is not worth the release at the time. So I begin to restrict myself. I think, What would be an appropriate way of responding to the anger I feel for the situation? What would be appropriate in terms of the flak I would have to take from someone coming in who needs to express it?" I guess I find that as an administrator I don't get my needs satisfied on the job in terms of releasing myself. So I find other answers.

Ed:

I guess I'm not saying that you always have to communicate the feelings you have on the job. But it's important to be aware of them. I agree with your appropriateness comment. There are times when it's very appropriate for me to be angry and to show my anger and, damn, I better be or I'll be hanging on to that anger when I leave the building. And that's no good. Other times it's inappropriate and I have to deal with that in a different way.

What I'm saying is that it's okay to have feelings. A lot of people say, in the role of the principal, "I have responsibility for this building. I should not have feelings. I should not be angry."

It's really an issue of one's basic humanity. Teachers say to me, for example, that they can't be friends with kids. They have to be "teacher." It's an either/or situation with them, either being a teacher or being human or either I'm an administrator or a human being. It really isn't so. Appropriateness is a good word.

Paul:

> I know that when I stub my toe it's appropriate for me to say "Damn!" I think if I stub my toe *on the job* I would think about whether I say "damn" or not. That's a restriction that frustrates me.

Our question of how they dealt with their needs for warmth gave rise to the following discussion:

Paul:

> It's with the kids. I've consistently found that the most expressive area for me is with kids. If I want to hug somebody I really get off on that—the interaction with the children—which is why I thought I was in education.
>
> That's not to say you can't be warm with the staff. Today we played volleyball. I thought that was important because when we do that we're all in another role, and it helps build morale, particularly in a year like this when everybody's down and we don't know whether the school is going to last. You make avenues for doing that. But there are problems with warmth. I have problems having friends on the staff.

Marie:

> Yeah, me too.

Paul:

> I tend to shy away from that. I think friends find it harder for you to change roles. If you take a job as an administrator, you have to accept the fact that a time will come when you have to call the shots, when you'll have to say you're not satisfied with what's going on. I know I try not to come on too strong in those situations. And if it's someone you have a personal relationship with, it becomes even more touchy. If I come down hard on a friend, I have a tendency to want to make it up. If it's a staff member who's not a personal friend, I leave it and simply expect that fair is fair.

George:

> I had an interesting insight about this. We've had teaching interns for a number of years. I found that my relationship with the interns was always a lot different than it was with any other new teacher. There was one particular intern. We had a particularly high regard for each other and we talked about it. What it came down to, was that I knew I'd never have to hurt that person. I'd never have to evaluate them or get rid of them.

And quite naturally, it seems, the discussion drifted to one that dealt with the problems that principals have simply in being themselves as they preside over a school:

John:

> Don't you get the feeling sometimes, I know I do, that you're not allowed the luxury of your feelings? I think it's really the way I was trained into the position. You don't have the luxury of being rattled; you're supposed to be decisive; you're supposed to be under control. I guess sometimes it's acting; because you

don't always have the answer and you're not really running under control. Sometimes you're running out of fear. But yet the image of control has to be consistent. At times I walk out of that building at night and it's very frustrating.

Marie:

Drained.

John:

Yeah, sometimes you're just not allowed the privilege of behaving like you really want to.

Marie:

Like walk across the desk and get flippy. That's what I'd like to do someday.

George:

Sometimes my flippiness will just come out. Like at times I'll go over to the air raid cord in our office and just yank it. I guess I do it about once a year after the kids have left. Everyone shrieks. It's stupid but it makes me feel good.

If I get mad I try to tell the person I'm mad. I don't seem to feel as bound by the role as you do. If something scares me I'll say, "Hey, that idea scares me and this is why."

Marie:

The first year I was on the job I felt I had to be under very tight control and that I was being watched so carefully. Every weekend I would get on a plane and just go somewhere. It wasn't that I went and did flippy things or anything like that. It was just that I could sit with a group of people who didn't know who I was and wouldn't care anyhow. It was down time. I could just be me. I was tired, wiped out.

George:

I see myself pretty much in a box, pretty much self-contained. It's the small town stuff. Wherever I go I'm known for what I am and I can't get that need for friendliness satisfied. But somehow things work out. I haven't gone crazy yet.

Marie:

It's the same with me. I don't make friends in that town. And there are some days when I'm so sick and tired of that goddamn school and everybody in it that I won't even go to the local grocery store. It's mostly emotional drain. It's dealing with kids who are upset and parents who are in tears. You have to have tight control. I can handle the situations effectively but it takes a lot out of me. Also, I guess it's that I'm highly visible in the town. I'm very aware of it and I'm not comfortable with it. And I'm a single female and that makes me much more visible. I'm aware that people know me, whom I don't know, and that people watch me that I don't know are watching me. You know, I get the stories back. And they are so way out, so ridiculous. And I know I'm susceptible to it all, but it's the one thing that will get me out of it all. I want my own world and I want to be able to share it with a few people whom I choose. Being public property is uncomfortable.

Ed:

I'm a bit different in the role. What you see and hear right now is basically what I am at school. School is my livelihood, not my life. In school I tend to be as warm, human, and genuine as I can be in that role.

The question I ask my teachers quite frequently is, "How do you allow the children in your classroom to nourish you?" Because I've seen them drained at the end of the day, and yet they have to replenish themselves and come back the next day. I ask myself the same question, "How do I allow the teachers in my building to nourish me?" Dammit, if I can't get hold of that and find some way of allowing them to do that then I, too, am going to feel drained. And like Paul, I get a lot from the kids, but I also have three or four teachers in the building that I really feel close to. I can sit down with them, reverse roles and say, "Look, this is the way I feel—listen." The big question is, who helps the helper? The helper, in many ways, has no one to turn to.

This dialogue speaks rather eloquently to the human concerns that these school principals had about themselves in their jobs. It also speaks, for the most part, to the loneliness of the position and points out a serious lack in the thinking and planning of school districts relative to providing support systems for school principals. How curious it is that schools—organizations whose *raison d'être* is the development of people—seem to ignore the problems and needs of those people whose responsibility it is to see that the job gets done. Double messages get sent. One is usually articulated clearly, "Pay attention to, try to understand, and deal with the learning and emotional needs of children." One that is unarticulated but clear nonetheless is, "Make it on your own. You can expect little or no help from the system relative to your own needs as a human being." It is not, of course, that there are no school districts that provide this help. There may, indeed, be some. It is abundantly clear, however, that if such arrangements do exist in some districts, they are aberrations from the norm.

People could take a hard-nosed position about the emotional problems that these principals faced as they tried to deal with themselves and the demands of the job. "Tough," the response might be. "That's part of the job. If they didn't know it when they became principals, they should have." But that view misses the point. That is, the test of a good principal is not the extent to which he/she can endure emotional stress. If that was all there was to it, we could simply select people who were terribly thick-skinned and had little or no insight into or caring about their own needs, precisely the kind of person who should not be a principal. Further, our group of principals could not, by any stretch of the imagination, be considered weak or complaining. To the contrary, they exhibited a tremendous amount of personal strength among them, and they talked about the concerns they had for themselves as people and the people with whom they work.

The job of a school principal is emotionally taxing. It wears people down. The wonder of it, from our position as professors, is that they continue to do what they do with enthusiasm—and that they seem to have fun doing it.

12

Toward a Theory of Leading a School: Action in Context

INTRODUCTION

The title of this chapter conveys our two concerns regarding the principal-ship: leading, rather than administering, and activity. We use the verb form "leading," not the noun "leadership," which suggests a thing or a position.

The focus on leading rather than administering reflects Katz and Kahn's (1966) three types of organizational leadership behaviors: ". . . (1) the intro-duction of structural change, or policy formulation, (2) the interpolation of structure, i.e., piecing out the incompleteness of existing formal structure, or improvisation, and (3) the use of structure formally provided to keep the organization in motion and in effective operation, or administration" (p. 308). Administering, then, means maintaining things as they are, on the assumption perhaps that the system will produce what it is intended to produce if things simply run smoothly. This means that the schools are structured in a functional manner, the teachers are all competent, and the curriculum and teaching methodologies are functional and relevant to the learning needs of the students. What remains for the principal to do is to administrate, to keep things running.

The principals we describe in this book obviously did not see themselves as organizational maintainers whose job was merely to see to the "structure formally provided to keep the organization in motion and in effective opera-tion." They had to perform certain routine administrative functions; but, according to the way they described themselves, their interests, joy, and frustrations, they focused their energy and time on other things. They were proactive. They all tried to make their school a different place from the one they found. To use Katz and Kahn's formulation, it seems that for the most part they engaged in "the interpolation of structure." They frequently tested the boundaries of their authority and influence to make the structure work for them and their needs. The issue, for most of them, most of the time, was not "We don't do that because things aren't done that way." Rather, the issue appeared to be simply "How should we go about doing it?"

We depart, then, from the notion of equating administration with organizational "leadership." Although it is critically important for schools to be kept in motion, merely to do so is not to lead. The process of leading involves influencing others to do things differently. The process of administering also involves influencing others, that is, organizational members—in this case, teachers and students—to not deviate from established norms in any significant way so that structured operating procedures and interpersonal relationships are not upset.

Choosing the verb "leading" rather than the noun "leadership" may seem like semantic nitpicking. There is a tendency in education, the social sciences, and government to *reify*—to take ideas, processes, and abstractions and give them names as if they were things. For example, we have things called progressive education, basic education, individually guided education, accountability, clinical supervision, and so forth. Once a thing is made out of an idea, people must follow certain procedures before they can say they are doing that "thing." Our concern in this chapter is not with a thing called leadership, but with trying to explain the dynamics of the process of leading—the principal exerting influence in a school setting. The title of this chapter begins with "Toward a Theory . . ." Our meaning of the word "theory" is similar to Cremin's (1976): a "common sense meaning as a systematic description or general state of a field" (p. x). Thus in the rest of this chapter we propose some notions that seem to us to make common sense, rather than to state facts or a set of rules.

To explain and analyze the behavior of an individual, one must conceive of that behavior as a function of the person's perceiving of and interacting with a particular situation. This statement of the classical Lewinian (1951) concept provides the backdrop for our discussion. It makes the point that, in a school, attention must be given not only to the principal as a person but also to the structure and dynamics of the school as an organization and to the larger social system (the school district) of which the particular school is a part.[1] Our discussion is not a full-blown analysis of schools as organizations. (For such an analysis, see Bidwell, 1965.) Instead, we focus on those facets of school organizational life that seem to have a direct impact on the school building principal—his or her emotionality and ability to exert influence or lead.

The chapter is divided into three sections. The first, "School Systems— The Larger Setting," describes some of the features of the larger system within which the school functions. This initial discussion of the broader aspects of the school situation concludes with a comment on the school's

---

1. The broader community is omitted from this discussion, although we acknowledge its impact on the schools and ultimately on the behavior of principals. Our data do not permit discussion of the diffuse linkages involved between the community and the school.

sense of its institutional being: that is, the school's sense of threat or security in relation to its mission, activities, and external environment. It is not intended as an all-encompassing description of the social structure or culture of the schools, but rather as an indication of the socio-cultural terrain we believe a principal must negotiate in order to lead successfully.

The second section, entitled "Elements of Principal Effectiveness," briefly describes three broad elements which we feel capture the common threads of adjustment to the school situation, as reported by the eight principals we interviewed. While each had its distinctive orientation, these three elements reflect the essence of their responses to their respective school situations, and hint at the personal qualities and character of these men and women.

The third section, "Principals Who Would Lead—Some Speculations," proposes some specific qualities and personal orientations of the people we studied which we believe help explain why they were noted as "principals who make a difference." Our comments are intended to focus attention on what might be termed the "character" of the principal and its importance, given the initial description of the school setting within which the principal must work.

Finally, a word of caution. In this chapter we intend to describe, not prescribe. That is, we do not intend to tell our readers how things "should" be, in some ideal sense, but how we think things "are," in a real sense. To the extent that our observations are valid and we believe they are, they constitute a basis for further study and action.

SCHOOL SYSTEMS—THE LARGER SETTING

In a somewhat tongue-in-cheek metaphor (Blumberg, 1974), the structure of school system organization is seen as feudalistic. There is a castle and a king or queen. Spread throughout the royal holdings are numerous estates, each of which is presided over by lesser royalty. The function of the king or queen is to provide overall direction, to see that peace is kept within each of the surrounding estates, and to help resolve problems and conflicts that may arise between their rulers who, at regularly scheduled intervals, pay fealty to their superiors. On occasion, if there is trouble in a particular estate—with the people who work in it or the populace in general—these lesser rulers will be called to account for an explanation. The king or queen may offer some hard-to-get resources to help resolve the problem. Or it may be decided that the person involved is unfit to rule, despite his or her title, and that person is removed for incompetency.

The ruler of each estate, besides keeping the peace and paying fealty, also must organize the estate, for both work and protection, within the general guidelines that emanate from the castle. The specifics, however, are left up to each individual ruler; and as long as the peace is kept and due obeisance given, there is rarely any trouble.

The amusing feudalistic metaphor is a useful tool for communication: people do seem to find it easy to understand it and to relate to it. However, it hardly rates as a highly sophisticated concept when it comes to describing the complexities of organizational life in school. One such concept has been discussed by Weick (1976). It proposes that organizations may not be composed of tightly woven networks of relationships and that it may be more productive to think of them as loosely coupled systems. By "loose coupling," it is Weick's intention

> . . . to convey the image that coupled events are responsive, but that each event also preserved its own identity and some evidence of its physical or logical separateness. Thus, in the case of an educational organization, it may be the case that the counselor's office [Central Office][2] is loosely coupled to that principal's office. The image is that the counselor [superintendent and other Central Office personnel] and the principal are somehow attached, but that each retains some identity and separateness and that their attachment may be circumscribed, infrequent, weak in its mutual effects, unimportant and/or slow to respond . . . loose coupling also carries connotations of impermanence, dissolvability, and tacitness all of which are potentially crucial properties of the "glue" that holds organizations together. (p. 3)

The notion of loosely coupled relationships between and among positions in school organizations can be expanded to suggest that the relationships between subsystems within the organization are likewise loosely coupled. The relationship between policies initiated at the Central Office and the activities in a school that result from that policy tends to be vague. In large districts the Central Office is frequently referred to by the amorphous title, "downtown." "The decision was made downtown" or "Someone downtown spread the word" communicates the loosely connected and tentative nature of the relationship. Even more pronounced is the looseness of the couplings among individual schools in a system. The feudal metaphor clearly illustrates this. Each school is a more-or-less self-contained fief. Its concerns are its own constituents and its own territory. The relationships among principals are transitory, based mostly on interpersonal liking. When they are in contact with each other, issues generally concern interpretation of Central Office policy. There is rarely a voluntary joining together on problems of mutual program development.

Crucial to understanding this acollaborative situation is to recognize that the issue is not the personality of principals. No data suggest that they are predisposed to be loners. On the contrary, even casual observation reveals that they are fairly gregarious individuals. Rather, the issue is that the behavioral conditions described are largely a function of the goals, values, and structure of the system. For instance, there is no eleventh commandment that says to school principals, "thou shalt not consult, collaborate, or join

---

2. Words in brackets are the authors'.

forces with other principals in your system." Such behavior simply reflects the prevailing role expectations (ambiguous to start with) for principals. Further, since this behavior is not explicit in the role, the rewards a principal may expect for engaging in it are likely to be small, if present at all. The system, then, which is loosely coupled to start with, reinforces itself by its priorities, although this reinforcement is not by design. Rather, no one ever gives much thought to it.

From our interview data and observations of principals at work, three primary characteristics of the principal's role seem to emerge from the nature of the system: (1) Principals operate under conditions of ambiguity relative to their relationships with other administrators outside of their school, whether in Central Office or in other school buildings. (2) Their position is one of relative isolation, particularly in regard to work relationships with other principals. (3) They experience a sense of powerlessness, deriving from and relative to their ability to exert influence on the larger system. Further, the work life of a school principal, particularly with respect to others in the larger system, seems to be congruent with Weick's observation that a characteristic of loosely coupled relationships is that they ". . . are somehow attached, but that each retains some identity and separateness and that their attachment may be circumscribed, infrequent, weak in its mutual effects, unimportant and/or slow to respond. . ." (1976, p. 3).

The upshot of it all is that the principal's energies get turned inward on his/her school, which is perhaps the way it should be. That is, although the feudal loosely coupled structure could never have been deliberately created, it does seem to have the effect of pushing people away from involvement in the larger system and toward almost exclusive focus on the individual school.

The piper, of course, must be paid. Although the nature of the system does seem to narrow down the focus of energy and control to the principal's own school, it also results in some costs, both to the system and to the individuals involved. The costs for the individuals are their isolation and inability to influence the system. The system, too, incurs costs from the isolation and powerlessness that it has induced in the principals. That is, the system tends to cut itself off from the collective wisdom and deliberate capacity of its principals. It is important to emphasize the word "collective." Individual principals are involved in matters pertaining to their own schools, but they tend *not* to be involved in broad educational policy and program matters that affect the total system. The problem is not the authoritarianism of the Central Office, although this may be the case in some circumstances, but rather the behavioral and attitudinal norms that develop as a function of organizational structure.

We have described some central features of school system structure that rarely receive the attention they deserve. In addition, we have highlighted some of their consequences for the everyday work life of the school principal. Our purpose is not to criticize school systems or to suggest ways they could change but rather to pose a question. If what we say here accurately, if briefly, describes the reality of school system structure, what are the implications for the work life of the principal?

Organizational Value System

Schools, like other organizations, are permeated by a value structure. Some of the values are public and committed to writing; for example, valuing each child's individuality. We tend to think that these publicly stated values are mostly intended for community consumption. Those that impact most strongly on a system and its participants, however, are the values observed in the day-to-day behavior of organizational members, often reflected in teachers' conversations about the uppermost concerns of administrators and supervisors. Over and over again the theme is repeated: "Are things going smoothly?" An implicit and pervading value in schools, then, is "keeping the peace." Concurrent with the value of peace-keeping is that of loyalty. It is very important for school principals to be loyal to their Central Office administrators and for teachers to be loyal to their principals—at least publicly.

The problems for leaders in school systems that place a high priority on peacefulness and loyalty are great. The process of creative leadership, of change that makes a difference, is not necessarily a peaceful business and may involve some disloyalty in creating a facade of maintaining things as they are. Leaders must communicate loyalty (and hopefully a peaceful scene) and simultaneously attempt to restructure ways of thinking and acting, perhaps creating, in the process, a not-so-peaceful scene.

Pressures to maintain peace and display loyalty in the schools are reinforced by another system value, maintaining the status quo. This value is reflected in the types of changes that are supported and encouraged. Those supported changes, which tend to be additive, and which usually take the form of a newly developed technique or shift in methodology, are ones that do not disturb some basic element of the system. Changes that reconceptualize and/or restructure some basic element of the system—the curriculum or the manner in which the school is organized, for example—receive little support.

There are many cases that illustrate this point. They may be found in individual classrooms or in school buildings. For example, an elementary school teacher had decided to restructure her classroom, to change it from a teacher-centered interaction plan to one that focused on interaction among students. The result was highly satisfactory to the teacher. The students seemed highly involved. There was much discussion among them and a lot of "doing." But there was also more noise in the classroom than there had been before. The principal of the school took a dim view of this. He saw it as disruptive to the peacefulness for which the school had been noted, and he made his views known to the teacher. The classroom was restructured to its original (more peaceful) form.

A high school principal wanted to restructure the decision-making process in the school from what had been a unilateral mode to one that heavily involved the faculty. The plan was put into effect, but it failed. The explicit message from the teachers was "you get paid to administer, we get paid to teach." The change involved learning new skills, a heavy commitment of time, and thoroughly rethinking the meaning of collegial governance of the school. The costs appeared too great for the perceived benefits.

These examples are not meant to criticize but to illustrate, to help explain, the manner in which system values foster the stability (some would call it inertia) of schools as organizations. Part of this resistance to restructuring, or second order change (Watzlawick, Weakland, and Fisch, 1974), can probably be attributed to the public character of the schools. Schools are quickly susceptible to parental and community pressure. After all, everybody has been to school. Thus everybody "knows" how they should be run. When a youngster goes home after school and tells his/her parents about something new that is happening, and possibly of his/her discomfort or bewilderment, the principal is apt to have a questioning or complaining parent at the doorstep in short order. Caution, indeed, becomes the better part of valor. Life for all is simply easier if efforts to change do not disturb the regularities of the system, do not interfere with a smooth operation.

To some extent, of course, these points are true of any social system. Reconceptualization of problems and restructuring of settings are not easy processes, and they do disrupt things. The issue, though, is more complicated and involves the central, powerful, normative value-thrust of the school—to maintain what presently exists in smooth running order.

THE SCHOOL BUILDING SYSTEM—A SETTING OF IMMEDIACY

We have implied throughout that the effect of the larger system on the principal's behavior is relatively diffuse and not immediate. The norms of the system do indeed put pressure on the principal, but the pressure is felt in subtle ways. Further, the demands that the larger system put on the role of principal are of a global, long-term variety, not for day-by-day or hour-by-hour interaction. Certainly there are times when Central Office calls for an immediate response by a principal, but such demands are infrequent and tend not to be an everyday or every week occurrence, particularly in larger systems.

The principal's relationships and interaction with the human system of his/her school building are quite different. The school building is a setting of immediacy; that is, demands placed on the principal by members of the school building system—teachers, students, custodians, parents—are frequent and varied during the course of a day and call for quick response. Principals rarely have the luxury to contemplate their actions during the school day. Irate parents cannot be told to come back in a day or two because the principal has other things to do. Nor can a teacher, upset because his/her classroom is out of control, be put off with "go get a good night's sleep and it will be better tomorrow." On the contrary, the principal is pressured or expected to act immediately, even if the action involves something as simple as listening.

The notion of "a setting of immediacy" connotes a reactive stance on the part of the principal, and indeed this is so in most cases. Most of a principal's day is spent reacting to situations that arise, in most cases unpredictably. Principals never know, for instance, when the telephone will ring, when a parent will enter the office, when a teacher will become disturbed, or when a fight will start in the hall. Some principals are completely exhausted at the end of a day, having dealt with one problem after another from the moment they arrive until the moment they leave. Then there are some principals who, perhaps to protect themselves from the emotionally draining experience of having to continually react to human problems, spend much of their time in their office dealing with routine paper-and-pencil mattters. What seemed to separate the principals we interviewed from most of their colleagues, however, was their proactive stance. Although they dealt with immediate demands on their time and took care of administrative details, the essence of their own role definition was that it was proactive. Their position seemed to be that they were educational leaders; that it was their job to make an impact on the school; and that they had a personal stake in making a place conducive to better teaching and learning.[3]

To help understand proactivity in a setting that puts a high priority on reactivity—immediacy of response—we turn next to a discussion of some systematic organizational characteristics of schools that are related to the ability of a principal to adopt and maintain a proactive position regarding the faculty and the educational program. The point of this discussion is similar to the one made earlier concerning the larger system of which the individual school is a part. It is not possible to understand the behavior of a person in a particular role unless attention is also paid to the social (and sometimes physical) environment in which that behavior occurs.

Individuated Nature of Teachers' Roles

The structure of the larger school system has been characterized here (following Weick, 1976) as much more loosely coupled than tightly woven. This pattern appears to hold for relationships within the individual school organization as well, at least in most of the cases we've observed. What occurs between a teacher and a principal relative to the teachers' work, for example, or what occurs between a teacher and his/her students, is not

---

3. We suspect most principals would choose to look at themselves in this light. But our experience suggests that this proactive stance is not a common one. In fact, in discussing this book with colleagues and friends, and indicating the kind of principal we were studying, the most common reaction was "where did you find them?"

necessarily relevant to events that develop elsewhere in the school. Further, the relationship between the principal and the teacher is loosely coupled, and the common ground that might relate them in a combined effort is hard to discern. Weick approaches this circumstance in his discussion of the relationship between intentions and action, perhaps another way of saying that "the road to hell is paved with good intentions."

> There is a developing position in psychology which argues that intentions are a poor guide for action, intentions often follow rather than precede action, and that intentions and action are loosely coupled. Unfortunately, they spend much time on planning, and actions are assessed in terms of their fit with plans. Given a potential loose coupling between the intentions and actions of organization members, it should come as no surprise that administrators are baffled and angered when things never happen the way they're supposed to. (1976, p. 4)

Weick strongly suggests that the very nature of schools as organizations places major constraints on the ability of a principal to influence the school as an organization or the individual members of the faculty in a way that administrators (and others, too) find baffling.

In a paper written prior to Weick's, Blumberg and Schmuck (1972) spoke more specifically to some school structural patterns that systematically create barriers to efforts to induce change in the school as an organization. Their analysis nicely parallels Weick's notion of schools as loosely coupled systems. It includes a concern with the individuated nature of the teacher's role and the dyadic nature of the principal's role.

In Woodward's (1958) terms, teaching is a single unit, or small batch, type of technology. Teachers are responsibile for total production within the classroom, including planning, operating, and evaluating. Even though specialized roles develop around areas of psychological and subject matter competence, for most purposes how well one teacher does his/her job is not related directly to how well another teacher does his/her job, even when they are working with the same students. At least the effect of one teacher's work on another's work is not easily perceived. Indeed, the teacher's role in the classroom tends to be organizationally nonintegrative. Teachers can do what is expected of them, for the most part, without ever communicating with one another. It seems reasonable to think that this lack of integration in teachers' roles influenced the development of the norm of low collaboration in schools. Perhaps a better term is "acollaborative." While school staffs are not necessarily against collaboration and integration, the point is that such norms tend not to be at all salient in most schools.

The primary orientation of a teacher to his/her school, then, is one of individuation, and not in the direction of what might be called organizational membership. The school, for a teacher, is the building in which he or she teaches. It tends not to be the social organism that provides the goals, relationships, and setting within which a teacher is able to produce in concert with others. Teachers are not concerned with the school as an organization, so the idea of devoting energy to improving the organization seems vague and irrelevant, especially for teachers who are having a satisfactory experience even as the walls of the school come tumbling down.

Dyadic Nature of a Principal's Role

The single unit or small batch technology that encourages individuated teachers' roles also influences a principal's behavior. The principal is confronted with the nonintegrative norms of the staff, and his or her behavior often reinforces these norms. As in the case of the teachers, the principal's view of the school tends to be oriented toward interpersonal relations and not toward the organization as a whole. Thus, the principal's concerns for change and development move him or her in the direction of improving communications with individuals and not with organizational norms and group problem solving. The principal tends, from this point of view, to be an organizational manager who has only a limited view of the concept of the organization.

On a behavioral level, what seems to happen is that principals make many decisions with only an occasional consultation with teachers as a group. The principals spend a large amount of their time developing good relationships with individual teachers, not with groups of teachers. The norms of school staff legitimize and sanction this way of working; it is not the fault of the principal alone. With the exception of adherence to system-wide policies, each school tends to be the private domain of the principal and the noninterdependent teachers. The principal's socialization into that role began when he or she was still a teacher. What was learned in that situation often tends to be repeated when a teacher becomes a principal. In this way, the organizational pattern of dyadic relationships with individual teachers on the part of the principal is circular and reinforced.

The principal, then, who would lead a school—who would help teachers do a better job, induce changes into the curriculum when appropriate, and create a searching, collaborative, and open organization—is confronted with an organization which, though bearing similarity to organizations that are structured in a hierarchical manner, is also markedly dissimilar in some crucial ways.

The Schools' Sense of Their Institutional Being[4]

It is probably true that, aside from governmental institutions, few systems have come under more attack from a wide spectrum of groups than the

---

4. The following discussion of school organization dynamics is adapted from A. Blumberg, "School Organizations: A Case of Generic Resistance to Change," a paper presented at the International Conference on Social Change and Organization Development, Dubrovnic, Yugoslavia, February, 1977.

schools. For example, conservatives complain that there is not enough emphasis on the basics; liberals criticize because the schools do not offer sufficient alternatives; newspaper editorials focus on too much permissiveness; blacks attack the schools because they don't take into consideration black children; and public advocacy groups take the schools to task for not adequately paying attention to the needs of handicapped youngsters.

For our purposes, the substance of these attacks is less important than their effect. One observable effect is the creation of a sort of siege mentality in many schools. It's as though administrators and teachers find it continually necessary to be on their guard. In addition, there seems to be a spillover effect of distrust that is directed at strangers, at people who are not directly involved on a daily basis in trying to do the job of schooling, whatever the job may be. Perhaps a more important result, though, of these criticisms and attacks is that, legitimate or not, they induce a feeling of goal ambiguity among teachers and administrators who work in the schools. "What is it we are all about? I thought I once knew, but now I'm not so sure," is a not uncommon reaction of school people. These reactions typify what Laing (1969) has referred to as a condition of ontological insecurity, a person's being unsure of him or herself and his or her essential raison d'être.

Laing uses the concept of ontological insecurity to account for individual psychoses. The transfer of the concept to the schools does not suggest that they are psychotic or that there are such things as psychotic organizations. However, the behavior of schools as organizations frequently communicates a strong sense of insecurity as to what it is they are all about. This does not necessarily mean that individual teachers or administrators are not ontologically secure. But the whole is different from the mere sum of the parts, and it is the whole that is of concern here.

Like many of our colleagues, we have held untold numbers of conversations and work sessions with individual administrators and teachers outside the immediate context of the school as an organization. These situations were usually pleasant and productive. It was as though the people involved wanted to relate, wanted to work, learn, or change. On the other hand, on many occasions we attempted to work on similar problems within a particular school but found the experience much different. We were confronted with lethargy, defensiveness, and an attitude that might best be expressed as "ho hum." The startling thing was that the same people were involved in several of these cases.

Why the difference between our experiences with individuals and with organizations? It is only possible to speculate, of course, but the differences may be these: The individuals involved were fairly secure in their sense of being an individual. They seemed not to be threatened by the prospect of new relationships for themselves. However, as they behaved under the constraints of institutional identity, they seemed to be much less willing to engage in thinking about prospective change. There may be a myriad of other factors that enter the picture—factors that may be related to our own lack of skill or, at times, inability to communicate adequately, or factors that may attach to the system's previous experience with people from the outside. Nevertheless, over and over again, the school systems and faculties, by their behavior, communicate that they are unsure of their essential institutional being and react accordingly.

ELEMENTS OF PRINCIPAL EFFECTIVENESS

The preceding discussion is not intended to suggest that schools are organized in an irrational manner. It may be, to the contrary, that they are organized in precisely the best way possible. After all, schools in their present form have existed many years and, though there have been many criticisms of schools and what they do, few criticisms have to do with the way they are organized to perform tasks. It is the task performance that is in question, and so we must go back to the principal, the nature of the demands that are placed on him/her that emanate from the organizational structure and value system, and the kinds of personal needs system and skills that might enable a person to lead. Given the school conditions described thus far, are there specific personal dispositions that appear to be associated with effectively leading schools? What personal qualities do the eight principals we studied share, and what specific personal orientations appear to be necessary to lead school? It is to these questions that we turn next.

In coming to understand the many similarities and differences among these eight principals, we identified three factors that partly explain their on-the-job success. While they seemed to hold fairly idiosyncratic perspectives toward their work worlds, and while these viewpoints appeared to condition their manner and style of behavior as principals, all eight were also (1) desiring and eager to make their schools over in "their" image; (2) proactive and quick to assume the initiative; and (3) resourceful in being able to structure their roles and the demands on their time in a manner that permitted them to pursue what might be termed their personal objectives as principals. We elaborate on these three factors in the discussions that follow.

Holding a Vision for the School

First, it is important to understand that they all had definite ideas regarding what they wanted their schools to be like. Fran said:

> What I don't want it to be is a single-minded approach . . . I want to be able to accommodate the different learning styles of different kids and teachers, the different strengths of different teachers. I think if we have that rare person who is an excellent lecturer, I say let that person lecture, and in fact, encourage that person to lecture . . . capitalize on those strengths.

While Fran talked in terms of creating a set of schoolwide norms to facilitate diversity of learning and teaching styles for students and teachers, Fred had a vision that was less broad. It centered on his being able to establish enough good rapport with teachers, children, and parents to make it easy for them to use him as a resource. He stated:

> I see myself as giving direct service to the teachers in the sense of getting them involved and helping them in areas where I have expertise, or finding resources for them, or trying to work with them in solving problems . . .

In a more direct statement he noted that he "created an atmosphere in the school where people feel comfortable coming in and talking about problems . . ." For Fred, this "service" image pervaded what he and teachers did within the school as well as the close relations the school had with community members and social agencies in the school's neighborhood.

Ed's image of himself and his school was similar to Fred's. Ed's primary concern was "developing a climate in the building where children feel good about being there and teachers feel good about working there." While he was concerned that all the children in his school acquire needed skills in reading, writing, and arithmetic, he was especially interested in creating conditions where children and teachers could express their feelings and learn about the affective/emotional aspects of their lives.

Paul differed from Ed, Fred, and Fran in that he envisioned a school situation wherein teachers and parents in the community were integrally involved in developing educational and administrative policy for the school. Paul saw this cooperative activity as the best way to secure the kind of educational program needed to serve a poor, urban, predominantly black school clientele. For example:

> I think you have got to look at the parent group as the key group that's going to keep you on the job. . . . If you want to make a change, it seems to me that has to be your key group to get together.

Paul recognized that he was in a politically and organizationally vulnerable position. The primary way to achieve his educational objectives was to build an alliance of teachers and parents, putting the parents themselves on the front line, so to speak.

John held an image of his school that was somewhat complementary to Paul's, except that it was a high school rather than an elementary school. However, John's image of an inner-city high school with few student behavioral problems and high academic achievement was never quite realized in his view:

> . . . when I went in there . . . I think the essential thing was to make calm out of chaos. . . . For the most part we were successful in doing that. . . . I don't think I was successful in turning around the educational program . . . in terms of scholas-

tic acievement. . . . We had too many kids graduating with "D" averages, just barely minimum, and that was the failure that I saw from my standpoint.

George faced a different situation from John and Paul, and he held different objectives for himself and his high school. For George, it was vital to develop a school situation that actively involved students and, ideally, parents. In his words, he "was interested in getting students into the working of the school." In reference to parents, he said, "I want them involved and I can't get them involved." George's vision was to create an educational environment that would facilitate the intellectual and social growth of the children in his charge. If he saw events occurring that he felt would be detrimental to students' interests, he'd intervene.

Marie was much different from the other principals in her vision of developing a more worldly and enlightened faculty. She was concerned that faculty in her high school had become insulated from the outside world, and frequently from each other, and that students ended up engaging in an academic program that not only lacked internal integrity but also bore little relevance to the world outside the school. Marie expressed her frustration this way:

> I figure if the staff gets educated, and gets exposed to new ideas, they'll transmit them to kids . . . and I found it very frustrating in the beginning to realize where they were, because I kept thinking they were here, and I'd get more data and find out they were even further back than that. . . . They're flying by the seat of their pants. They don't know what they're doing, they don't know why they're doing it.

Joan had a concern similar to Marie's regarding the school faculty, but her vision seemed more encompassing because it extended to helping both faculty and children build more positive images of themselves, their school, and each other:

> What we're really trying to work with at school, all of us, is trying to build a positive atmosphere—schools for a long time have been built on very negative kinds of things. . . . The first year I touched the instructional program indirectly; like teaching with teachers. But really, my big focus was on human relations—trusting kids, being a model for the kinds of behavior I expected from adults. The second year I really zeroed in on the instructional program—really individualizing the instructional program.

Each principal had an ideal vision of what he/she wanted the school to become. In some cases, the focus was on students, sometimes parents. Frequently their vision involved teachers and the school curriculum in some major way. Whatever the vision, it went well beyond merely continuing the status quo. While each principal attached some importance to the need for maintaining and stabilizing the organization, they all held personal educational visions that went beyond the bureaucratic dimensions of their job. In our view, this personal commitment to a particular educational or organizational ideal, their willingness to articulate and work for what they believed in and felt, was vital to the success of the students and teachers in their schools. It was one of the three critical personal orientations that distinguished them from many of their administrative peers.

Taking the Initiative

A second factor related to their personal effectiveness was their propensity to initiate activity and to assume a proactive stand toward their job situation. They did not allow themselves to become bogged down in "administrivia." Excerpted below are selected comments made by each of these men and women which we believe reflect their proactive work-world orientation:

> I see myself as an organizer. . . . I gather the information . . . and I put the ideas together. I like the word "initiator," but "pusher" may be the idea. Yeah, am I aggressive—yes, I am! (Joan)

> I like running things. . . . I know me and I know I always wanted everything to happen yesterday. . . . I have high expectations . . . you can get the building run the way you want. (Marie)

> If I get an idea in my head, right or wrong, I try to pursue it, and convince other people. . . . I get involved . . . . (George)

> . . . you have got to involve people. . . . I see myself as facilitating . . . that's my function as an administrator—to put everything together and make it go . . . . (John)

> . . . I try to coordinate things and I try to identify those things that I need to get involved with . . . and those I don't need to get involved in. . . . I try to check out perceptions . . . . (Fred)

> . . . I keep hoping that I'm going to be the savior, or that I'm going to make the breakthrough with people who happen to be resisters. . . . I will take pains not to involve the board in the administration of the school . . . . (Fran)

> . . . I am not willing to let the change go on without my being there . . . with the staff, I took leadership and I don't think after that first year that I ever relinquished the fact that I was their principal. . . . The most important thing to do is to define your own role. (Paul)

> . . . For the most part, the expectations I respond to in my position are my expectations of myself rather than someone else's expectations of me . . . . (Ed)

Each of them was sensitive to the need to be proactive and to structure their role, the school situation, and the expectations others held of them. All eight principals were careful observers and listeners. They seemed to us to have a very keen ability to determine what was necessary to adjust successfully to the requirements of particular situations—when to sit back, when to push, how to secure the involvement of others, how to search for and to evaluate alternatives. By actively and continuously initiating structure in interaction with others, they were able to keep their respective organizational systems moving in productive directions, not so much in leaps and bounds as by a shove here and a nudge there. They were sensitive to the changing character of their school environments and consistent and persistent in taking the initiative.

Being Resourceful—Not Getting Bogged Down

A third factor relates to their success in the principalship: their ability not to become consumed by the organizational maintenance requirements of the job. They did not ignore these demands, but rather satisfied them either with a small portion of their own personal time and energy or by capitalizing on other capable personnel. For example:

> . . . the key thing for me would be to pick out four or five people whom I could count on, who are upwardly mobile . . . short-sighted, but very consistent every day . . . they are going to be there every day; they are going to do the job every day . . . . (Paul)

> . . . I find that spending maybe 25 to 30 percent of my time on work such as budget, scheduling, transportation, cafeteria, and so forth, is plenty. (Ed)

> I think ultimately the principal is responsible . . . even though somebody else might do it. (George)

> In a large high school, you can't do it all . . . you need a vice principal who is a good detail man, who is good for the organization, who is good on scheduling, who is good on doing the things that schools have to have—bus schedules, all the paperwork that gets shuffled through a school office . . . someone who is good on students. (John)

> I never got any strong messages from upper levels of administration about what I'm supposed to do. . . . I often let the "Mickey Mouse" stuff go by and try to develop the instructional aspects of the school. . . . I've got a fantastic secretary . . . she saves me. I never have to get anything done, report-wise—I give it to her . . . so I've got a lot of other time. (Fred)

> I think we are unskilled in lateral thinking. . . . It amazes me how little thinking administrators do in terms of solving problems. . . . Maybe they solve problems for teachers by taking on the problems themselves—but that doesn't help the principal. . . . And I think that's what gets people so overwhelmed with their jobs—they take on so many other kinds of responsibilities that might not necessarily be their own . . . . (Joan)

> I have one assistant who just loves dealing with plant maintenance. He's just super with numbers, and he's dead accurate. He just loves that stuff and he's there till 5:00 every night—and takes it home . . . as far as the nitty-gritty details, he just loves doing it. (Marie)

> I try to shove the paperwork to the periphery of the day. I get there at 7:15, so I do paperwork from 7:15 to 8:00. . . . I try to relegate those kinds of tasks to times of the day when I don't have a lot of people around. (Fran)

While some spoke more directly than others to the problems of becoming consumed by organizational maintenance activities, each assumed that he/she and not the demands of the job *per se,* determined his/her on-the-job behavior. The four high school principals were in a somewhat more advantageous position. They had administrative assistants or vice principals to whom nitty-gritty, routine administrative and clerical tasks could be delegated. However, the four elementary principals also found ways to avoid becoming bogged down by day-to-day maintenance. In the final analysis, if some of this work couldn't be handled by secretaries, volunteer parents, or upwardly mobile teachers, it either didn't get done or, if it was important enough in the eyes of the principal, he/she would come to work very early, stay late, catch up on Saturdays, or take it home in the evenings—practically anything to avoid letting it interfere with what he or she considered the leadership dimensions of his or her role.

They approached their work in this way, not because of any organizational mandate or guidance from superiors, but because they did not want these routine maintenance activities to interfere with what they individually considered their top priority—the realization of their personal vision. Thus, their on-the-job "time" was left "free"—free in the sense that they could use it to exercise personal initiatives related to the realization of their particular educational or organizational goals. To reiterate, their success in approaching realization of these goals seemed related to the following personal orientation:

- An individual commitment to the realization of a particular educational or organizational vision;
- A propensity to assume the initiative and to take a proactive stance in relation to the demands of their work-world environment; and
- An ability to satisfy the routine organizational maintenance demands in a manner that permits them to spend most of their on-the-job time in activities directly related to the realization of their personal vision. They do not allow themselves to become consumed by second-order priorities.

PRINCIPALS WHO WOULD LEAD—SOME SPECULATIONS

The elements of vision, initiative, and resourcefulness, which characterize the general dispositions of the eight principals we studied, inspire us to speculate about some more specific qualities of principals who would lead. These additional qualities stem primarily from our talks with the principals in our study, but also from discussions with teachers and observations of other principals in action.

The remainder of the chapter thus builds upon the general orientations of the eight principals and offers a series of more focused propositions regarding the personal qualities of principals who would lead.

Goal Clarity/Goal Oriented

Principals who lead have clear goals and are highly goal oriented. The two go hand in hand: it is not enough to have clear goals if these goals are not a continuous source of motivation. Further, the substance of the goals is important. As noted earlier, it would be difficult to uncover a school principal who did not espouse clear, substantive goals, but in many cases the mere espousal of goals substitutes for continual action in the service of those goals. Such was not the case with the principals we interviewed. These people were continually alert for opportunities to make things happen, and if the opportunities didn't present themselves, they created them—all in the service of their goals. Principals must be capable of making their goals operational through both long-term strategy and day-to-day action. It is of little worth to be able to articulate aims if a person has no notion of how to go about implementing them.

Personally Secure

Principals who lead possess a high degree of ontological security and a keen sense of themselves and what they are about. It is not a matter of concern to them. These principals confront day-to-day relations with others both inside and outside the system without feeling threatened. The superintendent need not be treated with kid gloves. Parents are not seen as a threat but as people who are concerned and who may have something to offer. New ideas are welcomed and tested, not brushed aside as potentially upsetting to the school. This is another way of saying that principals who are secure with their own sense of being are able to be open and to be themselves with others, and to permit and encourage the testing of a wide variety of new ideas. If the new idea fails, it is simply seen as an idea that didn't work, and does not have consequences for the integrity of the people involved.

Tolerance for Ambiguity

Building upon this last point, principals who lead have a high tolerance for ambiguity. In a system as loosely coupled as the school is, this ability, relative to both the task and relationships with others, would appear to be highly important. Theoretically, this quality may well be related to the individual's ontological security. That is, if the system is ambiguous and a principal's personal sense of security is low, then ambiguity is likely to cause tension. If he/she is not on solid ground, and the system itself does not provide it, the result will provoke anxiety. One would expect principals whose tolerance for ambiguity is low to avoid specifically those situations and ideas that might contain the seeds of productive change in a school, precisely because those situations and ideas may create more ambiguity.

Also, such principals probably spend a great deal of time in routine administrative affairs and do not attempt to lead.

Testing the Limits

Principals who lead have a marked tendency to test the limits of both the interpersonal and organizational systems they encounter. They seem to be proactive copers and confronters. It is as if they were continually searching and probing in order to establish greater degrees of freedom for themselves and their school. That is, they take risks, but do not embark on projects that, if they fail, would result in catastrophe. They have a feel for what is possible, but only after they have tested the limits of the situation. They do not assume *a priori* what can or cannot be done. This latter point is critical. Sarason (1971) speaks to it when he notes the "regularities" of school system operation; ways of doing things that have been developed over time, for which there is no particular rationale except the integrity of the regularity itself. Principals who lead don't accept these regularities as hard and fast rules, as illustrated by one principal who wanted to schedule regular weekly time for grade-level team meetings. The assumption was that it couldn't be done, because the "regularity" specified that children had to be in school for a certain number of hours each day. He tested the limits—and it was done. Children were dismissed an hour and a half early one day a week.

Sensitivity to Power Dynamics

Related to testing the limits is the notion that principals who lead apparently are very sensitive to the dynamics of power both in the larger system and in their own school. Although they don't conceptualize the system as "loosely coupled," they seem to understand the behavior that results from loose coupling—for example, the difficulty of arriving at a collective decision that results in desired action. They understand the necessity for seeking out sources of power in the informal network of relationships and are adept at cultivating them. It is not so much that they are political, though they may be, but rather that they understand and are able to work with the requirements of the situation. They know they need to establish alliances outside school in order to get things done or, if this proves unfeasible, to establish a power base in their own school that will enable them to make successful demands on the larger system.

Analytical in Approach

Principals who lead are analytical in their approach to problem situations. They are able to stand back for a moment and do not allow themselves to become immediately consumed by the situation. Is their initial impulse to try and objectify the problem and analyze its substance (some of which may be interpersonal), or is it to deal first with the interpersonal aspect of the problem and then with its substance? The inference we drew from our talks with principals was that analyzing the substance of things comes first. Thinking through the consequences of the analysis on personal, interpersonal, and organizational outcomes is second. They first figure out what is happening; then they determine the meaning and the consequences.

Origins, Not Pawns

Principals who lead behave in ways that enable them to be in charge of the job and to not let the job be in charge of them. They are not pawns of the system. They seem to be adept at playing games on which their survival depends, but they don't let the game consume too much of their energy. These principals are well aware of the minimum requirements concerning routine administrative functions and are able to fulfill these requirements with dispatch. Thus they free themselves for more exciting (for them) activities.

People Oriented, and in Charge

A somewhat different perspective on principals who would lead concerns their interpersonal need system and the needs upon which they base their approach to their job. Our discussion, which reflects the theoretical formulation of interpersonal needs developed by Schutz (1958), derives both from our interviews with these principals and from some casual research we engaged in from time to time.

Schutz suggests that each individual has an interpersonal relations orientation that is composed of a mix of three needs: inclusion, control, and affection. Further, each of these has two dimensions: one that deals with expressing the need behaviorally toward others and one that suggests what the individual wants behaviorally from others. A person may have, for example, a high need to be included by others in activities but a low need to include others in his or her activities. Our data suggest several notions regarding the interpersonal needs make-up of principals who would lead:

1. They appear to have a high need to control a situation and a low need to be controlled by others. They rather like being in charge of things, proposing ideas, and initiating action. They strongly dislike it, and tend to reject it, when constraints are put on their prerogatives or when their freedom of action and initiative are restricted in any way. They prefer to find their own solutions to ambiguous problems than to be told how to do it by others, particularly their organizational superiors.
2. These principals seem to have a rather high need to include others in projects or in problem solving, and a moderate to high need for others to include them. Part of their analytic stance toward problem solving is to make sure that those involved in the consequences of decisions are

involved in making them. Thus they are not "loners," controlling things and making decisions from the confines of their offices. More often than not they can be found around the school talking with teachers and students. It is fairly important for them to be asked by others to join in on projects. They tend to become upset if they are not involved by others, particularly when they think they have some expertise germane to the problem.

3. Principals who lead tend to have rather high need to express warmth and affection toward others and to receive it. It is not so much that they are "warm fuzzy-wuzzies" to the exclusion of anything else. Clearly, this is not the case. But when they interact with teachers in their school there is a large amount of friendliness and good-natured fellowship. These principals are not standoffish.

How do these principals compare, relative to their interpersonal needs, with those who might be categorized as not leading? A data base for making such a judgment is not available. However, Schutz (1967) did report data on a sample of 104 school administrators simply as an example. On the whole, the mean scores were quite moderate and distinctly different from our hunches about the principals we studied. Something out of the ordinary seems to be operating among those principals who lead.

A FINAL NOTE

The chapter began with the idea that, to explain the dynamics of the process of leading a school, one must see that behavior as a function of the person's perceiving and interacting within a particular situation. The discussion focused initially on what we believe are salient characteristics of the school situation and concluded with a consideration of the principal as a person and of the character and predispositions of the principal as he/she functions within the school as an organization and interacts with the individuals who work in it.

Our study has led us in the direction of thinking that there are certain definable personality and behavioral differences between those principals who are able to make a difference in their schools and those who are not. The idea of a "great man or woman" view of the principal-who-would-lead is not advanced to suggest a new Machiavellianism. Rather, the concept is this: It seems to be true that most people can learn the necessary attitudes and skills that enable a group of people to function adequately. And it seems true that groups can learn to accept influence from a variety of people and to assign group functions accordingly. What seems *not* to be true is that *anyone* can assume the role of leading an organization—a school—in the direction of making itself better than it is. Other things besides ideas and democratic functioning have to occur, and the suggestion here is that these other things start with the character of the person involved.

The intent of this chapter has been to recast our thinking about the process of leading a school. We suggested that the nature of schools as social systems requires that renewed attention be given to the person of the principal, and we offered a number of propositions concerning the character and style of some principals who engage in leading. This chapter is not a plea to return to a trait theory of leadership. However, we do suggest that, in our headlong rush toward the greater development of social technology as the answer to the problems of creating more productive learning environments in the schools, we may have neglected the essential humanity of the people who preside over them. And this humanity is, after all, much of what schools are all about.

A final point. The reader may infer a prescriptive tone in the foregoing discussion of the characteristics of school principals who are somehow able to creatively influence their school and, in a deliberate fashion, to lead. Description, not prescription, has been our intent. To the extent that our observations have credibility, and we believe they do, they constitute a basis for further study and action.

Part II

As It Became—
and a Bit More

13

The Principals Revisited: Those Who Stayed

In the Preface we suggested that even when the last page of a manuscript is finished the book itself is not complete. This, we think, is especially true when a book such as this one deals essentially with the lives of people at work. Time, indeed, does not stand still. And certainly the thoughts and feelings that individuals have about themselves and their work do not remain static over time.

This chapter and the next, then, fill out the first edition of this book a bit more, though we know that even with their inclusion the book will still not be finished. What we do in these two chapters is to provide a different glimpse into the life and times of the school principals about whom we wrote in the early chapters. It is a glimpse that might be entitled, "The Principalship in Retrospect."

Seven years had gone by since, in the fall of 1977, we started talking with the school principals whose perspectives on their lives at work lent focus to earlier chapters. Much had happened to them as it has to the rest of us. We were interested in the content of that "much." How had things gone for them? How did they view their work now? What changes have occurred in their careers and why? These were the questions we had, centrally.

The idea of talking with these people once more takes us beyond the original aim of this book. It was an opportunity, that is, to learn more about the *principalship* as a form of work and to inquire a bit about the currents that may move principals in one direction or another as they engage their careers. It will become obvious, we think, that, though schools appear from the outside to be stable, sometimes immovable institutions, the lives of some of the people who work in and try to influence them are anything but stable and immovable.

Of our eight principals, we knew the whereabouts of seven. One, Fran, The Rationalist, resigned as a result of a bitter conflict in her district that whirled around her superintendent and ultimately engulfed her. She moved to another part of the country and we lost track of her. Of the others, four are still principals, though one will soon resign in order to open his own school; two are superintendents; and one has left the field of education.

We made contact and scheduled brief interviews that began with the simple thought that it had been some time since we had last talked with them about their work. We asked, "Talk about how things have gone for you." Much as the original sketches of these people stood by themselves, so will our presentation of them here. Their stories are presented in the form of edited protocols of the interviews that were held.

This chapter is devoted to the four people of the original eight who, as of this writing (November, 1984), are still principals. First we consider the three who have remained in that role continuously. Then we discuss one who left the principalship only to return after about five years. Chapter 14 will deal with the three who are no longer in that position.

GEORGE, THE VALUE-BASED JUGGLER

George remains the high school principal in the small rural town in which he worked when he first became a subject of our study. During that time, he studied for and received a doctorate in educational administration. He is now about forty years old.

I guess it's like a curve. If I could go back a couple of years, I was very disenchanted with it, very upset. I felt that I spent too much time on it. I was frankly sick and tired of it and had to expend too much energy to keep myself up in order to do the type of job that I would want to do. And yet for a variety of reasons, I wasn't able to move. Either personal choice, or whatever, and at this point, I feel over that hump and maybe I've given up on the idea of moving. I think it is more than that. I think it's being very careful about what I'm leaving the principalship for. I also have a feeling that there may be other things. Being in a principalship gives me an authority and a knowledge that right this minute I'm not willing to forsake. I think that's where a lot of things in education are happening now and I'm there. I don't know if I want to be outside looking in and saying, "Jeepers, if I were principal." Or losing all the daily contacts with teachers, with kids, with parents, with specific issues at school that I think you withdraw from if you go somewhere else.

There was a time, though, when I really felt boxed in and there was no door that I wanted to open. I guess if there was a door, I would have gone through it. I would have been out. The door would have been a superintendency. I suppose if somebody had offered me a job, I might have said "Yes." I was very careful. Various superintendencies were available. I only applied for certain ones. I applied for an assistant superintendency in a big city and thought I had a very good line on that and I think I might have been happy in that position for a very short time. It would have been a very interesting stop-over. If that door opened, I would have walked through and out.

It wasn't that I wanted to be a superintendent. It was that I wanted out of the principalship and going to a different school and being a principal didn't make any sense. Going to a bigger school as a principal didn't make any sense because I was sure the job would be the same, the problems would be similar. It was the continuous hassle, the sameness of the hassle, the predictability of the hassle, the "here we go again." One of these days I'm going to have graduation with all the kids coming with pogo sticks. How many graduation ceremonies can you administer, organize without getting sick and tired of graduation? Or award ceremonies? There comes a point where the individual students involved become a blur and it's just one more process.

I'm feeling a bit differently now. I don't know if I have any answers as to why. I struggle with myself. I'm almost in a research mood in a way. It's almost like the management of the school, the process of the school is being done automatically. And now I'm sitting back more reflectively, especially in light of the new reports and what people are saying about education and so on. And I'm examining these in light of day-to-day practice and coming up with my own ideas. It's almost like I'm an observer of the scene.

One of the things that the University made me very guilty about was the idea that I had to be a change agent. And you couldn't stay in one place too long because there will be changes if you go in for three years but if you stay more than three years, you become co-opted and your ability to impact change diminishes. I didn't find that true. We organized an alternative school last year, for example. Started a whole school in March and it ended up with around fifty students and seven staff members. Went back for more funding this summer and got funded again. We're running the school again this year and we have forty students again. It's for street kids. Kids that are on the streets. Kids that have had it with the regular system and need a different type of approach. Two-thirds of the students come off the street and about one-third come out of the classroom.

I think that as a result of my "down" period, I actively looked for new things to do so that my job would change. Three years ago I began to personally direct a whole element in the school program involving the training of student leaders. Class presidents, vice presidents, secretaries, treasurers. Organizing workshops for them. That is where I was this morning. Conducting a workshop for this year's officers. The whole microcomputer thing has come about. Not only instructionally, but administratively, and having a microcomputer at home. It's learning how to integrate that into a system. Learning what happens when your secretary tells you to shove it some place because she is frustrated with it, and overcoming that and integrating it into the system. Perhaps also, I can remember some of the research talking about how administrators do their job in light of other aspects of their life. How central is their job to their identity? There are other things in my life. My family, hobbies. And I don't feel so guilty anymore. It's very interesting seeing that in yourself. And checking it against how you do, you judge your own effectiveness now versus what it would be ten years ago.

I think sometimes I work smarter, not harder, to use a phrase that seems to be current. I think experience does pay off. You can see the dead-ends and so you don't run down them. So in that way I think I'm able to maintain a certain level of effectiveness without all the hard work that went in before. At the same time, perhaps, it's at the cost of some enthusiasm. It's at the expense of some increased cynicism. You have to catch yourself being that way, and say, "Hey, wait a minute." My job used to be my life, I put an awful lot of energy into it. Maybe I could see myself as a workaholic. Work all day and come home with a bag full of stuff. Now I say "The hell with it." And I feel okay about it, not guilty as I used to feel.

I'm not disappointed that I didn't become a superintendent. I might still do that. But if I do it, I don't think it is going to be because I want out of the principalship, as it was before. I just wanted out. The problem with the principalship with me right now is the time it requires in light of other things that I want to do with the knowledge that I've gained both from the position and my studies. I want to talk about it. I want to tell people about it, in my own way. I don't think that way has been told. Part of the reason is not having the time and part of the reason is not knowing how to go about it. Part of not wanting to leave the principalship is the fear of moving outside of what I see as the bull's-eye of education. That's where I get my kicks. The decisions that are made. The crazy stuff you have to deal with every day. As mundane as dealing with a kid's future in terms of his assignment to teachers and courses and allowing variances from established rules and those kinds of things. It's too interesting to leave.

Some years ago, when I was coming out of my dark period, wanting to get out of the principalship, I was thinking about a person being a native in his own country. What being a native is. Maybe it's dialect, maybe it's language, maybe it's the way you dress, maybe it's feeling at home, maybe it's what people feel when they come back to the United States and see the Statue of Liberty. Then there are people who are tourists. Obviously, it's nice to be a tourist. You see things differently. You broaden yourself, you learn things you didn't learn before. There are things that accrue to a tourist. You see things differently than the native. But perhaps having been both and being a native in a principalship, I think there are certain powers and certain abilities that a native principal has that a tourist, first of all, never sees. It's an idea that there is a difference besides just burn-out, besides just longevity, in somebody who happens to stay in one spot. Another analogy I use. It's fun to be on the train. You see a lot when you are on the train, but I think the fence posts along the railroad tracks see a lot of things pass by too. In some respects, I've been a fence post in one school district too long.

ED, THE AUTHENTIC HELPER

Ed, now in his late thirties, is still an elementary school principal in the same district he was in when we first talked with him. He has, however, moved to a different school.

Well, I would say that seven to eight years ago, I was a new principal at that time, very young and enthusiastic, excited about making changes in that particular building that I had. Wasn't quite sure what the future would hold for me as far as education. I really didn't have any aspirations at that time to move on to a superintendency, so I sort of settled in to the principalship in the building, and approached that principalship more from the standpoint of an instructional leader than as a so-called administrator. I have spent the last seven to eight years, since we met and spoke, developing my own instructional skills and trying to transmit what I've gained to my classroom teachers, hoping to enhance their programs and the total program of the school. I'm still in the principalship. I've been transferred from one building to another. I feel that the transfer was beneficial to me in the sense that, in the other building, I had probably reached a point of making as many changes as I felt were necessary, and was really looking for something else. And now I've been placed in a building that has more responsibility to it, more children. A program that needs to be developed to a greater degree.

It has been kind of rejuvenating for me to come here. I was getting run down in the other one, a little tired, a little dull. I think after seven to eight years within the same building that it becomes a matter of routine and the challenge and the excitement of change begins to dwindle.

Once I thought about moving. I believe that the strengths that I hold are instructional, so the only consideration that I've had would be to maybe pursue a Central Office position that would deal specifically with instruction. I have entertained that thought. As a matter of fact, I followed through on that and made an application to a specific district regarding an assistant superintendency for instruction, but that position was closed out so the application was nulliified.

It's not really on my mind now that I'm in this new situation. It's only my second year and there is still a lot of fun here for me. There is still a lot of challenge, a lot to be done. But, it won't take me as long in this building to bring this building to the point that the other one was brought to in seven to eight years. Probably half the time. So I may find myself looking again.

I think my style has stayed pretty much the same. I try to be very realistic. I may have been more idealistic years ago. I try to be realistic in my dealings with people. Try to be honest and fair with them. Help them when possible. But I also have to recognize my limitations in terms of effecting change in certain people. There was a time when I didn't see myself with many limitations. But my experience has sharpened my sense of self.

I've switched and changed my perception of education a bit, but I don't say that I'm disenchanted. I believe that the majority of teachers that I've been associated with have a desire to do the best that they can. And I think realistically in any setting, in any profession, you will get a certain percentage of people who don't have that enthusiasm and that desire to do the best that they possibly can. So I'm not disenchanted. No, I think that in the last seven to eight years we have made great gains in terms of developing programs for children that are truly meaningful. Especially at the elementary level. I enjoy children. I try to spend as much time as possible with the children. To get out of this office.

I think it's fair to say that in a very real way what happened to me as a principal over the last several years is that my idealism has been tempered somewhat as I came smack across some of the realities of the world. I still enjoy what I'm doing. But there will come a time in this situation, as there was in the previous situation, where the sense, the challenge, and the excitement of it will kind of simmer down. I'll probably get a little restless to do something else. I'm not quite sure where I would go. But I think that in a couple or three years, I'll be looking for some kind of change. In all probability, it will be something different.

JOHN, THE HUMANIST

Like George, John, in his late forties, is still principal of the high school at which he worked when we first interviewed him.

I'm very tired. Just reflecting briefly. I've been a high school principal now six years in the city and going on ten years here. So sixteen years, and that is a long time in the front-line position. I've contemplated making some career moves and I'm at the point, you know, where I really have to decide now because of my age, if I want to legitimately pursue that or not. The problem is that I like where I am in terms of geographical location and my family and kids are all born and raised here. So I really don't look forward to relocation geographically. In terms of salary, I'm up on a salary schedule so that if I did land a District Office position I might find myself having to take a cut in pay. Which at this point in my career is also not that distasteful. Money is not everything. So I find myself in a quandary right now in time, trying to decide should I or should I not make a career change in terms of a Central Office position. As I look around the county, of all the people that I've known who were principals when I started, only I and one other person still remain.

In a district to the west of us, a quality school district, in the length of time that I've been here, I think they have had four or five different high school principals. So the position is really one of high mobility. I would think there is a very high burn-out rate in this position, as I said, I'm getting tired. People don't seem to stay in this position. I guess what I'm saying is that somehow I find myself fairly rare without using that as any puffing or bragging on my part. High school principals generally don't last a long time.

There is continual pressure in this position. It is front line. While we were sitting here this morning, I received a phone call from an assistant superintendent who wanted me to come to a meeting in his office right now and you heard me say that I'm talking to a professor. He has a set of parents down there who did not like the way something was handled here on Friday and they have a lot of serious questions. So he is very concerned as well as they are, so I've had to reschedule a meeting for them for 11:30 a.m. Before he called, I got a call from the superintendent and at 8:30 he would like to have me at a meeting and I said, "I can't meet at that time. I could give you 10:30," not knowing how long this interview would take. He also had a parent who wants to talk to him and me and the vice principal about a situation that apparently she feels is occurring within the school concerning her son. So your work world is a world of spontaneous interruption. It is a work world of processing a thousand bits of information.

Yes, I think I'm getting tired. And I wonder sometimes when I leave at the end of the day just what it is that I have done. I talked to the principal at that district to the west of us. He is leaving for another position and he said that after three years, the principalship has left him emotionally and physically drained. He is really looking forward to a new position as an assistant superintendent. So, as I reflect on it, I think it is very hard, very difficult and getting more difficult as you perceive the rise of teacher negotiations and fighting situations that are distasteful to you that sometimes you have little power to change.

There are days that I do enjoy the job. There are days when I don't enjoy it. I guess what you have to look at is, when you think back on the years, did you enjoy it more than you did not enjoy it? If you are generally satisfied, will you stay with it? I do not feel trapped. I feel I still have many options, and I'm in a career quandary right at this point. It's that I'm not really sure I want to continue *this* job for another ten years or so. I just don't know . . . I mean not having worked in a District Office, I don't know. It might be worth exploring. People that do work in District Offices seem to like that situation better than what they had as a school principal. The ones that I have talked to—there have been a number of people that I have talked to about it—a lot of conversations that I've had would focus on the high school as a very aggressive environment. After a while, they'd had it.

One guy, who was a principal for three years and now is an assistant superintendent, put it this way. He said, "When I opened my door, there would be five more problems standing there. I just got extremely tired of that treadmill to the principal's office. Whether it was teachers or students." I guess that's close to the way I'm feeling now.

What, then, can be learned from these stories of the three principals who have remained in that position? The reader, of course, will already have sensed the issues, so that in this discussion we attend to some overall comments.

One of the things that can be learned from these people takes us back to the statement we made in Chapter 1. We noted there that the recent focus on the importance of the principalship was a "rediscovery of the obvious." The "obvious" here, though, is of a different nature, a phenomenon we have known about for some years—that being a principal, particularly of a high school, can, over time, be very costly to an individual's sense of well-being. Both George and John spoke of being tired and, in the case of John, "very tired." The adjectives they used to account for their feelings conveyed a similar meaning. For George, it was the continuous "hassle" that he had to confront; and John's descriptor was that of a "front-line" position. There was always some kind of skirmish going on, it seems. Someone always wanted a piece of your time, frequently on short notice, as was the case with John. What he seems to be saying here is that it is literally impossible for him to plan and carry out a day's work as he conceives it. And this condition, one must suspect, has led him to question the efficacy of his work. "Am I doing anything that makes a difference?" his query might be.

Another dimension of his job contributed to George's feelings of being "down" and disenchanted; that is, his sense of the sameness of things. Graduation and honors ceremonies, which once held meaning for him, had become ritualistic. The faces of the students he saw on these occasions were blurred. Added to this was that he found himself having to "expend too much energy to keep myself up" in order to do the kind of job he wanted to do, a thought that several years ago seemed not to have entered his consciousness.

How does a person deal with a situation that once brought a great deal of excitement and satisfaction but that now does not? We have similarities and differences, of course. Both George and John considered moving into a Central Office position. Interestingly, neither of them had this in mind earlier. That is, their thoughts about moving seemed motivated by a desire to escape from a situation they found emotionally toxic. For John, the prospect of a reduced salary in a Central Office job was not one that would stand in the way of his leaving. It was a question of when the right situation would develop for him.

George appears to have approached his job malaise by engaging in his own job-enrichment program. Having apparently made the decision to stay in the principalship ("the bull's-eye of education"), he seems to have sensed that he needed to take his own bull by the horns, lest he perform a simple run-of-the-mill custodial function for the rest of his career. An alternative school, a leadership training program, the use of microcomputers—these were the things that seized his imagination. Our hunch is that on some level he simply needed to engage in these things in order to avoid a high school principal's "death at an early age." But also, as he put it, " I think sometimes I work smarter, not harder. . . . experience does pay off."

The case of Ed, an elementary school principal, bears a similarity to his high school colleagues, but it is different as well. His feelings of needing a change derived not from being continually harried but from his sense of having taken his school and its teachers as far as he could. The challenge he had originally encountered no longer existed, and his work-life seemed to be characterized by sameness and dullness. He, too, was interested in a Central Office position as a way out, but the problems of declining enrollments eliminated the position and with it, his escape. Ed, though, was fortunate. His job-enrichment program and also his rejuvenation as a principal came about through his taking charge of a different school, with all the problems, and more so, that were present in his earlier one. He is free and excited, then, at the prospect of plying his trade, so to speak, for a few more years with renewed vigor. But recall that he said he had become less idealistic and more realistic about what he might accomplish. It may well be that thought that led him to say, "It will probably happen again"; by which he meant that, having done what he could do in his new school, he will sense a similar type of sameness on the job that will lead him to think about moving, to another school, an assistant superintendency, or out of the field of education altogether.

We return to the question we raised earlier in this chapter: What can we learn from the stories of these principals? There is no single answer to that question, of course. It is a mixed bag, and whatever response one makes to it may well depend on what perspective one brings to it as well as to anything else. For example, one may draw the conclusion that being a school principal, particularly one who desires and has the skills to "make a difference," is ultimately a debilitating job. There is so much you can do; after that, things become dull and routine. Or one may conclude, "That's life" or "No one ever promised you a rose garden," or "Life has its ups and downs and where is it written that it's all ups?" or "You win some and you lose some."

Elements of truth are found in each thought. Undoubtedly there scarcely exists an occupation that does not have its boring, dulling periods, some of which may last over a considerable length of time. It is also undoubtedly true that many people, perhaps a high number, become mired in those situations, "throw in the sponge," and look for the earliest possible exit through retirement. Though each of these principals seems to have experienced being mired, they did not surrender, but sought or are seeking other ways to continue making their life at work mean something. For George, it was inventing and doing new things within his school; for John, it is the effort to move into less of a "front-line" position; and for Ed, it was a move to a new school.

The point we make is this: It would be the ultimate fantasy to imagine that, particularly in this day and age, being a school principal over an extended period of time is not wearing on an individual. How one reacts to and deals with that condition, though, seems to be very much related to a variety of things: what one senses is needed to make life interesting, one's age, one's family situation, one's concept of self, for example. These do seem to be the types of things our principals thought about as they considered their situation.

A final point is in order. For some people, reading the vignettes may be depressing. Our conversations with the principals did not suggest that they were depressed, however. Most important, it seemed clear that they were not thinking about staying on the job and taking early retirement at the same time.

PAUL, THE POLITICIAN

Though presently an elementary school principal, Paul, now about forty, has not been in that position continuously since we first talked with him. He left his first principalship for a Central Office position in his district where he worked for about a year. Then he took a job in a federal educational agency in Washington where he stayed three years. About two and one-half years ago, after turning down an assistant superintendency, he accepted the principalship of an elementary school in a town in the same state but quite distant from the locale in which he started his administrative career.

> It has changed quite a bit for me, because I feel as though the tasks are quite different from what they were ten years ago. The task of trying to find out what worked is different. I think I know what works, and I'm able to set a different set of goals. For instance, I have a staff that has an average of nine to ten years' experience, so we're not talking about people who are fresh out of college. We're talking about a staff that when I came were apathetic and didn't believe in what the kids could do. They thought discipline was the key. So it's a different problem. And I'm different.
>
> One of the reasons that I went back to being a principal was that I hope to open my own school, which has been a dream that I've had and share with my wife. I think that I'm different because I'm looking for different things. I looked for a setting where there were very few outside variables affecting the school. Small district, very little political upheavals aside from those that would happen within any school district. And I specifically came here. In the interview, I stated what it was that I wanted to do, where I wanted to go.
>
> I went to Washington looking for some answers, and discovered that there are no answers. No one really has the key. There are things that work and you have to try them, and really the key word is hard work and I was willing to do that in a setting that I enjoy. So I have a school of 800 students. Kindergarten through fourth grade, and as I said, they thought their problems were discipline. I thought their problems were low test scores. So we worked.
>
> At the first faculty meeting, I gave them a list of what my goals would be and the time frame for when I thought we all were going to reach them. And I included in there the fact that they didn't know me from Adam. They didn't know if these could be done, and at the end I said that we're going to have a lot of fun doing it. I almost had to stop the faculty meeting two or three times because they were talking in the middle of it. They just totally disregarded an administrator and certainly any young fool coming in and thinking he was going to make a differ-

ence in that setting. Most of them lived there, had seen principals come and go. And then after that, I really had nothing to do with the staff, person-to-person, for almost a year. I dealt with the kids as I always do. I went on the playground, I took duty time.

But what I did do with the staff was that I looked into how they were organized and began setting the organization so that it allowed for some flexibility. Their big concerns were prep times and things like that. And I tried to rearrange the schedule that would include their concerns, but then would allow for some working together, because in that school everybody closed their doors and went off and did their own thing. The first thing that I did was put them into teams, I tried to find some people who were either taking some advanced courses or seemed to be upwardly mobile and made them team chairmen. And I started a newspaper. Got the kids involved in coming back to school activities on Saturdays. After a while they began to see that the kids were good. They started believing in them. I came thinking that we were going to have some really big discipline problems. But they weren't bad children. They were bored. They just didn't have anything exciting going on for them. All the extra money was spent on remedial education. One of the first things that I asked for was an enrichment program, and we started with a heritage program. We entered most of the contests they have academically in the region, and we began winning some. This was unheard of in a small black school in the area. I guess after about the third prize the school board started reacting. And the teachers started saying "Wait a minute! What's going on here? I want to get on the bandwagon."

I loved being back in school. Well, you know, I really do like the business. I learned to write in Washington, but I never learned to like it. Research, that was just not my cup of tea. I learned a lot. So it was exciting for me to get back to the children, plus I knew that my goal was to open my own school, so I had a purpose to being here. I wanted to see if I could really do some things that I thought I could do. I guess the real joy is in doing them, and they came so much faster than even I expected. I said five years, we would have 70 percent of the students on or above grade level. The time that I came, there were 30 percent. At the end of three years, 86 percent were on or above. I think that what happened was that the teachers started teaching.

I got them working together, instead of working separately. It was a bit of competition by putting them into teams. And we put on a few shows. They started competing with each other. You know, my team can do this, can do that. It wasn't very difficult, then, to turn some of that competition towards academics. For instance, the science fair, this type of thing. And I believe that as the school began getting calmer and a little bit more organized, when they weren't spending so much time trying to get free time, they started enjoying what they were doing. Teachers really just kind of caught hold.

Yes, it felt like home to get back. It felt like what I should be doing. I think I might get tired of being a principal in a public school setting. I'd like more control over curriculum and what happens. And I'm still an oddball for a principal. I don't look or act like a principal to most people. When I come to work on a motorcycle and speak jive occasionally, it doesn't mean that I don't know what I'm doing and I'm not going to do a good job. You know, that kind of thing. I run into that stuff every once in a while. I came to school with a suit and sneakers on. They said, "Why?" and I said, "I think when you come to school, you should be ready to work and you said the school was so bad I was ready to run around and take care of anything that needs to be taken care of." And I did that to make a point, for about a month. And they made a point about the sneakers, but I was making a point. After a while, I came back and said, "You don't need sneakers here. The school is not bad."

I think it's important to make it fun. I think we take ourselves too seriously. I think the first thing, too, I learned to do was to stay in my school and not to get involved in anything else. I didn't care what the politics in the area were, I didn't care what the superintendent was doing, the Central Office, I didn't get involved in anything other than the school. My goals were a bit different. I wanted to see if I still had the skills to move people. Actually, all the things that we've studied, to see if I could actually do them. And that's always been exciting for me. Survival was not an issue for me, this time. When I came, I told the school board that I would only stay two years at the most. I wasn't worried about surviving. If I didn't like it, I knew I could move on. I turned down an assistant superintendent's position for $10,000 more money. So I wasn't into that and I wasn't into anything political, so there wasn't anything to survive from. Calmer, the whole revolution died. There's another thing! One of the things that I did to assure that I wouldn't have some of the problems I did was to go into a totally black district, school board and kids. So there wasn't anything to battle, other than our own incompetence.

In a sense I protected myself. I didn't have to convince the people that our kids can do this, or that. They were already into that. They were just not expecting high enough standards. They have fought all of that and won. The control issue. They changed and got control of the school board. They had gone through all of that. They had a black superintendent and were looking for a change in administrators. And I got a nickname of "Simon Legree" for a while, but with a smile, still with a smile. I'm not quite as open as I used to be. I had to be more administrative. I had to get rid of about four people just as an example, just to let them know that I wasn't going to have that kind of incompetence. And they were totally incompetent. But once again, I didn't fire anybody. I got them moved, traded, retired. I'd like to think that I became a more skilled administrator.

It all feels kind of good. I know that this is what I want to do. When I left Washington, I had a lot of different options of where I could go. And one of the driving forces was to finish my retirement here in this state. I also had family concerns. So I headed this way. I was to the point of meeting a school board to accept a position as assistant superintendent of this little district. All I was going to do was put in two years as assistant superintendent and finish my ten years. And then I looked at this job and said, "Oh, that is what I'd really like to do." What I could do, of course, is keep notes and when I do open my school, I'd feel better because I wasn't sure I could apply my previous experience as a principal to other settings. And after having done this, I feel I could be a principal, anywhere, with any kind of kids, any kind of school.

Paul's experience seems about as different as it can be when compared to those of his colleagues. His "rerun" of the principalship is almost no rerun at all. It's almost as though this was his first job as a principal, if we can judge by the enthusiasm that seems apparent in the things he said. Or, perhaps a better analogy is that he almost seemed like a kid with a new toy.

How come? There seem to be some obvious reasons and some that may be a bit more subtle. On the obvious side, he had been out of the principalship for several years, though still in the field of education, before he became a principal once more. It may be that he had not remained in one school long enough to become wearied by the experience. Note, for example, his suggestion that he might indeed get tired of being a principal "in a public school setting," the issue being that he wouldn't have as much control over the curriculum as he would want. Another obvious point is that he made a deliberate choice to become a principal again, declining in the process an assistant superintendency that would have paid considerably more money. This choice, it must be understood, was instrumental for Paul: being principal of this school was to be his private proving ground. His ambition was to open his own school, and this was his opportunity to see if he could do what he thought he could do. His experience enabled him to answer the question affirmatively: "after having done this, I feel I could be a principal, anywhere, with any kind of kids, any kind of school." Feeling successful, and over a relatively short period of time, surely makes a difference, perhaps the main difference.

There are a couple of other reasons that may account for Paul's enthusiasm that seem a little less obvious than those noted above. First, this principalship was going to be a short-term one. Paul knew it, as did his employing school district. Survival on the job for a long period was not an issue. And this fact, one might suspect, left him free to be just the kind of person he wanted to be as a principal. He could make the joke ("I think it's important to make it fun. I think we take ourselves too seriously.") of coming to school in a suit and sneakers and not be concerned by what others might say about him not "looking like a principal." Additionally, he deliberately chose a school district in which he would not feel he had to fight political, non-educationally related battles. He was, once more, free to be what he wanted to be.

Perhaps the most important point of all about Paul's story was "Yes, it felt like coming home." This point notwithstanding, we need to add, "But not for long."

We need to make a few summary comments. As we noted early in the chapter, talking once more with these people was an opportunity to learn more about them as principals. Perhaps more important, though, it was an opportunity to learn through their experience more about the principalship as a form of work; though we understood that what we might learn would be somewhat biased because of the individuals involved. This limitation notwithstanding, what developed—particularly with the three people who had stayed in the role continuously—seems worthy of some discussion.

One almost gets the image of the principalship as a position whose effect is to grind people down, particularly people who wish to make a difference in the life of schools; or at least to create in them a sense of having been dulled. The caveat of "people who wish to make a difference" may be an important one. That is, it is possible to conceive of many principals whose primary role concept is to administer routine events and whose main engagement with teachers is to support them as individuals. It may well be that, for these people, the hassles, the interruptions, the routine of school life are not upsetting things. It is the life-blood of the job for them, and they get a good bit of satisfaction out of simply maintaining the school on an even keel. Matters educational—curriculum and instruction—are not central to their lives. (If this point strikes the reader as an incredible paradox, it does us, too. One must listen to lots of teachers to understand the validity of the statement.)

We think, then, that under the conditions just described, the principalship need not be a "grinding-down" type of work. A job is a job is a job. However, we think it is quite possible that, when the individual involved wishes to change things, to move a faculty, quite the opposite will develop. That is, the same hassles, interruptions, and routine will become debilitating. Recall the comments "It was the continuous hassle, the sameness of the hassle, the predictability of the hassle" and "I wonder sometimes when I leave at the end of a day just what it is that I have done." Perhaps this last point is the key. The principals about whom we've written have needs to *do* something and what some of them, at least, said is that the very nature of the demands put on them stood in the way of their doing. Their sense of achievement became limited and this was ultimately frustrating for them.

If our speculation bears any relation to fact, and we have little reason to doubt it, there is an important message in it for school policy makers. Put simply, they will need to start attending to the general welfare, growth, and development of their best principals—as they will likely lose them, if not in body, then in spirit. They will have to provide thinking time for them and resting time, as well.

14

The Principals Revisited:
Those Who Left

Of the three principals who are no longer in that position, two are now superintendents and one has left the field of education altogether. Paralleling the style in Chapter 13, we present edited protocols of the interviews, first with the two who became superintendents and then with the person who decided that the field of education was not one in which she wished to find her future.

JOAN, THE PROBLEM-SOLVER

Within a year or so after we first talked with her, Joan left her position as elementary principal to accept an appointment as administrator, with professorial rank, in a university-based, field-oriented professional development program. Its function was to organize, promote, and conduct conferences and workshops for a widespread association of school districts. Though she was quite successful at it, it did not offer her the type of "action" with school people and youngsters that she seems to thrive on, nor did it contain the possibilities for her to directly influence what happens in schools and classrooms. After about three years (during which time she received her doctorate), she resigned to become assistant superintendent for instruction in a small ex-urban district in another part of the state. She remained on that job for two years, and a year and a half ago became superintendent of another small system (1700 pupils) close to the one in which she had been working.

The principalship was the best job I ever had, for a couple of different reasons. First of all, if you want to talk about being a change agent, I think it is the only place to be. Contrary to what a lot of people believe about where you can make a change, and what policies are made, and the higher level and all that, if you really want to make an impact on education, on student learning, the place to do it is in the principalship. It's not at the teaching level, because there you don't deal with the whole system of the school.

Principals have a unique position. There is the principal sitting right in the

203

middle. You can make an impact on the Central Office and upon policies that are being made. And you can make an impact on the teaching and the students and the parents. So there are lots of direct relationships. In the case of the superintendent, things are very diffuse. Absolutely! If you look at the superintendency, you are looking at a whole different world. You are looking at a political world. I'm not saying the principalship wasn't political. In part, it was, but when you talk about building relationships or making an impact on teachers and kids, as a superintendent, you are too far removed to do that.

I guess I changed jobs for different experiences, for different opportunities. I left the University because I knew I wanted to go back and work in public education with students and, in truth, the assistant superintendency wasn't so bad. I was still making an impact on principals, who then could make an impact on teachers. So I still had those two relationships that were strong. I think the principalship also is a place where, if you are a people person, if relationships are important to you, then the principalship and assistant principalship are good places to be.

Now, would I ever think about going back to being a principal? Well, I would think first about going back to the assistant superintendency. I may do that, by the way, in the very near future. I'm now negotiating and I may go back.[1] But if the opportunity were there in the absolutely right place, I would go back to the principalship. I feel like I'm in a really good position right now. I can pick and choose the places that I want to go. I've had a lot of experiences. I know now what I like and what I don't like and I can make those decisions and I don't *have* to go any place.

You know, I was a principal for four years and I never wearied of it. Maybe four years wasn't enough time to get weary of it. I don't really know. I went to the University for an opportunity. Not necessarily because I was tired of the principalship. I went there, I guess, for another reason, though when I think back, I really thought that we had made a significant number of changes in a very short period of time and that perhaps the teachers couldn't take any more change . . . and that they might need a little more stability than what I knew I could give them because I would continue to want to make changes. So I thought maybe we had moved too fast in too short a period of time and they needed time to digest and practice those kinds of things.

I really thought about it at that time. From the third through the fourth year I thought a lot about it. Now since I've left I still keep in touch with probably 60 percent of the teachers that were there. We send our once-a-year letters, and in between I either come down or I see a lot of them and talk to them on the telephone. And now that I've talked to them, I think it is probably not true. They probably could have taken even more; they were stimulated, they were still ready to move. But at that point, I really thought I'd done about all I could do.

My life has been one of, kind of moving and looking for new kinds of experiences all the time. I've used a lot of what I've learned in the past, though, and applied it in different ways to the new experiences. As for the future, I want to get more directly concerned with instruction. The assistant superintendency is a good spot for me, I think . . . in a smallish district, no more than 5000 students. I felt the superintendency in a small school district could afford me the opportunity to do what I wanted. But not only to sit there being responsible for the policies, but also to make an impact on teaching. But it hasn't worked out. A political environ-

interesting!

1. Since our interview, a matter of three weeks, these negotiations bore fruit, and Joan will once more become an assistant superintendent for instruction.

ment doesn't allow you to do that. I've talked to a lot of people in the same position and it just isn't done.

FRED, THE BROKER

Shortly after our initial interview, Fred accepted a position as superintendent of a small (1000-pupil) town school district about twenty miles from the city in which he had worked. He is still there and is currently completing his doctoral work in educational administration at a nearby university.

It's been nine years since I left the principalship. The impression that sticks with me the most is that I remember the principalship as being very, very intense in the relationships that existed between me as a principal and the staff members, and the interaction between me and the students. I still recall that as being the thing that stands out most in my mind. And that intensity was a daily kind of intensity. The problems were there, you had to react to them, it was a very immediate sense because it required an answer. Not necessarily a solution, but people are always expecting answers to some immediate thing. And again it was always that dilemma that I recall. Reacting to those immediate concerns and trying to push for an overall change in terms of some of the directions we were going in, some of the goals that we might want to have for improvement. That constant tension between the immediate and the long-range. That for me, I guess, was something that I recall. I see it from my present position, and the administrators that I hire and the expectations I have of them.

The same things that made it, the principalship, difficult, made it happier in some ways, because I enjoyed those relationships. I enjoyed seeing improvement in teacher skills, and teacher behavior and being able to change some of that. It was frustrating when I couldn't. Also being able to solve problems and work with kids, and maybe become more effective learners. Not always. But being able to intercede and work out and solve some of the problems.

In my present job, I don't have that kind of closeness with the individual students. Usually by the time that you meet with parents, you're at the second or third level of dealing with problems. More than dealing with something immediately, you get it second and third hand. I happen to be in a building with junior and senior high school kids. My office is there. I enjoy the interaction that I do in that office. I miss that kind of thing.

There are a couple of reasons I became a superintendent. I think that there is a broader base of influence there. I think that that is one reason. I think the other reason is that I would have had reservations about how long I could emotionally survive in the principalship. Because of the pressure, the intensity and in order to do the job well, in my estimation, you have to keep that kind of intensity up. I would think that it would be very difficult to maintain that kind of intensity over a long period of time. The frustration would seem to set in and I think that some of the changes I've made—were made in the period of three or four years, maybe institutionalized and a few more years after that, but beyond that I think you'd have to either switch buildings, or take up a new challenge. I think the principalship for me would have been a dead-end at that point, for me and the way I see my life. I'm dealing with broader issues at this point. In a sense of, the school district goals and the political problems that are in the school district. Selling the school district if you will. All the various different aspects of communicating at a district level which you don't get in an individual building.

I wouldn't want to go back and be a principal. There are times that I miss parts of the job, but overall, as far as my satisfaction with what I'm currently doing, I'm generally satisfied. And I would not be satisfied being a principal. The horizons are too limited for me. I want to have a broader influence on the schools than just a building position.

I think I also like, in a sense, to be my own boss. I think I liked that as part of the principal's job at that time, being your own boss to a certain extent. I was accountable to some people and having some range of control, or some control over some of your behavior. Being able to influence some things is important, and is now at a broader level. Again, being able to deal with principals and board members and parents and have some greater influence with those people. At least, more people perceive it that way. My work world is larger.

I think I have a more supportive group of colleagues that I'm working with now and that has been a real positive thing for me. We have one of the strongest support groups and that wasn't always true. I look back. There weren't a lot of people to whom I could go for help. Just a couple. Collegial support was practically nonexistent.

I have pretty much of a personal style and I think that maybe that is one of the reasons, among others, I feel good about being in a small district. A thousand kids is not a big district and I know most of the kids and parents. Even as I look beyond my immediate horizons for other jobs, I look to have a position that is manageable in that sense. Being able to know most of the elements in the system. That's important for me. It's part of my make-up.

In a way, I see myself replaying the principalship in a different context. I see that in a couple of areas where I've gotten involved with kids and advocated through kids with principals. And I think sometimes the principals wonder why would I take an interest in that kid. But they have been very kid-oriented themselves so we've worked well together that way. Yes, that has carried through.

I think being a principal helped me develop a lot of confidence working with problem-solving skills. A lot of confidence working with a variety of problems with teachers. I just had a lot of confidence in my problem-solving skills as a result of that. It was like winning a tough football game. It was a confidence builder. Yes. It really was. There wasn't anything that I wouldn't be willing to take on as a result of that. I mean I have been successful in difficult situations and it wasn't a cockiness, it was just that I felt a quiet confidence that I could handle anything.

There is no evidence we are aware of that suggests that, when people start their work-career in education as teachers, those who eventually become Central Office administrators have that aspiration in mind when they start to teach. Undoubtedly some do, but for most we suspect the decision to try and become a superintendent or assistant superintendent as a career goal gets made slowly over time and for a variety of reasons. In the last chapter, the cases of George, Ed, and John provided us with some rich data about the process. With them, the issue seemed to be to seek a way out of a situation that was taking its toll of them as human beings.

The cases of Joan and Fred, though, present us with differences; and we are fortunate indeed that these differences exist because they provide us with another perspective on the careers of our principals, and in a way on the principalship.

Joan held several positions before becoming a superintendent and didn't remain in any of them more than a few years. Two things seemed to characterize her moves: a need to learn more (and we don't think her saying that was merely for the sake of appearance); and a need to be in a position where she could directly influence what was happening in schools and classrooms. With regard to the latter, her university position was frustrating. It was too removed from the action, but learn a lot she did. Her move into the position of assistant superintendent for instruction proved satisfying, and she was good at it. So good and comfortable was she, that it did not constitute a major conceptual leap for her to think of herself as a superintendent. And so she became one.

Illusions do become shattered at one time or another for all of us. Joan's illusion of the superintendency as a position from which she could exert direct influence on the quality of education in her district was not long in the shattering. She said, ". . . things are very diffuse. Absolutely! . . . a whole different world . . . a political world." And at a point after the tape recorder had been turned off, she said, "I hate it!"

But what about the principalship after eight or nine years in three different positions?—It "was the best job I ever had" and "If the opportunity were there, I would go back to the principalship in the absolutely right place." Whether or not those conditions will ever develop and, if they do, whether or not Joan would once more become a principal, is unanswerable, of course. In the meantime, there is her new position as an assistant superintendent, one month off from the date these words are being written.

What we seem to have, then, in the case of Joan, is an extremely energetic and active person for whom the principalship, even though she now describes it as her best job, apparently did not hold enough for her at the time. It was a good fit relative to her skills, but alone did not contain either the challenges or the opportunities for the learning she needed. It did not appear to have tired her (though she was only a principal for about four years); rather, and curiously, she seemed concerned that her pace had tired her teachers. So it was on to other things, looking all the time, it appears, for the perfect match between her skills, her needs to learn and influence, and a school situation that would complete the other side of the bargain. Seasoned superintendents might smile, thinking her naive to ever have entertained the idea that her idiosyncratic needs could be met in the superintendency, or might counsel her to think in terms of a longer time perspective. Moving a total system is different from moving an instructional program or creating staff development initiatives.

The issue concerning Joan's reactions to being a superintendent, then, was not that there was no action attached to the position. There was plenty of it; but of the wrong kind, as far as she was concerned. Being a manager of the political structure of a school-community system, even though she did this successfully, took time and energy away from that which she valued most. So it was back to matters educational for her by way of the assistant superintendency. Joan seems to be rather an exemplary case of "once a teacher, always a teacher." Further, on some level, sensing the importance of this idea to her intellectual and emotional well-being, she appears to have had the wisdom to make the change "back" (in the sense of a "lesser" position, but we doubt she saw it that way) to a place where what she is asked to do fits well with what she wants to do. For her, there is no such thing as being "locked in."

Fred's reflections on both the principalship and the superintendency differ markedly from Joan's. For him, the idea of the principalship being "the best job I ever had" doesn't fit. But that is less important, it seems, than some of the things he talked about when we discussed the principalship. His recollections of the intensity and immediacy of demands stood out, as did his elegantly analytical "it was always that dilemma I recall. Reacting to those immediate concerns and trying to push for overall change." It was that yin and yang of the principalship—the tension that developed between needs to devote energy to the immediacy of daily demands and needs to think and do things about long-range change—that made an impression. Further, and still in retrospect, that tension and intensity of being was responsible for Fred's comments that "I would have reservations about how long I could emotionally survive in the principalship." Still it was an enjoyable time, and Fred, like Joan, got much satisfaction from the relationships that developed as well as from being able to see the direct results of his influence on his school.

It seems clear that Fred's move to the superintendency was motivated by needs similar to Joan's—to be in a position of broader influence. There, as we have seen, the similarity stops. Joan will be shortly out. For Fred, to this time, being a superintendent constitutes a satisfying and productive work-life. We may only speculate on this difference, which seems to rest on the personal "baggage" each brought with them to the position. For example, Joan had difficulty tolerating the daily, weekly, never-ending accumulation of superintendency "garbage," which had to be "hauled away" before she could turn her attention to the matters most dear to her. Fred sees that same accumulation as something that has to be taken care of as smoothly as possible so that other things can happen. Perhaps there is something called a "garbage toleration quotient" involved. Or perhaps Fred does not conceive of the highly political milieu in which a superintendent must work in those terms.

But note two final things about Fred. First, he is in a small-town, fairly homogeneous district, where "I know most of the kids and parents." And second, "In a way, I see myself replaying the principalship in a different context." Fred seems to have made his school district his school. And why not? Put another way, it's not ill-advised at all to stick with a winner. We note, however, that leading a school and leading a district present different problems, and that, as systems increase in size and complexity, these differences impact both the nature of the problems presented as well as the means by which they can be addressed. We don't think Fred means to suggest that larger school districts be run on an elementary school model.

MARIE, THE CATALYST

Marie stayed on as principal of a suburban high school for two more years after our first interview; after four years in that position, she resigned, though not to move into a Central Office position. Hers was a complete break with the field of education. She went into the field of interior design.

The first two years were fine and exciting. Then—well, we fired a teacher at the end of the second year. We had a board that had been there for a long time and they hired the superintendent and they hired me. Well, I think the firing of that teacher did them in. One of the men said to me, "My wife said that she could divorce me and if she did she would name twenty-one correspondents as a result of the hours and nights that he spent in the hearing of firing the teacher." It was an open hearing. It was really very grim. Anyway, they left, the bulk of that board. Left at the next election and I think that was the straw that broke the camel's back. We got a new board and their median age was about thirty-eight. They attacked everyone and everything, but they particularly went after the superintendent. So the superintendent changed from being fairly easy to get along with to being super defensive. He would get attacked by the board at night and he would call me at 8 a.m. and he would start on me. A different issue and often irrelevant. I don't know. I was the first administrator he'd talk to because I had the high school.

It really kind of got grim because the board didn't know what they were doing. They were not functioning as a cohesive group. He could not control them, and they would go off on their own tangents. They would wander in and out of the schools. They would send their wives in the school during the day. The wives would go sit in the classrooms in the schools and report. With no data, no background, no understanding of anything and go and report back to the spouse about what had happened in the classroom. You can't believe it. It was just totally out of control to the point where I would not allow them in my building. The husbands or the wives. We had been a very open school, no matter who wandered in and out. We didn't care who wandered in and out of classrooms, it never bothered any of us. But we began to be more closed. That was also at the point in time when there was Proposition Two. So that those two years were during the budget thing. The budget thing would go on for six months. It would start up in January and usually wouldn't be over till June and the meetings were three to four nights a week and they would start at 7 to 7:30 and they would be over 11:30 to 12:30, and then I'd go home so mad. It wasn't that I was involved necessarily. I was there to answer any kind of questions. I had already presented my budget. The board made decisions and cuts. They knew *nothing*. They owned a store, they worked for different companies, they were young, they had no children in the high school. It was unbelievable!

It wasn't as much interference with me as they interfered with the superintendent, who then interfered with us. It was direct fall-out. They tried to interfere but they were focused more on him. Because some of them really hated him. They perceived him as being very Machiavellian and essentially wanted to get rid of him so they were attacking in order to collect data on him. They weren't doing it too cohesively. And they weren't doing it constructively. Some of those board

Very angry with new Bd of Ed

meetings were very damaging to people. They would just attack. And the super-intendent and nobody else. The chairman of the board did not say, "This will stop, we'll go into executive session." It just went on and on and it was grim. It was a kind of situation where you started having working papers with dates and times and you told your leading staff members who were being attacked to also make sure they had working papers with dates and with times.

It was bad. The system was getting very paranoid. The staff were also being individually attacked. The staff and I were fairly cohesive. My department chair-men were too. I had some really good people, some really sharp people. I had begun to be able to move them into decent positions or positions of power. And I also had some little boys and some just plain jerks.

Generally in firing people you can do it, and do it quietly. You could get rid of staff that weren't doing the job. But after that, I wasn't too inclined to go after staff in terms of firing anybody. On the other hand, I had been there enough years that we unloaded a lot of staff so that there wasn't—there were still some people left, there were a couple that I thought needed to go. But again, it takes hours and days and years to collect data in the first place. If I walked into their classrooms, even though I knew what was going on and I had reports from other people, they would clean up their act. Any of the administrators walked in. It was very, very hard, particularly after firing that teacher. I mean they were very careful about having their acts together in the classroom when we were around.

I was exhausted. Absolutely exhausted and the end of the fourth year, the budget business was even worse than the year before and by this time I had had a year's worth of the superintendent acting that way. I sat down, looked at it and thought, "What is a nice girl doing in a place like this? This is no fun. I'm putting in fifty to seventy hours a week."

In the first two years, I had a lot of fun. It was still a lot of stress and a lot of hours, but it's fun and so then the stress and the hours, they are okay. But it wasn't fun. So the only thing that I missed when I left was the kids. They were fun. It really is upsetting sometimes to think about it. It got so bad.

There were ongoing personal attacks on me. And I was highly visible and I hated it. I never was comfortable. I'm not that kind of personality.

I don't know, if I'd still be a principal if all that stuff hadn't started. There were some other things that entered into it. I had no time for me. None. My youngest child needed an enormous amount of time. He needed me not to be with him every minute of the day, but to know where he was and to keep track of him.

During the day it wasn't too bad. I found that for me to have relationships, there wasn't time. You can't build any kind of relationship if you are working those kind of hours. You can't—how can you have a husband or anything if you are out every night? It wasn't the way I wanted to lead my life. So the only other thing that would have been any kind of fun would have been an assistant super-intendency. But I was too tired. Too tired to do anything in education. I had to get out for my own survival, my own sanity.

Marie got caught, apparently, in circumstances not of her own making. Never at issue was her performance as principal. Rather the community, it seems, through the personae of a newly elected school board, set in motion forces that had the effect—for Marie, at least—of making her position no longer attractive to her. And not only that, since the ultimate result was her decision to leave the field of education entirely. We have no evidence to suggest that this was the school board's intent. We doubt it, but it's not beyond the realm of possibility.

The intent of the school board, of course, is not the issue. What is the issue is that a situation was created in which what had been a good fit between Marie, her school, and her school system became just the opposite. Things got too costly. The long working hours were no longer balanced by the fun of working. In fact, working simply ceased being fun; and, as we have seen, Marie not only became disenchanted with her own work situation but also with the possibility of a future in the schools.

It is not an unfamiliar story. But it is a sad one for at least two reasons. On the personal level, when Marie said, "So the only thing I missed when I left was the kids. They were fun. It really is upsetting sometimes to think about it," her voice broke. Though the circumstances occurred several years ago, the memories of the fun and excitement of working with the kids won't stay buried.

The story is sad on a much broader level, as well. Apparently the political conflicts and tensions within one school system were eminently successful in depriving that system and the field as a whole of the kind of person it seemed desperately to need. The issue, we think, is not that schools should not be part and parcel of a community's political structure. In our society they most appropriately are. Rather, what Marie's case seems to illustrate is a situation where the balance between political concerns and matters educational became upset. Unfortunately, as the history of education tells us, it is not a new story.

We close this chapter by reflecting briefly on our recent conversations with these principals. With only one exception (Joan), they revealed a common theme. Stated boldly, or sometimes by inference, was the idea of becoming tired; fearing that one would become emotionally strung-out or that the constraints of policy would, over time, make the principalship an undesirable place to be. As expected, people dealt with these feelings idiosyncratically. They made their own peace in their own way; and each of them, with the exception of Marie, remains in the field, highly committed to improving schools. But what does seem to have happened is that each has added a dimension to their thoughts and feelings about their jobs that was not present seven years ago. That is, a tempering process seems to have taken place through which they say, in effect, "The job is still as important as it was. But I and my sense of self are important, too." We can only think of that as a healthy development, even though some trauma may be a necessary prelude to it.

A final comment is this: One cannot fail to be impressed with the quality of the thinking processes of these people as they went through this tempering process. As they dealt with themselves, their weariness, excitements, and disappointments, it seems they also became more mature. Apparently they were able to develop a finer sense of what they were all about and, perhaps, of what life itself is all about.

15

Dilemmas about Values

As the reader now understands, Chapters 13 and 14, about the work-lives of our principals and their views of themselves, carried a more profound message about the nature of the principalship itself. In this chapter we take the discussion further as we focus on some value dilemmas that seem inherent to, unavoidable, and in some ways idiosyncratic to the principalship.

Our working hypothesis is that the essential meanings of the principalship, or of any type of work, lie below the surface, sometimes just below, sometimes at great depth. They may take the form of high peaks of self-fulfillment, of great disappointments, of deep anxiety about one's competence, of moments of hilarity and others of sadness. Or they may take the form of implicit unspoken expectations that a school board has for the behavior of its administrators and that are internalized by them. For example, when the job description of a superintendent specifies responsibility for the personnel function, it never says "Don't form too close a relationship with the union president or the school board will figure you are 'giving away the store.' " Similarly, principals, whose function is to supervise instruction, are never told that part of performing this function means that they will have to agonize over their own inability to do very much about less-than-adequate teachers who happen to be tenured. Part of this view, then, that essential meanings of the principalship lie below the surface, is that, for most intents and purposes, they are rarely the subject of any public forum. In a sense, they constitute the undiscussables of the job.

In summary, the point we make here—and it is an obvious, but unexplored, one—is that any adequate understanding of the behavior of principals and the principalship cannot rest on an organization chart or a list of functions in a job description. Things go much deeper than that.

Understanding that the subsurface life of school principals is apt to be a many splendored thing (due to a book of its own, no doubt), we chose to get a sense of that life by inquiring into the dilemmas principals face that involve their value set. Given the post-Watergate concern with the ethics and values of public service, and given that some initial inquiries of principals indicated that the topic was one they considered important, the choice was an apt one with which to close this book—and to study further.

Our sample of interviewees was expanded to include, ultimately, seventeen principals beyond the seven that we had re-interviewed. The interviews were relatively brief, usually lasting twenty minutes or so. It was not our intent to explore these dilemmas in depth, but only to get a sense of their variety and substance. Though what follows surely does not represent the universe of value-oriented problems principals confront, the broad categories that developed are ones to which most principals would have little difficulty relating.

On the broadest level, there appear to be two kinds of situations principals get involved in that entangle them in problems with their own values. First, there are situations in which a principal is party to the conflict; it involves her or him directly and unambiguously. Mostly, it seems, this type of circumstance evolves as a principal confronts the substance and/or process of the school system's decision-making or policies. There are times, as well, when a principal becomes directly involved in a value-oriented conflict with a member of the school faculty. Second, and more frequently we believe, principals become involved in value conflicts when they are called on to play a third-party role—an arbitrator, mediator, ombudsman, and so forth. That is, simply being a principal implies that one will inevitably become part of circumstances that stem from confrontations between other people: teachers, parents, and students, for the most part.

Both types of situations are generic to any organizational type. At one time or another administrators in any setting will have a conflict over values with the system in which they work or with the individuals in it. And certainly, regardless of the nature of their employing organization, they will also be called on as a third party to help resolve differences that arise between people who work under their supervision.

As an inherently conflictual position, what, then, sets the principalship apart from an administrative or supervisory position in any other work setting.? Our thinking and our conversations with principals suggest that the critical difference emerges as one begins to understand the unwritten law of the principalship, which many principals espouse, sometimes publicly, but possibly more often to themselves as they assume that role—"Thou shalt be an advocate for children." Our notion of what seems to happen is this: As a person moves from being a teacher—with direct, face-to-face influence over children in classrooms—to being a principal, where such influence can be only indirect, the need to be influential in the life of the school at times takes the form of child advocacy. This stance is most often not a formal public one but rather a part of a principal's informal private concept of his or her role.

It is true, of course, that principals become enmeshed at times in value conflicts not based on child advocacy. A decision must be made on staffing or facilities, for example, and the principal is sworn to secrecy about it until the superintendent decides the time is right to go public. In the meantime, when subjected to questioning about what might happen, the principal must pretend ignorance—lie, and feel uncomfortable about that. Or a principal may disagree with a particular district policy, pretend to implement it, do what he or she wants—and feel uncomfortable about the subversion. Or a principal may bow to upper administrative pressure to hire or not hire a particular teacher for what he or she sees as the wrong reasons—and feel uncomfortable about that.

To be sure, such circumstances are vexing. They are, however, relatively common in the life of anyone who works in a bureaucratic organization. Whatever costs they exact, in terms of one's ethical self, tend to be seen as part of the dues one must pay to the organization, albeit not without some occasional trauma. Such matter-of-factness seems not the case, we sensed from our interviews, when a principal must deal with a situation in which a youngster has to pay a price—get a raw deal—because of what some adult did or did not do. These are the times, it seems, that are most perplexing and agonizing for principals. Further, they imply a uniqueness to the principalship, in the sense that it is most often the principal who feels called on to defend the particular problems of youngsters against the general, though not spelled out, demands of the system to which loyalty is owed. To put it squarely, if perhaps too simply, situations arise that call upon the principal to balance the demands of two opposing dicta: The first is a personal mandate to see that youngsters get a fair shake in matters both educational and disciplinary; that their teachers do a good job of teaching; and that, when behavioral problems arise, children are not treated like members of an oppressed minority. The second is the unspoken expectation that principals, publicly at least, will always support teachers, staff members, and the system itself.

It is a neat balancing act, then, as principals negotiate themselves through circumstances in which these conflicts take place. "Negotiate themselves" is an apt phrase because, as we shall see, they seem to hold "reflective conversations" (Schon, 1983) with themselves about what is happening. Following are some examples. By no means do they represent all that occurs in the value-oriented part of a principal's life at work. Our purpose is just to suggest the flavor of things, not to propose any general laws of the principalship. We are quite sure that readers who are principals, and those who have been, will find the anecdotes and remarks familiar and will be able to add some of their own.

A PARENT, A TEACHER—AND THE PRINCIPAL IN THE MIDDLE

Principals are universally drawn into differences between parents and teachers that involve children. A parent may perceive that a teacher is not doing a good job of teaching—and the principal gets a complaint. Or a pupil, in the parents' eyes, has been unjustly accused of misbehaving. Though the misbehavior is not questioned, the severity of the punishment is—and the principal gets a complaint. We have some examples.

> So, a parent comes in and complains about a teacher and you think, "Maybe the parent is right." As an administrator who really tried to support her teachers, I tell you that sometimes it's a really difficult thing to do. I have questions about the teacher's adequacy, the parent does too, and there's not too much that I can do. I don't acknowledge to the parent that the teacher is less than a good one. I think what I try to do is to say to the parent, "I understand what you are saying. I agree. I wouldn't want that happening to my child. Let's see where we go from here."
>
> When I get that kind of complaint and I feel the parent is on target, I just can't come right out and say to the parent, "You are absolutely right. That teacher is the worst thing going. Not only do I have your example, but I can name you ten other cases." I can't do that, I'd be destroying the school. Absolutely! So I listen a lot to the parent, support the teacher, and then work with the teacher.
>
> Oh, yes, I've been in situations where I knew the parent was right. I usually have a conference with the teacher and let them know that I don't accept what they've done, that when I have a meeting with the parent, I'll support them, but I want them to understand that it cannot happen again. It's happened many times. I don't feel good about that at all. And there are some people who just never learn a lesson. And sometimes I will let a teacher be confronted by a parent and go ahead and hang themselves. Because it's happened enough times, I say "you have to start handling it yourself."

Notice that several things are happening in these brief accounts. First, it is the principal who is initially called on by a parent to right a wrong, or a perceived wrong, in the "service" that is rendered by the school. On the face of it, this seems like a not-unreasonable position for an administrator to be in. Aren't administrators or supervisors in any organization frequently called on by clients or customers to make adjustments in services or to accept for return damaged or unsatisfactory goods that were sold? The similarity stops right there, though. What is being called into question in the latter case is the quality of a tangible service or a defective product. The supervisor has more or less direct control over the remedy used to satisfy the customer. Further, we would expect that little in the way of deep-seated values is involved in the transaction.

These circumstances obviously don't hold in the cases we are concerned about here. What is in question is not a tangible service or product, and the principal's control over the remedy is diffuse, to say the least. Further, deep-seated values are indeed involved, primarily those that put a principal's concern for youngsters (are they getting "full value" out of their school experience?) in conflict with a need to be seen as supportive of teachers, thus maintaining good relations with them.

A disinterested observer might conclude that this is no conflict at all. Kids come first. Aren't they and their education, after all, what the schools are all about? But the role of a school principal is not that simple. The principal is not a free agent, whose only charge is to follow the dictates of a single message of conscience. Indeed, other voices of conscience (Green, 1984) intrude regularly. So that in the comments above we can almost visualize the battles that go on: one voice saying "Protect the kid"; another, "Shield the teacher"; and another, "Protect the school."

Life for the principal, then, is not easy. Choices have to be made that focus on a sort of general strategy of (1) Pacify the parent; (2) Support the teacher publicly; (3) Go to work on and with the teacher. It is important that each party to the conflict be left feeling that they are still "okay." This means that the principal must become a rather skilled tightrope walker.

None of this, even when the balancing act is pulled off with aplomb, leaves the principal feeling very good about him/herself. That is, if peace is maintained and everyone saves face, there is still the knowledge that, quite possibly, kids are not getting what they should and the principal is relatively unable to do too much about it.

There is also lingering knowledge of another sort. It is the principal's private knowledge that a public position was taken—supporting the teacher—that was contrary to what he or she really believed. Two unwritten value-oriented job expectations have come in conflict, and the resolution involves some sort of compromise of self, an uncomfortable position to be in, to say the least.

Some principals evade being caught in the middle between parents and teachers, at least initially, by adopting a personal policy: Parents who are upset about youngsters' experiences in school should be encouraged to see the teachers involved. Some principals insist on this as the first step in conflict resolution. It all seems reasonable. If you have a problem with a person, go see that person.

Things are seldom that simple, however, in the kinds of situations we are considering. What seems to be involved for the principal is a shift in the concept of the role he/she holds vis-à-vis teachers, particularly in the circumstances we have just described. The role shifts from overall protector of teachers to a somewhat removed consultant to both teacher and parent, particularly when the problem is vague. One principal described his actions this way:

> I have basically stopped maintaining teachers in instances where I know I don't have any framework for the problem. I've moved to bring the teacher and parent together. That's where the conflict originated. I told all my teachers at a faculty meeting that this is what I was going to do. I said, "Look, when a parent comes to me and complains, you can count on me bringing them up to you. It doesn't mean I've made up my mind one way or another. It means I think it's best to resolve it between you and the parent, with me available." That is nice and clean. The teachers shook their heads. But it puts the problem and the pressure exactly where it belongs. And teachers know they're going to have to defend their actions.

Now that's a change for me. Seven–eight years ago, I would have gotten involved with so-and-so and so-and-so and I would have balanced both ways, trying to get them without giving this other person knowledge of where I got the information about them. I'd try and manipulate it so I could get control.

He changed his concept of how he should structure these types of conflicts and of the role he should play. The shift paid off. He is no longer the go-between. No longer required to manipulate the situation, he is still there to see that "justice" is done—in the event that teacher and parent can't resolve their differences. In effect, he treats teacher and parent like the adults they are by expecting them to resolve the problem. It is not a bad model to present to the school community.

Note that this shift in role from protector to arbitrator carries some risk with it. Abundant evidence (see Blumberg, Greenfield and Nason, 1978, for example) suggests the preeminence of teachers' expectations that the principal will support them in conflicts with parents. It is not exactly a case of "my country, right or wrong," but it bears a strong resemblance. So when a principal eschews that position, he/she runs the risk that the move will be seen as violating a strongly held school norm. Recall our principal saying that the teachers "shook their heads," the implication being that the "buck has passed" to them. So it is possible that, by designing a system he thinks deals with these conflicts more equitably, he sows the seeds of another one that will pit him against his teachers. The risk, he apparently thinks, is well worth it.

WHO'S RIGHT?

Many shades of gray are involved when, as in the previous section, a teacher's adequacy is called into question by a parent. The spectrum is narrowed considerably in discipline problems, particularly those cases where a youngster maintains innocence in the face of an accusation by a teacher or other adult. Two complicating factors are involved. First, cases of "Who's right?" almost always occur in the absence of the principal's direct observation—in a classroom, the hall, lunchroom, or on a schoolbus. Thus, the principal is called on to adjudicate a situation where the issue is simply, Whom to believe? This is the same question that gets dealt with in courts of law, a comparison that makes us feel uncomfortable when we talk about the schools. The major difference, of course, is that in court both the accuser and the accused bring witnesses to try and make their case. In schools this is not likely to happen, at least publicly. It is the adult against the youngster— and frequently vice versa, we might add.

The second factor—more complicated than differences over the adequacy of teaching—is the demand by teachers for unwavering principal support in matters of discipline. There is a certain legitimacy to this demand.

If principals do not support the disciplinary actions of teachers, or if they are inconsistent in dealing with cases that are brought to them, teachers experience a loss of face and control and a sense of having been cast adrift.

Part of a principal's role is to be responsible for the general condition of the school and the morale of its faculty (including other members of the staff). So the answer to this very forceful demand for support in matters of discipline seems simple: When disputes arise—support adults! Simplicity, however, seems not to be part of the principalship. Furthermore, these situations are complicated by another mandate: Protect the kids!

What seems to happen in most of these situations is that principals make decisions that favor the adults, but not, we add, without some gnawing doubts about the rightness of it all. For example, a boy was accused of deliberately throwing a ball at and hitting a teacher. The boy, admitting that he had been playing ball, steadfastly denied aiming it at the teacher. Regardless,

> He ended up serving detention last night. It was a real conflict. I really don't think he threw it. So here I am penalizing him for something I really don't think he did. But I believe in the concept that I have to support my staff, whether it's a teacher, a custodian, a cafeteria worker who's involved. I don't feel good about it. I wrestle with it. I wrestle with it even more when there is a suspension pending. A student is going to be suspended and he or she sits there saying, "I didn't do it. I didn't do it." And I sit there having to say to them, "I'm sorry. I wasn't there to really verify whether you did it or didn't do it. All I can do is base my judgment on what I have here before me from the staff." You can bet I don't feel good about that.

A similar theme was struck by another principal:

> It's the whole thing of loyalty and support. Even when incompetent teachers make bad judgments. The kid calls him on it; the parents call him on it. And I have to support the teacher. Or, you are in a lunchroom with 150 kids and a teacher is the only one there. You can't withdraw that person's authority and strip them bare. You have to allow them authority and back them up, even if, at times, they misuse the authority and a kid gets hung out to dry. The kid may have been incited to do what he did. That gives me problems, real problems.

We cite these two anecdotes, not because they illustrate discipline problems over which principals have value conflicts, but because they illustrate very clearly a central dilemma inherent in the principalship. In a sense, they are prototypical, and principals seem to sense that they have less freedom of action in cases involving these kinds of problems than they do in those that relate to the efficacy of a teacher. That is, demand for support of the adult in matters of disciplinary action is truly an unwavering one. To do otherwise, at least so most principals seem to think, would be too disruptive of the authority structure of the school. Perhaps they are right; but possibly they are not. Regardless, for our purpose, to gain some deeper understanding of the principalship, it's important to understand that these circumstances exist irrespective of the individuals involved. They occur daily in schools all over. Put another way, as noted earlier, they "come with the territory." But not, we should say, without exacting an emotional toll of each school principal.

THE SPECIAL CASE OF SPECIAL KIDS

Another type of situation calls forth the child advocacy and "fair shake" values of principals in a manner somewhat different from the one we have just discussed. It is related to the growing concern for handicapped children. Prior to the passage of Public Law 94-142, the Education for All Handicapped Children Act, in 1975, handicapped children, *if* in school, were tucked away and generally not considered part of the mainstream of school life. That condition no longer holds. While there are still segregated special education classrooms, many of the youngsters formerly in them are now "mainstreamed" into the regularities of school life. This fact alone causes problems of conscience for principals and teachers alike as they wonder about and struggle with the problems of trying to integrate and provide a good education for this population of young people.

There is another concern, though, that fits with this chapter's focus on the value dilemmas associated with the child advocacy role of the principal. As we shall see, it pits the principal against the bureaucracy of the school system. That is, there are no personal villains involved, but, as in many other situations, individuals can easily fall between the cracks if no one is there to look out for them. Here are some ways that principals become involved:

> A parent will make a specific request and I feel they are exactly right, yet the District cannot provide that kind of service. For instance, I have a little boy in this school who is multiply handicapped, who has nonverbal skills, who really should have a computer. I mean that is the way this child is going to communicate. I would think that it is the District's responsibility to provide him with this material, and if we had the computer he might not need an assistant standing over him all the time writing for him. It would make the child much more independent. I'm told we don't have the money. I understand that. So I end up backing the School District against the request of the parent and the needs of the kid. It makes me mad. I go to the District, but they can't take my word or the parents' word for it, that this would provide a good education program for this kid. The District is much more concerned with what the outlay is going to be.

> It's the whole idea of being honest and fair in dealing with these children. I feel responsibility for their programs. I don't like overlooking things or doing what's expedient. So there were some mainstreamed kids in the school who were just not making it in a regular classroom. They were successful when they had resource room time in a very small group. So we recommended a full-day program and sent the recommendation to the Chairperson of the Committee on the Handicapped. He stonewalled the recommendation and I ended up not getting the program for these kids. I was told that it would be educationally unsound, that

we were just trying to pull these kids out of classrooms and not deal with their problems. I was frustrated and mad. And the kids ended up not getting the best we could give them.

We are under no illusion that these two brief anecdotes cover anywhere near the range of problems principals confront as they play child advocate for handicapped youngsters. That was not our intent. Rather, our intent was to indicate that, as we try to understand what the principalship is all about, we cannot neglect the value-oriented problems that come into play when these children enter the picture. Again, it is not that anyone is conspiring against them with evil intent. It is more that the principal's view, as it should be, is particularistic with regard to the needs of an individual student and so comes in conflict with the system's need to maintain itself, to follow specified procedures, and to generalize its policies with regard to all concerned. It is a familiar organizational problem—a professional norm opposed to one that is bureaucratic. But that doesn't make it any easier for the principal who must daily observe kids getting less than what he or she believes they deserve. The issue, it seems, becomes deeply personalized. One principal put this and the other value dilemmas he faced in the following perspective:

> It's always a battle between what you think is best for the child, best for the school, and best for the adults. Basically, I don't think you can be in this job and be a self-serving individual. You can't think what's best for you if you really want to do what's best for children. I try to look at each child in my school as *my* child. If I can, I'll ask myself the question, "If this child were mine, what would be the best thing to do?"

We close this chapter by returning to its beginning. Recall that our position was that, if one really wants to understand the essence of the principalship, one has to go beyond the view of that office conveyed by any organizational chart—as an office charged with seeing that things run according to system-wide policies and procedures. To the contrary, our view is that the principalship is best understood through the thoughts and feelings principals have, which rarely become the subject of public discussion. We chose to focus on dilemmas of value by way of illustration. Unavoidably, as we did this, we had to make the point that the principalship is a position that makes one a child advocate for most intents and purposes. To put it more plainly, it may well be that the last sentence of the above quotation says it all: "If this child were mine, what would be the best thing to do?"

That question reflects both a lofty principle and a heavy burden, if it is to be taken seriously. But perhaps that's what being a school principal really means. But perhaps, at the same time, that is too simple a way to put it, because what we are writing about here is concerned with value-oriented dilemmas of the school principalship, not role perceptions for people who occupy that position.

With that point in mind, the issue becomes broader. For principals, even though they may take their child advocacy role very seriously, it is not simply a matter of deciding what's right and working single-mindedly for the good of the child. Schools exist to serve many interests beyond those of the children, difficult as this thought may be to stomach. Among these interests are those of the family, the community, teachers, the state, the school system—and the principal, her or himself. The dilemmas arise as a principal, almost in a cost-benefit way, because indeed every benefit gained costs something, wonders about the balance that must be achieved among these frequently competing interests. What seems, then, to be a basic question for principals in these situations is, "In what ways must I behave so that, while serving one interest (that of a child, family, or teacher, for example), I do the most good or the least harm to others?" In their own way, the experiences of the principals we discussed in this chapter dealt precisely with that question.

16

... As the Principal Goes, So Goes the School ...

The title of this concluding chapter takes us back to where we started. The reader will recall the Valentine's Day anecdote that opened Chapter 1 and the implication we draw about the subtle influence that a principal's behavior has on the character of school life, another way of saying,". . . As the Principal Goes, So Goes the School . . ." In this chapter we elaborate on that theme. We pay particular attention to a principal's decision-making and the way his/her values and moral judgments about decisions provide clues as to what a principal is all about and thus—where the school is going.

First, though, a historical footnote. "As the Principal Goes . . ." has its roots in the early days of American education, in the days when there were no principals in schools, only teachers. In the *Annual Report of the Superintendent of Common Schools of the State of New York* (1845), the superintendent of Wayne County wrote, " 'As the teacher, so the school' has already passed into proverb . . ." (p. 415). Of course, this superintendent was writing about the influence of a teacher's ability on the level of student learning, not about the broader leadership and management function of a latter-twentieth-century principal. The concept, though, remains the same. The tone of schools as organizations, for good reason and for better or worse, seems to be heavily influenced by the attitude and behavior of whoever sits in the principal's office.

We must draw back a bit, however, lest we give the impression that everything that happens in a school becomes a function of how its principal thinks, feels, and behaves. That is, although the notion of "As the Principal Goes" is important, it is also oversimplified. Things are much more complicated than that. Yet we believe it captures the essence of much that we have learned in our effort to understand the views these eight principals have of themselves and their work, the dilemmas and frustrations they have experienced personally and professionally, and the various ways in which they have come to grips with those realities. Principals do make a difference in their schools, and the principals we studied were selected precisely because they had that kind of reputation among teachers, colleagues, and members of the larger educational community. However, they did not do it all by themselves, nor could they be effective without considering the multiplicity of complex and often interrelated elements that make up the fabric of school life—and which frequently become problematic to effectively leading and managing schools. So, while we note that "As the Principal Goes, So Goes the School," we by no means intend to suggest a "White Knight" (Bridges, 1977) conception of the principalship. Leading and managing schools effectively is more complex than that, evident in both the viewpoints these principals shared and our efforts in Chapter 12 to describe the complex web of elements shaping their work world—the larger system, the character of the school itself, the culture of schools, and the contextual constraints shaping the activities and perceptions of principals and teachers.

In a fundamental way, our study has led us to a new appreciation of the importance and power of the culture of schools and the ethos of educators as an occupational group. We certainly did not set out to study culture and ethos *per se;* but, in bringing this phase of our inquiry to momentary closure, we are struck by the "embeddedness" of the principalship in that culture and by the notion that being a principal essentially means coming to terms with the culture of the school, the larger system and community context of the school, and the ethos of teachers as a social group. The remainder of the chapter addresses our notion of the importance of school culture and its implications for principals, the connection between values and actions, and the importance of vision to effective leadership. We conclude with some speculations about the preparation of school principals and offer a few suggestions for further inquiry.

THE SCHOOL CULTURE

Organizational culture "is the pattern of basic assumptions that a given group has invented, discovered, or developed in learning to cope with its problems of external adaptation and internal integration, and that have worked well enough to be considered valid, and, therefore, to be taught to new members as the correct way to perceive, think, and feel in relation to those problems" (Schein, 1984, pp. 3–16). School principals can choose to accommodate the existing school culture and affirm the ethos of teachers or, if they believe the existing order is less than desirable and possible, can work to achieve a vision of what is best for children and for the educational program.

These are, of course, overly simplified choices, for the world of the principal is shaded in grays; there are few clear-cut issues. The principal exists in a political milieu constrained by the realities of limited resources and conflicting preferences over means and ends; and, while the principal can be instrumental in exercising power and authority and thereby shape the school and the meaning it holds in the experiences of children, teachers, and members of the community, one is forever confronted by the necessity to balance the good that might be achieved immediately with that which might be obtained. One must decide when to advance and when to retreat, constantly aware of the balance among short- and long-term costs and gains. Winning the battle hardly ever wins the war, as some battles are more critical than others—and so goes the principal who would be effective.

While we did not at first conceptualize it in this manner—perhaps we were too close to the details of the accounts provided by the eight principals—we believe that their fundamental aim was to change aspects of the culture of the schools in their charge—in effect to run "counter" to the existing culture, to make changes of the "second order" (Watzlawick et al., 1974), which would bring them closer to realizing the "vision" they held regarding what constitutes a good school, a good education. They were not interested in changing for the sake of change, or in making a "splash" to insure their promotion or career advancement—instead, they sought to make changes of a more fundamental nature, informed by the standards of what constitutes a good school, a good education—as reflected in the larger normative community of educators. In short, their aim was to narrow the gap between what they perceived to be *current* practices and what they believed to be *good* practices—to reduce the discrepancy between their experience in the *empirical* community and their knowledge about and commitment to what the larger and historical *normative* community of educators maintain as the possibilities of good practice.

And this brings us to the centrality of values—the moral component of action and decision—and the importance of "moral imagination" in effectively leading and managing a school. The closest we came to these ideas in the first edition was to call attention to the importance of "vision" and to discuss the centrality within the larger school setting—the larger system of which the school is a part—of the valuing of activities intended to "keep the peace," to maintain the status quo, and to otherwise not "rock the boat." We feel the observations made then hold true today and that they require further elaboration in order for us to more fully understand the work of principals who "make a difference."

VALUES AND ACTIONS

In an early and still fundamental treatise that conceptualized administration as a cycle of interrelated decision-making processes, Herbert Simon (1957) observed that decisions follow from two sets of premises, one grounded in facts and another grounded in values. This is to say that completely objective decisions, in the sense that we know the meaning of the idea of making a conscious decision, always involve the assignment of value to facts and the exercise of judgment in arriving at an alternative; that is, making the choice between one decision alternative and one or more alternative courses of action. Thus, while decisions are usually informed by some understanding of the "facts of the matter" (whether the facts are valid and reliable is another issue), they are in the end always subjective. That is, they always reflect a judgment that one alternative is to be valued more highly than another.

We are in the midst of a technological revolution of sorts. Computers and other bits of sophisticated gadgetry are becoming increasingly commonplace in schools (and on the desks of school principals), and prepackaged learning "modules" and "teacher-proof" curricula are being produced at a faster and faster rate by publishers with an eye on the "education" market. Yet school principals and teachers are still faced with the necessity to make decisions. That is, they still must assign values to the facts as presented and in the end make judgments regarding which decision alternative is to become the chosen course of action.

We note the centrality of values to making decisions not only because it is a valid and important observation but, more critically, because it is a work-world reality that has been ignored by educators and researchers; even though making decisions is so central to the work of principals and teachers—decisions regarding curricula, methods of instruction, school goals and objectives, and policies and practices regarding student conduct and development. The list could go on *ad infinitum*. Making judgments about alternatives introduces a moral component to action, to the activities of teaching and to the activities of leading and managing a school. Values held by individuals therefore not only reflect but also sustain and sometimes change school culture.

The moral component to action and decision-making requires that a judgment be made. It thus carries with it the possibility, often a high probability, that one standard of goodness may be sacrificed for another. We cannot always have our cake and eat it too, so to speak. The world of the school principal, as illustrated in the examples given by those we revisited, and others as well, is characterized by many a moral dilemma—that is, the necessity to make a judgment that one set of valued alternatives is to be preferred over another. In one instance, for example, a principal had to decide whether to support a teacher against a student—and thus validate and reinforce a criterion of goodness central to the ethos of teachers as a group ("principals support teachers, right or wrong")—or to subscribe to a criterion of goodness held central by the normative community of educators as to what constitutes good teaching or good educational practice; and by this standard support the child against the teacher, knowing in the particular instance that, by the standards of good teaching, this teacher did not behave appropriately.

Thus, not only do decisions require assigning values to facts and making judgments regarding courses of action, but also often include a moral component involving the application of *competing* standards of goodness. That is, what standard of goodness should we apply in making a judgment as to which course of action is best? Should the principal use a standard of efficiency, of good educational practice, of convenience, of political expediency, of friendship, or some other standard of goodness? Actions are embedded within the context of school culture, and often the school principal is faced with a value dilemma—the problem of competing values and thus the problem of deciding on a course of action.

In this sense, then, there is a moral component to the activities—the decisions—involved in leading and managing a school. We believe this is illustrated in both the original set of data on our eight principals and the observations they shared during our visits with them some eight years later. Clearly confronting and managing or resolving moral dilemmas was central to their day-to-day work as principals.

MORAL IMAGINATION

We noted earlier the idea of "vision" as a critical factor in their view of themselves and as one of three major elements associated with their effectiveness as principals. Each held a vision of what he/she wanted to achieve, and, generally speaking, this vision concerned making changes in educational and organizational arrangements that would, in their view, serve the best educational interests of the children in their school. Stimulated by their comments regarding the moral dilemmas they face as part of their work, we believe the idea of "vision" deserves more attention. We thus go on to discuss the concept of "moral imagination" in order to more fully understand the meaning of "vision" as it bears on the activities of leading and managing a school.

In a treatise entitled *The Formation of Conscience in an Age of Technology,* our colleague Tom Green explores the ideas of conscience of craft, of membership, of sacrifice, of rootedness, and of imagination (1984). We draw upon these ideas because the voices of conscience of which he speaks reflect important aspects of the qualities of character which earlier we argued were central to principals who would lead a school well.

Urging the reader to explore the full range of the voices of conscience described by Green, we limit our discussion to what he refers to as the conscience of imagination, because that is the quality that distinguishes the principal who would lead and manage a school well:

> Persons who count themselves well educated because of their technical skill and their professional standing, but who lack vision, who do not dream, who assume that the world as it is is as the world must be—such persons are not morally educated, however much we may count them to be "good men and women." Lacking visions and lacking dreams, however rooted they may be, they cannot lead. Where would they lead us? (1984, p. 24)

The principal who would lead a school well is characterized by a quality we wish to call "moral imagination," the capacity to help us see the discrepancy between how things are and how they might be and in so doing invite us to act on those imagined possibilities and, through our actions, transform the present—to move closer to the imagined (and possible) future. It is *moral* imagination because the possibilities envisioned, the standards that serve to illuminate the discrepancy between the present and what is possible, are rooted in an awareness of and a commitment to the standards of good practice that characterize membership in the normative community of educators.

So when we speak of "vision," or of "moral imagination," we refer to that quality of character that distinguishes the morally educated person, that gives that individual the ability to see that the world need not remain as it is—that it is possible for it to be otherwise, and to be better. It is this quality that differentiates the school principal who leads from those who do not; and, while it is a quality found in other persons as well, it is especially critical for principals, because principals must bear the greatest responsibility for, and hold the greatest potential for, determining what sort of school a school is or is to become. Again, As the Principal Goes, So Goes the School.

Vision, the capacity to exercise moral imagination, is the foundation upon which the moral authority of the principal rests. It is what enables the principal to lead a school well. While authority of position provides the principal with an institutionalized base for influence, this is not sufficient to lead a school; yet too often it appears to be the only basis used by principals, and thus many attempts to improve the school (by "somebody's" standard) are resisted or aborted. Thus, in order to lead a school well, one must have a vision of what is desirable and possible in that school's context; one must be knowledgeable about and believe in the standards of good educational practice, which are the gift of a normative community of educators extending throughout history. Finally, one must have the ability to communicate those possibilities to others and to move others to action to realize those possibilities.

RUNNING "COUNTER" TO THE CULTURE

As we noted at the beginning of this chapter, our revisitation with these principals led us to a new appreciation of the importance and power of the culture of schools and the ethos of teachers as an occupational group. Leading a school involves changing aspects of the school culture—in a certain sense, running "counter" to the current school culture in the process of sharing and acting upon one's "vision" of what is possible. This is difficult because schools are characterized by weak normation; that is, the norms that form the school culture are primarily instrumental, having to do with the technicalities of day-to-day practice, and evolving in response to contingencies associated with the organizational structure of schools and with the fact that public schools must accept and attempt to teach all students, regardless of their ability or motivation to learn (Green, 1984; Cusick, 1983).

The norms serve an instrumental purpose in securing conformity to certain patterns of behavior by teachers and students. But behaving is not believing; that is, the norms do not convey any sense of moral authority; violation of the norm does not evoke any feeling of guilt or outrage. Teachers can teach poorly, students can fail to learn, and principals can shirk their responsibility to manage and improve the instructional program—and no one seems to get upset. This is so, as we suggested, because there is not strong normation in the school; the norms that do exist are primarily instrumental, and they do not carry any sort of moral authority (Green, 1984). The norms that prevail are the operational norms of the day-to-day practice; these norms have their roots in the teacher and student subcultures and reflect the assumptions, adjustments, and adaptations that have evolved in response to the social conditions in schools.

We do not offer any magic prescription for success in changing school norms, in building a school culture that reflects a strong normation informed by standards of good practice that have survived the test of time. However, based on our study of these principals and on our work in assisting principals and teachers with the challenges and problems of changing instructional and organizational practices, we do believe that changing norms is possible and that successfully doing so rests upon two fundamental personal qualities, or characteristics, of principals. First, one must have some sense of direction or purpose; a vision of what it is that one believes is desirable or possible in a particular school setting. Second, one must be able to communicate those possibilities to others and to engage various school constituencies and participants in an ongoing dialogue about that vision—what the gaps are between the present state and what is desired; why that which is possible is better than what is experienced at present; and what the various alternatives and strategies are that might serve to narrow the distance between today's reality and the dream of what is possible.

These observations lead us to two additional thoughts about the problems and challenges of leading and managing schools successfully. We noted earlier that the principalship is embedded within a school culture and that schools themselves are rooted in a larger historical and community context. While we suggest that effective principals often find themselves running "counter" to the existing culture (this, after all, is what fundamental change requires), internal constraints in terms of the ethos of teachers and external constraints in terms of the community context place limits on what is possible. Thus, when we speak of vision, or the exercise of moral imagination, we are speaking not of what is "ideal" but of what is desirable *and* possible, given the constraints of the situation. For example, a wealthy upper middle class community represents a school context that is different from one represented by one that is rural and poor; an urban school serving a highly heterogeneous student population represents a context quite different from one found in a large farming community. Good educational practices are found in both contexts, but what is possible in one school may not be possible in another school. Thus context is critical to what is possible to achieve in terms of instructional programs, educational practices, and learning possibilities for children.

A second thought regarding leading and managing schools and changing fundamental norms is this: The work world characterizing the principalship is marked by an endless series of interpersonal encounters and exchanges. To paraphrase a recent study of principals (Gronn, 1983), "talk is the work." The medium of work is verbal. It involves much face-to-face interaction among students and teachers and between principals, teachers, and members of the larger school community. Thus interpersonal skills of principals and their ability to build a climate of trust and open exchange of ideas are both critical to engaging teachers and others in an ongoing dialogue about the possibilities of good practice. Talking "at" teachers or parents is quite different from engaging them in conversations about the possibilities of good practice; memos and pronouncements do not constitute a dialogue. Continuing conversation and informed dialogue are thus the basis upon which constraints may be discovered and addressed; and they provide the medium by which principals may communicate their vision to others and through which commitment by others to particular courses of action can be developed and nurtured.

Engaging teachers and others in sustained dialogues about the possibilities of good practice, and then acting to realize those possibilities, takes time—and time is the very resource that principals and teachers most frequently mention in explaining their inability or their frustration vis-à-vis "good practice"—"there isn't enough time." "Enough time" is not the way to think about time. Unlike most other resources, "time" cannot be banked, or set aside, or saved up for a rainy day. Time is a resource that is forever behind us or ahead of us, but only with us for a fleeting moment. We cannot create any "more" time than already exists. All that is possible is to use time differently, to make more efficient use of it.

Recognizing this leads us to suggest that school principals have a special responsibility to manage time well and to consider how time might be used differently or more efficiently. If this is not done it is unlikely that meaningful conversations and a continuing dialogue regarding good practice will evolve—talk takes time; and, when discussions center on matters of what constitutes good practice, there are certain to be conflicting points of view and shades of difference which will take time to work through—and the character of schools as work settings is such that developing consensus and commitment to new norms of practice is extremely difficult. Our basic thesis, however, is that if teachers and principals do not take time to engage in continuing dialogues on good practice, normation in schools will remain weak, and imagined possibilities of desirable practice unrealized.

Addressing this challenge is not an easy task, and, while interim strategies associated with making better use of time spent in faculty meetings or in unit and department meetings may create some of the necessary slack, we doubt it will be sufficient. A further step might be more imaginative scheduling of instructional and extracurricular activities, so that time for such dialogue is actually built into the schedule—not merely "piggy-backed" onto time already allotted for instructional preparation and planning.

We conclude these observations by urging educators to consider a *basic* redefinition of their conception of the work of students, teachers, and principals; for example, a redefinition of the "role" of teacher that values the activities of reflecting upon and studying what one is doing and engaging one's colleagues in informed dialogue regarding the realities and possibilities of good practice. These activities should take place during the school day, rather than after school, evenings, or weekends.

The current "factory" model of schooling, ill-conceived at the turn of the century, has remained with us to this day, despite the fact that school populations and curricula have become increasingly heterogeneous and complex. Despite society's expectations of schools as vehicles for social reform, a virtual explosion in the breadth and depth of expectations regarding what students are expected to learn in school, and major underutilized advances in communication technology, the roles of school teacher and principal remain largely unchanged; the structure of school organizations and basic relationships between students, teachers, and principals have not changed in any substantial way. Students are still batch processed, teachers teach for most of the day, and school principals struggle to survive the press of immediacy in a work environment that is full of uncertainty, highly fragmented, with relatively limited support staff. It seems miraculous to us that principals and teachers survive these conditions, let alone be effective in their work. There are other possibilities, and we urge principals and teachers to engage one another in an ongoing dialogue to discover what is possible and to work together to realize that vision.

WHITHER THE STUDY OF SCHOOL PRINCIPALS?

There has been a slow but clearly evolving shift in the focus of research on the principalship during the past decade, and this reorientation promises to continue in the years ahead. While the public at large, as well as many professional educators, still hold a "White Knight" conception of the school principal (and this image of the principal continues to be reflected in much of the school reform literature), serious students of the principalship and of school improvement recognize the limits of this perspective—the problems of leading and managing a school, of improving instruction and the general quality of school life for students and teachers, are simply too complex, too broad.

To hold a "Great Man" view of the principal as leader simply misrepresents the facts of school life. It ignores the reality that school principals, like all people, have their limitations—they're not superhuman, nor should we expect them to be. While history illuminates the possibility of great accomplishments by individual men and women, as reflected by Mahatma Gandhi, Harriet Tubman, John Dewey, Martin Luther King, Golda Meir, John F. Kennedy, and Eleanor Roosevelt, it is simply unreasonable to expect every school principal to work miracles in his or her school. There will always be the "exceptional" principal; and a few, like Marcus Foster, will be remembered because of their great accomplishments in school improvement—but let's not delude ourselves with a false image. After all, principals are people, and some will be effective at their work and others less effective than we would like—very few, if any, can possibly live up to the "White Knight" (Bridges, 1977) image that we hold so dear.

What does this suggest regarding efforts to study and understand the work of school principals? One way to better understand the issue we are raising is to think for a moment what you would seek to understand, what you would study, if you put aside any conception you hold of "principal as leader"—toss aside, for the moment, the idea of effective leadership. What would one study, how would one approach the problem of understanding why some principals are more effective than others? By the way, this is very hard to do, because we are embedded in a culture where "leadership" reigns supreme—leadership is a cult, a religion, and we persist in our dreams that great leaders will emerge and become our salvation—and this is as it should be, for our future welfare largely depends on our hopes, aspirations, and dreams of what might be possible with great leadership.

One approach to reconceptualizing the images that guide our study of schools and school principals would be to ask more basic questions. Rather than attempting to understand "effective" principals (read "principals who lead"), we might merely try to grasp a more detailed understanding of what it is that principals do—what is their work, what are their activities, what do they actually do? Wolcott's (1973) study of one principal is an example of such research. The work-activity studies by Peterson (1978), Martin and Willower (1981), and Willower and Kmetz (1982) are other examples that use a different research strategy. The studies by Dwyer et al. (1983), Morris et al. (1984), and Lortie (1983) approach school principals from a descriptive rather than a normative viewpoint. These studies emphasize the actual work of school principals, rather than their effectiveness in the role. In addition, these researchers are concerned with a broader range of role behavior than is permitted by the concept of leadership.

In this vein, a much-neglected dimension of the role of school principals is revealed—and this concerns the managerial aspect of their work—in the day-to-day operational routines which serve to maintain and stabilize the school as a work setting. Routines that are functional and well managed provide the foundation upon which the work of students, teachers, and principals rests, and relatively little is known regarding these arrangements—what are they, which ones are most critical, how are they developed, and what are the purposes served by these routines? What are the regularities of school life, of the work of school principals? What threatens these regularities, and what are the consequences of those conditions for the work of principals?

Another avenue to studying the principalship might be to think of the school as a small society and to ask what it is that school principals do as members of that society. What does it mean to be a citizen of the school? What are the rights, duties, and responsibilities of citizenship? In what manner do other members of the society view transgressions of citizenship by the principal? And with what consequences for the principal? What are the civil (citizen) rights, responsibilities, and duties of teachers and students as members of the school community, and what is their relationship to those of principals, and to the work of principals? What are the threats to citizenship, to the school community, and in what ways are such concerns reflected in the principal's work? We suggest that much could be learned about the principalship and the nature of schools with such an approach . . . a description of the rights, duties, and responsibilities of citizenship in the school.

Viewing the school as a polity, and teachers as the legislative body (*de facto,* if not *de jure*), what problems of governance confront the school principal? This image illuminates the problem of authority in schools, and the use of power by the principal and other members of that assemblage. What is the structure and use of power in the school—or, from Pfeffer's (1981) perspective, what are the sources of "potential influence through which events can be affected" (power); and what are the political dynamics of the principalship—". . . those activities or behaviors through which power is developed and used in organizational settings" (politics)? Power and politics, or the use of power, are understudied phenomena in the organizational literature generally, and particularly as they manifest themselves in schools, and may be revealed in the work of principals and other actors on the school scene. Conceptualizing power as a property of the system at rest (Pfeffer, 1981) directs attention to the *context* of the principalship and views politics as a range of *activities and behaviors* undertaken to acquire, develop, and use power to influence events and outcomes in the school. Studying both of these phenomena would reveal much about the problems of school governance, the structure of authority, the potency (or lack thereof) of the person and/or office of principal, the language and activities surrounding the decision-making process, and the nature of the resistance, opposition, and self-interests of individual or subgroups within the school polity itself, or within the larger community in which the school exists.

These three "images" of the school and the work of principals are offered as alternatives to the traditional and overworked conceptions of the school as bureaucratic and of the principal as leader. If these alternative images are taken as the premises guiding study of the principalship, we believe a more complete understanding of the problems of the principalship, and hence the work activities and behaviors of principals, will be realized. There are additional images and metaphors that could be envisioned. We note only these three to suggest that there are useful alternatives to thinking of the principal and the work of that person only in terms of leadership or administrative effectiveness. The concerns regarding school "leadership" are not likely to be shunted aside completely, nor should they be abandoned. However, it seems fruitful at this juncture in the study of schools and of the work of principals to explore new avenues of inquiry.

A related set of issues, which we comment on only briefly in concluding this discussion, is the implicit assumption in most studies of the principalship (ours as well) that there is a cause-and-effect relationship between the work behavior and activities of the principal and the consequences and outcomes for students, teachers, and the effectiveness of instructional programs. Murphy et al. (1983) offer an excellent discussion of this and other basic (but questionable) assumptions guiding research on the principalship, and we build upon their observations in several ways. There are two specific issues we wish to address, and they are related in part to the manifest structure of authority in schools and to the cause-and-effect view of the principalship vis-à-vis the influence of the principal (cause) upon instructional learning and other school processes and outcomes (effect).

Society's preoccupation with both the cult of leadership and the hierarchy of authority (bureaucratic structure as the dominant structure of most work settings) contributes to a cause-and-effect assumption in the study of the principalship (principal as causal factor) and to a preoccupation with the leadership function of administration. Three things happen: (1) the principal or some associated set of behaviors, characteristics, or activities is treated as an independent variable and tends to be overly emphasized by researchers; (2) the interdependency or reciprocal character of social relationships, events, and activities is deemphasized; and (3) contextual variables are virtually ignored.

While we agree that a "White Knight" view of the principalship is fallacious, and that it is a mistake to always assume that a cause-and-effect relationship obtains between what principals do and what happens in schools, we urge the reader not to assume that the principal has no effect at all, or that the behaviors, characteristics, and activities of principals don't merit study. We believe there is sufficient evidence to support the importance of the character of the principal (knowledge, skills, attitudes, and beliefs) and the relationship between those characteristics and success in the activities of administering, leading, and managing a school. We do not advocate a return to the "traitist" approach, nor do we advocate a "Great Man" theory of the principalship. However, we do believe that a much-neglected dimension of the study of principals, as well as of their training, selection, and later career development, is the character of principals and their qualities as human beings, including their values and beliefs about education, teaching, and learning, their interpersonal skills and orientations, their skills of analysis and tolerance for conflict and ambiguity, and their knowledge regarding instructional and organizational processes. We refer to these generally as "person characteristics" and call attention to them here because they represent an understudied and, we believe, potent source of understanding regarding work activities and effectiveness of principals.

Regarding the interdependent and reciprocal character of social relationships and activities and events in schools, we urge researchers to pay more attention to (1) the social dynamics between and among students, teachers, and the principal and (2) the impact of school-structure characteristics on those relationships and processes and on the work behaviors, activities, and orientations of principals. Cusick's (1983) study of high school social structure is a good example. It illustrates the complex web of social processes and structures in schools, their interdependent and reciprocal character, and their consequences for students, teachers, and principals. The organizational processes and structures that characterize schools and mediate the work of principals and others represent an important set of variables and relationships that too often remain unexamined in studies of the principalship.

Finally, what contextual variables mediate the work and behavior of school principals, in what manner does the principal respond, and with what consequences? In addition to contextual variables associated with organizational structures and processes, noted above, the culture of the school, the ethos of students and teachers as separate but potent and interdependent social groupings, the character of the larger community environment within which the school resides, and the problems and work activities of individual teachers, students, and other members of the school all represent a broad set of potential influences on the work activities and orientations of school principals. These are noted because they are understudied (see Duckworth, 1983) yet represent a potent set of factors associated with the principalship—what is their effect on the work of the principal?

Understanding these elements will provide researchers with more knowledge about the nature of schools and the work and problems of teachers and students, and so can provide a more solid basis for identifying and studying the problems, hence the work, of school principals.

CAN WE "PREPARE" SCHOOL PRINCIPALS?

What are the implications of our findings for those responsible for selecting, preparing, and developing school principals? There's a fundamental obstacle to answering this question—neither the academic community responsible for graduate programs for administrators nor the professional school administrators themselves offer a very clear answer regarding their performance expectations for school principals. The reality in school districts we are familiar with is that principals are expected to do everything equally well—to provide instructional leadership, to manage instructional programs and re-sources, to administer day-to-day school operation, to monitor student be-havior and support teacher discipline, to manage all the support staff and to handle inquiries and concerns of parents, to attend numerous meetings during and after the regular school day—the list is almost endless.

Answering the question, Can We "Prepare" School Principals? requires some agreement regarding the nature of the work of school principals—is it art, science, craft, or perhaps some blend of all these kinds of work. We believe it is more like a craft than either a science or an art—though throughout the evolution of the field of educational administration the no-tions of scientific administration and the art of administration abound. Blum-berg (1984) conceives of "administration as craft," and we find this perspec-tive useful as a point of reference in commenting on the preparation of school principals. The brief comments to follow are intended to suggest the limits and the possibilities of preparation, and to direct attention to the locus and purpose of preparation.

FORMAL PREPARATION

The prevailing conception of preparation is grounded in a view of adminis-tration as science and hence tends to emphasize the acquisition of formal knowledge. While the social sciences clearly have much to offer in the way of ideas germane to the work of school principals, formal preparation pro-grams tend little to the problem of translating formal knowledge into action through practice. Although many graduate education programs do include an "internship" in course requirements associated with a professional prep-aration curriculum, it tends not to be a "practice" opportunity of much depth or intensity, and often it is disconnected from the formal curriculum which precedes it. This need not be the case; educational administration, we believe, would be well served in following the examples set by the profes-sions of medicine and psychology, for example.

A related question regarding the "formal" preparation of administrators is, "What knowledge and skills are required for the principalship?" This question has been debated much during the past few decades, and it is our observation that the debate has paid little attention to the actual work of school principals. What are the "materials," so to speak, upon which the principal applies the knowledge and skills that constitute the "craft" of ad-ministering schools? We argue that the "material" with which principals work is fundamentally social in nature; consisting largely of individual and group behaviors mediated by complex social processes, bounded by school culture and community contexts. Further, we suggest that formal prepara-tion programs basically ignore the centrality of the "social" character of the work of principals; and, while this might be rationalized as a sin of omission rather than of deliberate intent, we believe those charged with the formal preparation of school principals have a responsibility to redress this error. After all, it does not seem unreasonable to expect a fairly high degree of correspondence between the knowledge and skills that principals are taught in a formal professional preparation program and the problems of practice constituting their work as principals.

What might this entail? We have no grand sense of exactly how this issue might best be addressed but suggest that it is possible, in the context of a formal preparation program, for participants to acquire formal knowledge and to develop the associated skills of practice underlying effective interpersonal communication and effective group behavior. There is a substantial formal knowledge base related to the social dynamics of small groups and interpersonal communication, and there is ample evidence and materials informing the translation of this knowledge into good practice. Formal preparation programs do not address these "tools" of the craft, so to speak, but they could—and, obviously, we believe they should.

A second and related "curriculum" issue is salient to the work of principals but is not addressed by formal preparation programs. It centers upon (1) knowledge related to teaching and learning (the standards of good practice) and (2) skills related to identifying the "gaps" between current practice and that which is possible and those associated with examining, articulating, and developing commitment to the valued standards. While school teachers and principals find their work-lives inextricably intertwined around these issues, administration preparation curricula do not address these issues in any depth, nor is there usually any explicit effort during formal preparation to provide teachers and prospective school principals with opportunities to interact with one another or to collectively discuss and debate such concerns. If this occurred, we suggest that it would provide principals with opportunities to become more informed about the views of teachers and the standards of good practice and that principals would have opportunities to sort out their personal values regarding these questions and to practice articulating and discussing such matters with teachers.

INFORMAL PREPARATION

While efforts to professionalize the preparation of school principals have resulted in curricula that are broad in scope and grounded in a knowledge base that is reasonably generalizable (if not always on target, as suggested above), formal preparation program and related certification policies fail to recognize that much of the "role-learning" associated with the principalship occurs informally and often concurrently with formal efforts by graduate schools. That much role-related learning does occur informally fits the "craft" notion of the work of school administrators—almost as if an "apprenticeship" model of training exists to supplement or extend the "formal" model manifest in professional preparation. It is not conceived of as such, nor do we believe it functions in this manner, but the apprenticeship-like character of informal role training that currently exists could be capitalized on in efforts to improve the preparation of principals.

A basic limitation of the informal preparation process, as it functions in most settings, is that there presently are no mechanisms that help assure that prospective principals are exposed to models of good practice, or that they develop familiarity with the full range of problems and situations associated with the principalship, or acquire an appreciation of the implications for the work of principals of differences in school contexts. These limitations could be addressed, and we believe the result would be to structure the informal preparation process so that it more closely adheres to the "apprenticeship" model—both prior to and during the period of formal preparation, as well as after.

One who is "master" of his/her craft certainly has not acquired that status upon gaining membership in the guild (read "completed administrator certification requirements") but rather as a result of successive and successful years of practice. And so it is with good or effective principals—they have practiced the craft of administration over the years, developed their skills at working with "social" materials shaped by differences in school culture and context, and over time have learned how to work effectively with these differences in "social textures."

We note the importance of developing skills through practice, over time, and in the presence of good models, because too often efforts to reform and improve the principalship miss this essential antecedent of good practice—and instead focus almost entirely upon minor and frequently insignificant aspects of the formal preparation curriculum or the policy guidelines dictating administrator certification requirements. It often is as if one expects good practice to automatically follow from acquisition of knowledge *per se.* Knowledge must be transformed into action and skills must be practiced if they are to be developed. The existing models of administrator preparation ignore both of these points.

To summarize these observations regarding the locus and purpose of preparation, and by way of answering the question posed at the beginning of this section, Can We "Prepare" School Principals?—we offer several concluding comments. The principal's work is largely social, and interpersonal communication with individuals and small groups is the medium through which the principal works at the "craft" of administering the school. While formal knowledge is important and can provide principals with a broader understanding of the possibilities inherent in the materials with which he/she works, it is practice guided by good models and high standards that enables one to develop the skills and qualities of judgment that distinguish the effective administrator from others, just as the "master" is distinguished from the "apprentice" in the practice of one's craft. Finally, the purpose of professional preparation must bear some correspondence to the problems of practice to be encountered, and the profession would serve ıtself well to recognize that preparation occurs informally as well as formally, and that potent and complementary connections between formal and informal preparation processes hold the possibilities of better-prepared "rookie" principals who, through practicing their craft, can become more skilled and more effective over time.

"VALUE LEADERSHIP IN EDUCATION"

We conclude with some final thoughts about the nature of schools, the work of school administrators, and the person of the principal. Some seven years ago we embarked upon an effort to understand principals' views of themselves and their work, and, while the whole story will never be complete, this volume adds a few more bits and pieces as we grapple with the meaning of the principalship and its impact on schools and upon the lives of those who would be principals.

What have we learned? Aside from gaining additional insights into the complexities of schools and their implications for the work of principals, our follow-up study has heightened our awareness of the importance of school culture and context and has confirmed for us the importance of the character of the principal as a key actor on the school scene. While we eschew a "White Knight" conception of the principalship as overly simplistic, we do view the principal as a central and important contributor to what happens in school—whether existing practices are maintained or changed, whether the social and academic climate is or is not conducive to good teaching and positive student development, and whether organizational arrangements are or are not supportive of instructional programs and directives. In this sense, as the principal goes, so goes the school.

More so than in the initial study, our "revisitations" with these principals led us to more fully appreciate the significance of school culture, the ethos of teachers as a group, and the larger social and political context within which the school is embedded. In a sense, we have observed that principals engage in a kind of running battle with the school culture and that what one accomplishes as a principal is constrained by the limits of culture and context on the range of what is possible in that school situation.

The critical ingredients in all of this are value leadership, vision, and the capacity to exercise "moral" imagination. This is a much-understudied aspect of leading and managing the school, and it is a dimension at once intertwined with the character of the principal, the culture of the school, and the socio-political context within which the school is rooted. Value leadership essentially involves increasing awareness among teachers and parents of what is possible within existing constraints and then working with those constituents to develop the consensus and commitment needed to close the gap between what is, and what is not possible.

Related to the notion of value leadership is the observation that action is often constrained by competing value preferences. As we observed in Chapter 15, what sets the nature of the principalship apart from other administrative roles as an inherently conflictual position is that many of the conflicts with which the principal must grapple involve teachers and students or teachers and parents, and these most often occur outside the principal's perceptual field. Additionally, they frequently require that the principal perform a neat balancing act between one's perceived role as "advocate" for the child on the one hand and, on the other, the pressures to conform to a very strong message that is central to the ethos of teachers as a group—"support the teacher, right or wrong." From a teacher's perspective, one of the worst things a principal can do is fail to support the teacher in the face of conflict with a parent or a child. Value conflicts pervade the work world of school principals.

Finally, the materials with which the principal works are essentially social in character, and they are shaped by school culture and context. In this sense, the materials upon which and through which the principal practices the craft of administering a school are highly variable across school settings, and it is only through practicing the craft over time that one develops one's capabilities to be a good principal, to be effective. However, practice in the absence of good models and high standards of performance is not likely to yield the quality we desire and look for in school principals—just as good models or high standards by themselves are not sufficient for good practice. In the final analysis, one must act and, in the action itself, strive to apply good standards of practice—to close the gap between what currently exists and what we know is possible as good practice. As the principal goes, . . .

Suggested Readings

We noted in the Preface that, rather than include an extended discussion of the historical and research literature on the principalship, as we did in the first edition, we would instead provide a brief bibliographic essay for those who might wish to read further. By no means does it reflect all the relevant literature; however, we believe the sources discussed here do provide a useful starting point for readers who wish to explore the literature in depth.

The studies we've selected address three broad interrelated areas: (1) the culture, context, and structure of schools; (2) the perspectives and orientations of teachers at work; and (3) the viewpoints and work activities of school principals themselves. We include sources on the work of teachers and the nature of schools because without them one could only partly understand the principalship. Indeed, one useful way to think of a school principal's behavior is to view it as largely reflexive and accommodative—at times engaging in actions that turn back upon both themselves and other actors on the school scene, and at other times adapting and adjusting to the situation as presented. The essay concludes by noting several studies, which themselves are partial reviews of the literature, and by discussing ideas that suggest what has and has not been studied and what new avenues of inquiry might prove to be rewarding in providing us with further insights on the principalship.

The essential features of the principalship, as we know it today, are rooted in events that occurred during the late 1800s and early 1900s. Pierce's (1934) study, entitled "The Origin and Development of the Public School Principalship," traces its evolution to (1) the rapid growth of cities and expanding school enrollments during the late nineteenth century, (2) the grading of schools and accompanying problems in coordinating pupils and curricula, (3) the consolidation and reorganization of schools into a single administrative unit, and (4) the establishment of the position of head assistant to free the principal from teaching responsibilities. As schools grew larger and more complex, the role of principal evolved from that of "principal teacher" with assorted clerical duties to that of "supervising principal" with no teaching duties and a broader responsibility for the organization and general management of the school, for supervising staff and instruction, and for interpreting the work of the school to the immediate community.

Callahan's *Education and the Cult of Efficiency* (1962) provides further insight into historical developments influencing the principalship, tracing the infusion of business values and practices into the schools, the evolution of the "school as factory," and the circumstances shaping the vulnerability of school administrators to community contexts and pressures. The book focuses on America's growing preoccupation with "efficiency" and "scientific" management and describes the ways in which public schools and their administrators responded to those pressures. The idea of the "platoon school," seized upon by school administrators during the early 1900s as an answer to the public press for more efficient "businesslike" schools, reflects the basic pattern of organization and instructional scheduling underlying American schools today.

These historical accounts by Pierce and Callahan are rich in detail and provide a useful reference point regarding the interplay between schools and society. They are vivid reminders of how sensitive schools are to the economic and social contexts in which they are embedded. One only needs to recall the most recent public fervor for educational reform, sparked by the spate of "excellence" commissions and reports that emerged during the early 1980s, to grasp the vulnerability of educators to public pressure, and the consequences for principals and teachers who scurry frantically to implement the plethora of new cures for education's "failures." We note the notion of "failure" in quotation marks because the recent outcries tend to overlook many of the successes of education during its recent history and, more importantly, because the promulgated reforms, as in the past, tend to ignore the very conditions of schooling in America that make it difficult to educate every child to the level desired.

These conditions are captured most vividly in the earlier studies by Waller (1932), Becker (1951), and Bidwell (1965) of the work of teachers and the organizational characteristics of schools, and in more recent studies by Lortie (1975) and Cusick (1983). We note them here to call attention to conditions shaping the work and occupation of teaching and the social structure of public schools. While Pierce and Callahan provide insights regarding the external context and conditions influencing schools and the work of principals, many aspects of the principalship are in turn shaped by internal features of the school culture and social structure.

Waller's *Sociology of Teaching* (1932) provides a rich description of teachers, their work, the nature of their relationships with children, and the dilemmas they experience under the press of uniform expectations for student achievement in the face of a highly variable, and often recalcitrant student population. The frustrations and problems recorded by Waller more than fifty years ago are not very different from those reflected by teachers today—the problems of discipline and control, tenuous relations with parents and school administrators, and relative isolation from peers. Becker's *Role and Career Problems of the Chicago Public School Teacher* (1951) contains a vivid picture of teachers' views of their work and their relationships with principals, parents, and students, and provides numerous insights regarding the principalship—as viewed by teachers. Becker illustrates the ways in which the teaching role and the structure of the teaching career influence mobility patterns in the teaching occupation, and confront school principals with numerous frustrations related to rewarding and keeping good teachers, and developing, transferring, or firing those who do not reflect desired qualities. The study offers rich insights into the ethos of teachers and the culture of schools, and the reader desiring a view of the principalship from the vantage point of teachers will find the study illuminating and rewarding in terms of gaining a more complete understanding of the problems of leading and managing teachers. Lortie's *Schoolteacher: A Sociological Study* (1975) extends the picture of teachers annd teaching painted by Waller and Becker, delves more deeply into the day-to-day frustrations and rewards of teachers at work, and is particularly illuminating of the importance teachers attach to the psychic rewards of teaching, their sentiments and interpersonal preferences, the endemic uncertainties of their craft, its consequences, and the social environment in which they work.

The studies by Waller, Becker, and Lortie capture the work-world perspectives and frustrations of teachers illuminating the character of the work force and the associated problems of instruction, which shape the school as a social situation and thus provide a critical reference point for understanding the work of principals. While principals are vulnerable to and must be responsive to external pressures emanating from parents and the larger community within which the school is embedded, teachers themselves represent a critical and potent set of internal influences on school principals. The teacher's world is inextricably bound up with and influences that of the school principal, and while this is so, studies of the principalship tend not to reflect this condition. Understanding the teacher's world can thus provide useful insights into the principalship itself, because much of the work of principals reflects an accommodation of or an adjustment to the teacher's perspectives and work situation.

Similarly, the principalship in large measure cannot be separated from the social structure and the organizational characteristics of schools. Bidwell's "The School as a Formal Organization" (1965) and Cusick's *The Egalitarian Ideal and the American High School* (1983) provide useful observations regarding the structural properties of schools and their impact on both teacher and principal. Bidwell describes the dilemmas created by the pressure for uniform outcomes and by the recruitment character of teacher relations with students and the potential conflicts between professional and administrative authority in the school. The pressures on teachers and administrators are quite different, leading to different perspectives of the school situation and thus different views regarding what is problematic and how those problems might best be addressed. Cusick's portrayal reveals the organizational accommodation by teachers and principals to students with highly variable levels of ability and motivation to learn. Strategies by teachers to engage disinterested and unruly students and pressures by the school principal to maintain discipline result in a complex social structure that turns upon and reinforces itself. The consequence is a situation wherein teachers are evaluated on the basis of their ability to control students, students shape the curriculum and reinforce a highly eclectic and elective curriculum (wherein teachers pretty much teach what they want and students, in effect, decide what constitutes their "education"), and the school principal spends the majority of his or her time managing personnel crises and maintaining administrative routines. It is not an image of school one would point to as desirable—but it appears to be a valid picture of what high schools are like—or at least those studied by Cusick. Both Bidwell's and Cusick's work illustrate the impact of organizational arrangements and social structures on the role of principal and suggest that many of the behaviors and orientations of principals can only be understood in the context of the school as a social situation. Again, this is a much-neglected dimension in research focused on the principalship. It is as if we can't see the forest for the trees.

Now we turn to studies of school principals and their work environments. The studies reviewed reflect the social character of the school and its larger context. We based our selection on this criterion because we believe it is crucial to understanding the principalship and because too many studies fail to grasp its significance. Wolcott's *The Man in the Principal's Office: An Ethnography* (1973), Morris et al.'s *Principals in Action: The Reality of Managing Schools* (1984), Lortie et al.'s *The Elementary School Principal in Suburbia: An Occupational and Organizational Study* (1983), and Dwyer et al.'s series of four case studies of principals in different school contexts (1983) represent major contributions to the general literature on the principalship.

Wolcott's portrayal of the day-to-day work life of a suburban elementary school principal is the most in-depth study available. It captures a broad range of problems and pressures associated with the principalship—the endless stream of formal and informal encounters, the diverse range of activities comprising the "daily routine," and the highly verbal and interpersonal character of the work. For the principal Wolcott studied, every problem was important—and this seems to be one of the major dilemmas of the principalship.

Morris et al.'s study of sixteen elementary and secondary principals in Chicago reveals an endless series of brief interactions, a great variety of tasks, and a large amount of decision-making discretion associated with the principalship. School principals in this study reveal a considerable degree of freedom in terms of following rules and policies and in terms of responding to issues and problems in unique ways. While the social situation of the principalship presents numerous constraints on action, the principals studied by Morris et al. appear to possess and exercise a great deal of personal discretion in enacting that role, quite unlike the stereotypical idea that "the principal's hands are tied." The latter may well be a myth of convenience promulgated by principals themselves, one of many strategies principals appear to rely on in coping with their work environment.

Lortie et al.'s study of elementary and secondary suburban principals is quite extensive, examining the principal's relationship with Central Office personnel, teachers, pupils, parents, and peers. These researchers explore recruitment and socialization to the role, the role of the principal as a subordinate, principals' feelings about their work situation, and the impact of school differences on the principal's role. Major role differences associated with the socio-economic status of the school reveal the impact of situational differences on the work of principals; and the localized recruitment and socialization pattern and associated pressures for conservation illuminate some of the difficulties of assessing the effectiveness of principals and improving educational programs.

While Wolcott's study examines one principal in depth, Morris et al.'s captures the varieties of ways in which principals respond to constraints of the system and the immediate school situation, and Lortie et al.'s looks in depth at a broad range of social and structural conditions associated with the principalship, Dwyer et al.'s four case studies of principals in distinctly different school settings yield a close-up view of the triumphs and tribulations of principals and the problems of instructional leadership. The cases include four different settings: an inner-city elementary school, an urban junior high school, an elementary school in a stable urban setting, and an elementary school in a rural setting. The use and importance of routines, the principal's persistence in the face of conflicts between local school and system priorities, the centrality of the principal's vision, and the critical importance of being responsive to context are revealed in these cases. Each is rich in descriptive detail and offers a reasonably complete picture of different school situations and the impact of these differences on students, teachers, and principals. More completely than other studies of school principals, these four cases illustrate the consequences of differences in school contexts for the work of principals, and reveal the interplay between school contexts and the character of school principals.

We conclude this brief essay by calling your attention to several more complete reviews of the literature regarding principals and the problems and challenges of leading and managing schools. "Empirical Research on Principals: The State of the Art" by Greenfield (1982) reviews a number of early studies of the principalship and offers a number of recommendations for further study. Bossert et al.'s (1982) "The Instructional Management Role of the Principal" provides a good discussion of the multiple influences on school principals and offers a framework for understanding the role of the principal as an instructional manager. Murphy et al.'s (1983) "Problems with Research on Educational Leadership: Issues to Be Addressed" examines the limitations of traditional approaches to the study of educational leaders, and Peterson's (1984) "Mechanisms of Administrative Control over Managers in Educational Organizations" examines the ways in which superiors constrain the work of principals, the ways in which district size and school social status influence the pattern of control, and the consequences of these conditions and control mechanisms for principals.

The sources noted above and those discussed briefly in this essay do not reflect all of the readings one might pursue regarding the principalship, but we do believe they will provide the interested reader with a solid foundation for further exploration. The public school principalship is a complex and difficult organizational role, both to enact as well as to study, and there is much yet to be learned regarding this public school position.

As can be seen in these few pages, the literature on the principalship is broad and reflects a range of perspectives. Those who wish to pursue a line of systematic inquiry will find a rich assortment of puzzles to untangle; principals who want to understand their own work will find the accounts of other principals stimulating and useful as a reference point for reflection as they pursue their responsibilities in leading and managing schools; and teachers and lay people who simply want to learn more about the work of school principals will find these studies enlightening and helpful.

Whatever your interest or line of work, we invite you to read critically, and to share what you learn with others—and if your inquiry helps you or others understand the work of school principals in a way that is useful, then all of our interests will be well served. We hope this happens and that you'll find your own exploration as stimulating and as provocative for you as ours has been for us.

Bibliography

Annual Report of the Superintendent of Common Schools of the State of New York. Albany, New York, 1845.

Arendt, H. *The Human Condition.* Chicago: University of Chicago Press, 1958.

Argyris, C. *Interpersonal Competence and Organizational Effectiveness.* Homewood, IL: The Dorsey Press, 1962.

Argyris, C. *Personality and Organization.* New York: Harper and Bros., 1957.

Argyris, C., and Schon, D. *Theory into Practice. Increasing Professional Effectiveness.* San Francisco: Jossey-Bass, 1974.

Barth, R. "The Principal and His School." *National Elementary Principal* 56 (November 1976): 8–21.

Becker, H.S. "Role and Career Problems of the Chicago Public School Teacher." Ph.D. dissertation, University of Chicago, 1951.

Bidwell, C.E. "The School as a Formal Organization." In *Handbook of Organizations,* edited by J.G. March. Chicago: Rand McNally, 1965, pp. 972–1022.

Blumberg, A. *Supervisors and Teachers.* Berkeley, CA: McCutchan Publishing, 1974.

Blumberg, A. "The Craft of School Administration and Some Other Rambling Thoughts." *Educational Administration Quarterly* 20, No. 4 (Fall 1984): 24–40.

Blumberg, A., W.D. Greenfield and D. Nason. "The Substance of Trust Between Teachers and Principals." *NAASP Bulletin,* 62, 422, December 1978, pp. 76–88.

Blumberg, A., and R. Schmuck. "Barriers to Organizational Development Training in the Schools." *Educational Technology,* October 1972, pp. 30–34.

Bossert, S.T., Dwyer, D.C., Rowan, B., and Lee, G.V. "The Instructional Management Role of the Principal." *Educational Administration Quarterly* 18 (1982): 34–36.

Bridges, E.M. "The Nature of Leadership." In *Educational Administration: The Developing Decades,* edited by L.L. Cunningham, W.G. Hack, and R.O. Nystrand. Berkeley, CA: McCutchan Publishing, 1977, pp. 202–230.

Burlingame, M. "Some Neglected Dimensions of the Study of Educational Administration." *Educational Administration Quarterly* 15 (Winter 1979): 1–18.

Callahan, R.E. *Education and the Cult of Efficiency.* Chicago: University of Chicago Press, 1962.

Cremin, L. *Public Education.* New York: Basic Books, 1976.

Cusick, P.A. *The Egalitarian Ideal and the American High School.* New York: Longman, 1983.

247

Duckworth, K. "Specifying Determinants of Teacher and Principal Work." Eugene, Ore.: Center for Educational Policy and Management, 1983.

Dwyer, D.C., Lee, G.V., Rowan, B., and Bossert, S.T. *Five Principals in Action: Perspectives on Instructional Management.* San Francisco, CA: Far West Laboratory for Educational Research and Development, 1983.

Fromm, E. *Escape from Freedom.* Rinehart & Co., 1941.

Green, T. *Work, Leisure, and the American Schools.* New York: Random House, 1968.

Green, T.F. *The Formation of Conscience in an Age of Technology.* The John Dewey Society Lecture. The John Dewey Society and Syracuse University, Syracuse, New York, 1984.

Greenfield, W.D. *Empirical Research on Principals: The State of the Art.* U.S. Department of Education, National Institute of Education, Washington, D.C., 1982.

Gronn, P.C. "Talk as the Work: The Accomplishment of School Administration." *Administrative Science Quarterly* 28 (1983): 1–21.

Kahn, R.L., Wolfe, D.M., Quinn, R.P., and Snoek, J.D. in collaboration with R.A. Rosenthal. *Organizational Stress: Studies in Role Conflict and Ambiguity.* New York: John Wiley, 1964.

Katz, D., and Kahn, R. *The Social Psychology of Organizations.* New York: John Wiley, 1966.

Laing, R. *The Divided Self.* New York: Pantheon Books, 1969.

Levinson, H. *The Exceptional Executive: A Psychological Conception.* Cambridge, MA: Harvard University Press, 1968.

Levinson, H. *The Great Jackass Fallacy.* Boston: Division of Research, Graduate School of Business Administration, Harvard University, 1973.

Levinson, H. *Organizational Diagnosis.* Cambridge, MA: Harvard University Press, 1972.

Levinson, H., Price, C., Munden, K., Mandl, H., and Solley, C. *Men, Management and Mental Health.* Cambridge, MA: Harvard University Press, 1962.

Lewin, K. *Field Theory in Social Science.* New York: Harper & Bros., 1951.

Likert, R. *The Human Organization.* New York: McGraw-Hill, 1967.

Lortie, Dan C. *Schoolteacher: A Sociological Study.* Chicago: The University of Chicago Press, 1975.

Lortie, D.C., Crow, G., and Prolman, S. *The Elementary School Principal in Suburbia: An Occupational and Organizational Study.* U.S. Department of Education, National Institute of Education, Washington, D.C., May, 1983.

Maccoby, M. *The Gamesman.* New York: Simon and Schuster, 1976.

Marin, P. "The New Narcissism." *Harper's,* October 1975, pp. 45–56.

Martin, W.J., and Willower, D.J. "The Managerial Behavior of High School Principals." *Educational Administration Quarterly* 17 (1981): 69–90.

Maslach, C. "Burned Out." *Human Behavior,* September 1976, pp.16–21.

Morris, V.C., Crowson, R.L., Porter-Gehrie, C., and Hurwitz, E., Jr. *Principals in Action: The Reality of Managing Schools.* Columbus, Ohio: Charles E. Merrill, 1984.

Murphy, J., Hallinger, P., and Mitman, A. "Problems with Research on Educational Leadership: Issues to Be Addressed." *Educational Evaluation and Policy Analysis 5,* No. 3, (Fall, 1983): 297–305.

Peterson, K.D. "The Principal's Task." *Administrator's Notebook* 26 (1978): 1–4.

Peterson, K.D. "Mechanisms of Administrative Control over Managers in Educational Organizations." *Administrative Science Quarterly* 29 (1984): 573–597.

Pierce, P.R. "The Origin and Development of the Public School Principalship." Ph.D. dissertation, University of Chicago, 1934.

Pfeffer, J. *Power in Organizations.* Marshfield, MA: Pitman, 1981.

Polanyi, M. *The Tacit Dimension.* New York: Doubleday, 1967.

Sarason, S. *The Culture of the School and the Problem of Change.* Boston: Allyn and Bacon, 1971.

Schein, E.H. "Coming to a New Awareness of Organizational Culture." *Sloan Management Review* (Winter, 1984): 3–16.

Schon, D. *The Reflective Practitioner.* New York: Basic Books, 1983.

Schutz, W. *FIRO.* New York: Holt, Rinehart, 1958.

Schutz, W. *The FIRO Scales Manual.* Palo Alto: Consulting Psychologists Press, 1967.

Simon, H.A. *Administrative Behavior,* 2nd Edition. New York: The Free Press, 1957.

Steele, F. *The Open Organization.* Reading, MA: Addison-Wesley, 1975.

Waller, W.W. *The Sociology of Teaching.* London: Chapman and Hall, 1932.

Watzlawick, P., Weakland, J., and Fisch, R. *Change.* New York: W.W. Norton, 1974.

Weick, K. "Educational Organizations as Loosely Coupled Systems." *Administrative Science Quarterly* 21 (March, 1976): 1–19.

Willower, D.J., and Kmetz, J.T. "Managerial Behavior of Elementary School Principals." A paper presented at the Annual Meeting of the American Educational Research Association, New York City, March, 1982.

Wolcott, H.F. *The Man in the Principal's Office: An Ethnography.* New York: Holt, Rinehart, and Winston, 1973.

Woodward, J. *Management and Technology.* London: Her Majesty's Stationery Office, 1958.

Index

251